THE LEISURE CLASS
IN AMERICA

This is a volume in the Arno Press collection

THE LEISURE CLASS IN AMERICA

Advisory Editor
Leon Stein

A Note About This Volume

Neville's fascinating memoir is especially valuable for showing how a select society reflecting good taste, culture, exclusivity and a status system could flourish successfully despite the resistant features in a swashbuckling frontier area. In San Francisco the ascension to wealth and position was sudden and recent. In addition, frontier circumstances encouraged individual personality traits and political and financial daring. Neville, who died in 1927, remembers the life with loving clarity. "These rich and witty memoirs will provide an abundant pleasure for those who know well that San Francisco is one of the great cities of the world." "It is to be hoped that these memoirs will not be missed by those who generalize about frontier life as raw and crude and brutalizing. Here were charm and amusement, drawn together by a distinctive social character." — *The New Republic*

See last pages of this volume for a complete list of titles.

THE FANTASTIC CITY

BY
AMELIA RANSOME NEVILLE

ARNO PRESS

A New York Times Company

New York / 1975

Reprint Edition 1975 by Arno Press Inc.

Reprinted from a copy in
 The Princeton University Library

THE LEISURE CLASS IN AMERICA
ISBN for complete set: 0-405-06900-6
See last pages of this volume for titles.

Manufactured in the United States of America

Library of Congress Cataloging in Publication Data
Neville, Amelia Ransome, 1837-1927.
 The fantastic city.

 (The Leisure class in America)
 Reprint of the ed. published by Houghton Mifflin,
Boston.
 1. San Francisco--Social life and customs.
2. Neville, Amelia Ransome, 1837-1927. I. Title.
II. Series.
F869.S3N4 1975   979.4'61'00924 [B]   75-1863
ISBN 0-405-06929-4

THE FANTASTIC CITY

*Memoirs of the Social and Romantic Life
of Old San Francisco*

AMELIA RANSOME NEVILLE

THE FANTASTIC CITY

*Memoirs of the Social and Romantic Life
of Old San Francisco*

BY
AMELIA RANSOME NEVILLE

EDITED AND REVISED BY
VIRGINIA BRASTOW

BOSTON AND NEW YORK
HOUGHTON MIFFLIN COMPANY
The Riverside Press Cambridge
1932

COPYRIGHT, 1932, BY HOUGHTON MIFFLIN COMPANY

ALL RIGHTS RESERVED INCLUDING THE RIGHT TO REPRODUCE
THIS BOOK OR PARTS THEREOF IN ANY FORM

The Riverside Press
CAMBRIDGE · MASSACHUSETTS
PRINTED IN THE U.S.A.

PREFACE

AMELIA RANSOME NEVILLE was the daughter of Colonel and Mrs. Leander Ransome, of Connecticut, who established their home in California in 1856. She was born on November 25, 1837, at Columbus, Ohio, when her father was resident engineer of the Ohio Canal. In 1851, with her mother, she visited England and was presented to Queen Victoria at a drawing-room in Saint James's Palace. At Lord Hawarden's castle she met the Duke of Wellington, and among her friends was the Earl of Cardigan, who led the famous charge of the Light Brigade.

In Dublin the pretty, spirited American girl became a favorite at the vice-regal court, and in Ireland she was married to Captain Thomas J. Neville, of the British Army, a son of Brent Neville, Esq., of Ashbrook. He resigned his commission to come to America with his bride, and, with her, to accompany the Ransome family to California. Mrs. Neville's home was in San Francisco for fifty years, through Vigilante times, the reign of the bonanza kings, and later days rich in color before the old metropolis of El Dorado was destroyed by earthquake and fire in 1906.

Romances of early days in California rarely portray the life Mrs. Neville knew, yet it was more significant than that of gambling-palaces and dance-halls; and not less dramatic; the life of pioneers who were builders and who, with the Vigilance Committee, brought law and order to the 'wickedest city in the world.'

Mrs. Neville's later years were spent in the homes of her grandsons S. D'Arcy Rickard and Brent Neville Rickard, and she died at the latter's house in Helena, Montana, June 15, 1927. A short time before her death she completed the book of her memoirs, much of it having been written by her own hand in the last years of her life. It was left to her grandson Greville Rickard.

CONTENTS

CHAPTER I   1

The city of youth — A mission to California — We cross the Atlantic — A London season — Presented to Queen Victoria — The Great Exhibition — The Queen in Crystal Palace — Handsome Prince Albert — English house-parties — The season in Dublin — At the Guinness home — Reversing in the waltz — At the Irish Court — Lord Gough's Castle — Meeting the Iron Duke — Ex-President Van Buren's visit — Lord Cardigan of the 'Light Brigade' — Fanny Kemble reads 'Hamlet' — Married in Dublin — An Irish honeymoon — Back to America — New York in the eighteen-fifties — The first Peacock Alley — Washington Irving and Barnum — Rachel as 'Camille' — Sailing for California — The voyage to Panama — Fellow passengers — Kidnapped on the Isthmus — From Panama to the Golden Gate — A tragedy at sea — News of the Vigilantes

CHAPTER II   37

Through the Golden Gate — Landing in San Francisco — The International Hotel — A future diplomat — Velvet and diamonds — Fashions for gamblers — A Wild West scene — Street crowds — Ships in the streets — Mission Dolores — Lola Montez a bride — Adah Isaacs Menken — Montgomery Street parade — Raphael Weill — A flash forward, Melba at the Bohemian Club — Pony Express inaugurated — Popular resorts — Bishop Kip's Melodeon — Fear of fire — Richard Henry Dana's visit — Lady Franklin and the middie — Mrs. Wood plays at Maguire's — Julia Dean Hayne — Lotta's return — Tetrazzini at Lotta's Fountain — Colonel Ransome's surveying expeditions — The McAllister family — Ward McAllister, Jr., and Senator Clark

CHAPTER III   80

Balls of the eighteen-fifties — Belles and beaux — A sensational murder — At White Sulphur Springs — Admiral Farragut's dancing — A rattlesnake at dinner — Mare Island Navy Yard — A navy wedding — An international episode — Torchlight processions — Women and politics — Buchanan's election — The Wallacks play Shakespeare — General Frémont — First Mechanics' Fair — Sacramento and the gold country — The Overland stage — A generous highwayman — The Placerville Road — Memories of Sibyl Sanderson — Black Bart, knight of the road — In the High Sierras — Eaten by a bear — Covered wagons — Tragedy of a mother-in-law — Colonel Jack Hays makes an offer — Bret Harte's mother — A dark wedding

Chapter IV   116

Governor Weller's inaugural ball — A cold party — Dancing in overcoats — We celebrate laying of Atlantic Cable — Launching at Mare Island — Ball at the Presidio — Mount Vernon ball — An old romance — Broderick-Terry duel — Josie Mansfield's début — Lone Mountain — Hugh Whittell's epitaph — Growth of the city — South Park hospitality — Uncounted calories — Wine for President Washington — A dinner menu of the fifties — New Year calling — Isadora Duncan's childhood — A musician's romance — Bayard Taylor is guest of honor

Chapter V   142

Civil War declared — California uncertain — Mass meeting in San Francisco — Thomas Starr King speaks — The city for the Union — Tragedy and comedy — Rev. Mr. Scott is deported — A rebel flag waves — Bounty men — Billy Birch of the minstrels — Bombardment at night — A Gilbertian affair — General Albert Sidney Johnston — A Southern lady's relief work — Suspected of conspiracy — Silver in Nevada — Rush to the Washoe mines — Mourning for Lincoln

Chapter VI   151

After the War — New faces — Parepa Rosa's bracelet — Eccentric Dr. Coomb — Street characters — An earthquake — Interesting visitors — Shelley's nephew — Sir Richard Burton's disguises — Meeting the Mesdames Brigham Young — Duc de Panthièvre at Fort Mason — Mark Twain's lecture — Laughs at the wrong time — British admiral among Fenians — Divine service on battleship — Mrs. Paran Stevens — Mr. Kaird and the Alabama — Bret Harte a neighbor — Harte and Lawrence Barrett — Lord Charles Beresford helps buy a bonnet — The Duke in tweeds — A borrowed dress suit — General Beale of El Tejon — The old Cliff House — Driving days — D. O. Mills drives 'San Mateo' — Sutro imports eucalyptus trees — Fashionable equipages of the sixties

Chapter VII   178

Bonanza days — The $30,000 brass fence — Nob Hill palaces — The Big Four — Legends of the plutocrats — A royal dais — The Melting Pot's triumph — Through Spain to Italy — Old Taylor Street romance — A house that came around the Horn — Mrs. John W. Mackay — The hotel 'runners' — Old neighborhoods — Chinese peddlers — Chinatown scenes — Anti-Chinese feeling — The cook who was a hatchet-man — Sand-lot riots — Coleman's Pickaxe Brigade — The reign of Ralston — His extravagance — Belmont hospitality — Raiding the Mint — The Palace Hotel opens — Ralston's tragic death — Senator Sharon acquires Belmont — Entertains General Grant — Menlo Park and Major Rathbone's chandelier

CHAPTER VIII   210

Along the Barbary Coast — Memories of the theater — Ristori as Marie Antoinette — Opening of the California Theater — Barrett is host — McCullough in 'Money' — At Ben Holladay's — The popular pallbearer — A famous stock company — Gala night at the old California — General Barnes wins histrionic laurels — Mercantile Library Lottery — 'Dundreary' Sothern — Edwin Adams's Farewell — Mary Anderson at seventeen — In later years — Applauds Maude Adams — Adelaide Neilson talks of her rôles — Hawaiian royalty — A merry monarch — Death finds Kalakaua in San Francisco — Queen Victoria's cousin — First nights at the Baldwin — Rosina Vokes in comedy — Lillian Russell's golden youth — Mrs. James Brown Potter plays Juliet — Georgia Cayvan's glass dress

CHAPTER IX   231

When Patti sang — The diva meets a wit — Coquelin's art — Jane Hading and the 'Hading wave' — The Kendalls — French restaurants — A breakfast for Bernhardt — Clerical teas and delightful bishops — Moody and Sankey save sinners — A son of Charles Dickens — His discretion — The Victoria Regia blooms — Oscar Wilde is bored — His Fauntleroy suit — Irving and Terry — Wild enthusiasm — A great first night — Irving in 'The Bells' — Entertained at Bohemian Club — Stevenson in San Francisco — His quiet wedding — Mrs. Stevenson's independence — A monument to R. L. S. — Midwinter Fair — Grand opera stars — Julia Ward Howe — The Century Club — An advanced woman

CHAPTER X   251

The eighteen-nineties — Lunt's dancing school — Mrs. Langtry buys a ranch — *Fin de Siècle* — 'The Lark' and 'The Purple Cow' — Mrs. Atherton begins to write — The Trilby craze — The first long-distance call — Horseless carriages — Market Street parade — Poet of the Sierras — Ambrose Bierce — A blind political boss — Mr. Phelan as Mayor — Uncle George Bromley's wit — Mr. Chang of Korea — The Prime Minister from South Park — A lady from Seoul — Spanish War days — The new century — Leaving San Francisco

INDEX   267

ILLUSTRATIONS

AMELIA RANSOME NEVILLE	*Frontispiece*
CAPTAIN THOMAS J. NEVILLE	20
COLONEL LEANDER RANSOME	20
RACHEL	24
SALLY PELHAM	30
From an ambrotype made in Kentucky in 1854	
ARRIVAL OF CASEY AND CORA AT THE VIGILANCE COMMITTEE ROOMS	34
From a contemporary woodcut	
A MEETING OF THE VIGILANCE COMMITTEE ON PORTSMOUTH SQUARE, 1856	34
From a woodcut after a daguerreotype	
PANORAMA OF SAN FRANCISCO	38
From an old print	
VIEW FROM STOCKTON STREET IN 1856	48
From a reproduction of an old photograph	
RAPHAEL WEILL AS CHEF OF THE BOHEMIAN CLUB	58
From a painting in the Club by Joe Strong	
LOTTA	70
DR. R. BEVERLY COLE, PHYSICIAN OF THE VIGILANCE COMMITTEE	74
WILLIAM T. COLEMAN, OF THE VIGILANCE COMMITTEE	74
From a woodcut after a photograph	
MRS. HALL MCALLISTER	78
HALL MCALLISTER	78
CHARLES, LORD FAIRFAX	82
JAMES R. KEENE	82
ADMIRAL DAVID GLASGOW FARRAGUT	86
MRS. GEORGE PULLMAN	98
CONSTANCE NEVILLE, DAUGHTER OF THE AUTHOR, ABOUT 1860	116
NELLIE GORDON	130

MRS. JOSEPH TILDEN (JULIA FOARD)	134
JOSEPH TILDEN	134
MASS MEETING AT THE CORNER OF MARKET AND POST STREETS, MAY 11, 1861	142

From a reproduction of an old photograph

PIERRE D'ORLÉANS, DUC DE PENTHIÈVRE	152

From a photograph presented by the Duke to Mrs. Ransome, July 9, 1867

CAPTAIN JAMES CUTTING, U.S.A.	152
SIR EDWARD SHELLEY	158
LADY SHELLEY	158
MRS. CHARLES KEAN	162
CHARLES KEAN	162
BRET HARTE	166

From a photograph inscribed 'To Mrs. Neville with regards of Bret Harte'

LAWRENCE BARRETT	166
SIR ARTHUR FARQUHAR	170
LORD CHARLES BERESFORD	170
CLIFF HOUSE AND SEAL ROCK	174

From a woodcut in the Ford Collection

MRS. JAMES B. HAGGIN	186
JAMES B. HAGGIN	186
MRS. WILLIAM C. RALSTON	198
WILLIAM C. RALSTON	198
FLORA SHARON, AFTERWARDS LADY HESKETH	206
RISTORI AS MARIE ANTOINETTE	212
EDWIN ADAMS	218
EDWIN BOOTH AND DAUGHTER	218
ADELAIDE NEILSON	222
ALBANI AS ELSA IN 'LOHENGRIN'	246
HENRY IRVING	246
CLARENCE GREATHOUSE, ADVISER TO THE KING OF KOREA	260

THE FANTASTIC CITY

*Memoirs of the Social and Romantic Life
of Old San Francisco*

THE FANTASTIC CITY

CHAPTER I

SAN FRANCISCO has a vivacious past, all color and high lights, and some of the glamour of that other age, which was just yesterday in history, still hangs about her. It was part of my youth. As a young bride in the eighteen-fifties, I first knew the sparkling life of the new city: a fantastic city tossed together on sand hills, where I lived for many years to see it grow and finally vanish in the metropolis which stands now, with a certain pride of power and beauty, at the Golden Gate.

The California I knew had little to do with covered wagons. These rarely reached the lower coast lands of the Pacific, being bound for the mines and farming country of the mountains. San Franciscans came from the East and South by water — by way of Panama or around the Horn. Sons of Virginia and Carolina families were business and professional men of the day, with others from New England and New York come West for fortune or the sheer zest of living in a new land. Those who had brought or sent for their families lived in attractive homes, however unimpressive they were externally; two-story houses of brick or frame, with iron balconies or long

Southern galleries, that were ranged along Stockton Street and scattered over the hills, each with its garden.

Later there were stately, beautiful houses. South Park and Rincon Hill with its gardens might have been set in a city of old social tradition. In these something of the legendary hospitality of Spanish days blended, with that of the old South represented by so many families, into a manner of living indescribably generous and delightful, distinctively Californian.

This overlay the life of the streets and gambling-halls and all the drama of adventurous youth and reckless beauty that gave San Francisco its fantastic charm.

It was like some extraordinary play in a theater when I stepped into it from the quiet New England ways of our home and a year of living abroad. Now when I recall it I know that an original and vivid phase of American life passed when old San Francisco burned in 1906, with its foreign quarters, strange bazaars, and gay restaurants. But principally the verve of youth it had, with a pervading joyousness, made it unique among cities. No one was poor. Every one was happy. We lived at the rainbow's end and its colors shimmered about us.

My father went to California soon after the first gold rush to establish land surveys for the Federal Government, and it was decided that in his absence my mother and I should visit relatives in England. We sailed from New York for Liverpool on July 9, 1851, passengers on the Pacific of the Collins Line, sister ship to the Atlantic which had brought Jenny Lind to America that year.

The Pacific would look like a tender to one of the modern leviathans of the ocean, but we thought her very grand. Staterooms were all below deck opening on a grand salon and were considered the last word in luxury of travel, each with its strip of crimson carpet, white woodwork, and washbowl and pitcher held in place with firm braces.

Of our wardrobes I remember a tippet and muff of ermine lined with blue silk with which I expected to dazzle Mayfair, and white Swiss party gowns suitable for a very young girl. Mother always wore silk — soft plaid taffetas, black, and sometimes bottle-green with black lace flounces; a flowing black silk cloak lined with fur for traveling. In our trunks were many muslin petticoats, the starch all washed out of them for packing, but to be restarched in London to hold our skirts to a proper flare. Hoops were not yet 'in.'

We sat at the Captain's table and dressed for dinner on the Pacific, and after dinner gathered with fellow voyagers in the round-house, a place of many windows on the upper deck where passengers met in a friendly fashion long since lost to trans-Atlantic travel. Our diversions were primitive. I make no apology for them to young moderns. We asked conundrums, and all joined in singing songs. 'Juanita' was a favorite. Our riddles I've forgotten. Doubtless 'Who was the father of Zebedee's children?' was one of them.

A humorous gentleman with flowing side-whiskers would invent and propound elaborate posers, and when, after profound thought, some one would say, 'I give it up. Why is a rose tree like a nightingale?' — he would blandly answer, 'I don't know that it is,' which sent us into gales of laughter. Mrs. Deane, a pretty little bride, played the guitar and led the singing, or tried to; for singers would break into groups, each group starting its own selection, with a resulting choral chaos we found hilariously amusing. At the close of the evening we would all follow Mrs. Deane in the Canadian boat song, 'Row, Brothers, Row,' which we thought appropriate for an ocean voyage.

There were always to be met, traveling in those days, fragile, fluttering females who went out of fashion with crinolines — the sort that had 'the vapors' at slight provocation. One of these drove our amiable Captain Nye distracted. 'Oh, Captain, do you think it will rain?' she would ask. Or, 'Oh, Captain, shall we have a storm?' — until one day we did have a storm and Mrs. Flutterby was prettily terrified. 'Oh, Captain!' she cried, waylaying him, 'do you think the ship will sink?'

'Yes, ma'am. She'll sink to hell in ten minutes,' Captain Nye replied, with grim finality, and went on his way, leaving her silenced and uncertain.

The eleven days' crossing seemed short to me. Indeed, it was short for the eighteen-fifties. The Pacific was an ocean greyhound in her day which was to have a tragic end. She was lost a few years afterward, struck by an iceberg, it was believed. No word ever came from her or any soul on board. Our Captain Nye had retired then. Captain Asa Eldredge went down with the Pacific.

My aunt came from her English country home to meet us in London and we took a house for the season, an especially gay season because of the Great Exhibition lately opened by the Queen and Prince Albert in Crystal Palace. There were dozens of visiting royalties with lesser dignitaries from foreign lands, and an endless succession of parties. I was far too young for these, but longed to be in the gay rush of things and my aunt conspired with me. She suggested that I be presented at court for no year could be more auspicious and another season might find us back in America. It was our opportunity, she insisted, and mother was finally won over. I was tall for my age and with my hair done up could easily pass for seventeen.

Thus it happened that I reveled in balls and low-cut gowns — but not too low — all a joyous experience for a girl scarcely out of the schoolroom. In fact, there were still morning lessons in London when they could be arranged. I can still see the London ballrooms — with frescoed walls all Cupids and flowers, and chandeliers hung from the rosy sky of ceilings — filled with long-vanished dancers; gentlemen with side-burns, young ladies in full-skirted frocks garlanded with flowers or lace flounces, whirling decorously in the waltz. Only the toes of our slippers showed when we danced.

Chaperons were everywhere; banked at the end of a ballroom or in the small reception rooms that overflowed with them. They never danced, but chaperoned faithfully and sleepily to the end in an amiable, detached sort of way that interfered not in the least with many light flirtations and a degree of serious romance. For I remember pale young ladies of whom it was said they had been disappointed in love. Occasionally one went into a decline over an unhappy heart affair; or it was told of some flashing beauty that she had jilted young So-and-So, an unmaidenly performance generally condemned. It was a reprehensible thing to encourage suitors one had no thought of marrying and one must be careful to give a gentleman no hope if indeed there were none. Naturally these discretions barred friendships with men for any really conscientious girl, and naturally we sometimes agreed that married women had all the fun.

Yet, in spite of handicaps of manners and dress, we had a gorgeous time in the days of my youth. We were quaint and old-fashioned, but we did not know it then.

Consider our gloves. A lady never walked or drove abroad without them and they must be buttoned before she stepped out of her door. 'Always finish your toilet before you leave the house,' my mother told me. 'You would not think of buttoning your basque as you walked down the street. You should no more think of buttoning your gloves in public.' We sat through long evenings in them at the theater and danced all night without uncovering our hands. One-button gloves which left the arms bare were not bad, but when eight- and twelve-button gloves came in, they could be a trial, yet, imposed by fashion and etiquette, one to be borne as a matter of course.

Being 'presented' was an event approached through long anticipation. There was the excitement of fittings for gowns, and gathering all of the paraphernalia — slippers, feathers, and what-not; and for days mother and I practiced the curtsy, sweeping the length of our drawing-room trailing tablecloth trains, kissing my aunt's hand to get the proper bend.

On the great day we drove to St. James's Palace, sitting very straight in the carriage with furbelows all arranged just so. But we might have relaxed, for furbelows were all disarranged in the crush at the palace doors. I was finally shot through, my gown torn by the spurs of army officers and my bare arms scratched by their epaulettes. We were all in evening clothes, of course, although it was three in the afternoon.

A little preening and we approached the final portals. I gave my card to some one who thundered forth my name — the Lord Chamberlain he was — and started across the great room toward a group of royalties in richly colored gowns and glittering uniforms.

The Queen smiled and laid her plump little hand on mine and I brushed it with my lips as I curtsied low. The thought of the power that little hand represented, signing what historic decrees — raised in a gesture of negation heeded around the world, made me a little dizzy as I kissed it.

Genuflections to other royalties, and then I backed toward the door of egress praying that my train would follow me decently. Trains were great spreading things, in those days, far more difficult to direct in a turn than the narrow, trailing scarfs of later fashion.

Safely through the door, I had time to remark many dignified gentlemen in knee breeches trying to look unconscious of their costumes, and many elaborate ladies with plunging plumes, happily conscious of theirs. But it was brief reward for weeks of preparation, I thought, and we really had a better view of the Queen at the Crystal Palace, one day.

Mother and I had gone to the Great Exhibition, to see the American Display, and were depressed to discover it principally coffins and carriages. Funereal, we found it, and wandered idly over to the French concession. There an awed circle stood staring at the Queen. The center of a royal group, she was examining machinery with excellently feigned interest. She was pretty, I thought, with her large eyes, amiable expression, and the flowered bonnet tied under her chin. The little Prince of Wales and the Princess Royal, who was to be Empress of Germany and the Kaiser's mother, were with her. Victoria Adelaide was then ten years old, but full of dignity. The little Prince was more engaging. Both dutifully regarded the machinery.

I have no other vivid memory of the Great Exhibition save that of its closeness and heat. It was all under glass, in a sort of mammoth conservatory, and only hothouse plants could have long survived its atmosphere. Spectators simply wilted, and fainting ladies were carried out to revive on the lawns. But there is another vivid memory of the Queen: We were driving in Hyde Park late one afternoon when word was given that the royal equipage would pass and carriages in the long procession all drew to one side. Two outriders in scarlet livery came first, pacing grandly down the avenue, then two lords-in-waiting, also on horseback; following these the Queen's carriage, an open landau in which she sat, smiling, with Prince Albert at her side. He had not yet been given the title of Prince Consort. Her carriage passed very close to ours and she flashed her friendly smile at us while Prince Albert touched his hat. I thought her lovely, that day. She surely had great charm in her youth, and was exceedingly pretty in her white muslin dress with tiny rosebuds embroidered all over it. A white lace scarf hung about her shoulders, and her white tulle bonnet had rosebuds on it. She carried a white parasol. All this I noted with wide, eager eyes, and also the fact that Prince Albert was a very handsome prince. Just behind the landau were two more lords-in-waiting, then two more scarlet outriders, and the royal cavalcade had passed.

Victoria and Albert were all that a queen and a prince should be, I thought, but how shocked I was at first sight of one of the great English country houses! 'Knowsley,' seat of the Earl of Derby who was then Prime Minister, was my disillusionment. Stately and grand without, but within — well, naturally, having seen mansions of University Place in New York I expected something very fine, much more elegant than these; and found, instead, something distinctly shabby. Threadbare carpets, worn upholstery, and dingy hangings. Poverty-stricken, it all looked to me, and it was several visits later before I could reconcile the slightly dilapidated dignity of many of these places with my American ideas of how earls and dukes should live.

In a round of country-house visits, one was at the home of the Duncombes of Duck, a great house in a park where life was lived formally. Family prayers began the day. Guests were expected to be in the library at nine o'clock for this ceremony, and when we were all assembled, the servants entered, butler, housekeeper, footmen, maids, and valets, with maids and valets of guests, all in strict order of precedence. We made an imposing congregation. Solemnly Sir Philip read a passage from the Bible and made a prayer. Then the servants withdrew and we considered breakfast.

At the Duncombes', I think it was, we met Comte de Lintivie, French Consul-General in London, and his Comtesse, who is one of the figures impressed on my memory for no important reason whatever. She was large and florid and was followed everywhere by a small white poodle whose name was General Tom Thumb. 'Venez ici, Tum Tum,' were the only words I ever heard her say, and whenever she moved she thus addressed Tom Thumb.

Another unforgettable lady was the elderly songstress who would seat herself at the piano after dinner and tragically intone, 'Rome, Rome, Thou art no more as thou hast *ben*,' until I shook with smothered mirth, though no one else found it amusing.

Picnics were among our pastimes, and the Duncombes' coaches, with four perfectly matched horses for each, would swing up to the main entrance about eleven in the morning. Servants with hampers of food would be stowed inside while we climbed on little stepladders to the seats on top. Some favored belle would be invited to sit next the driver, who was usually one of the guests noted for his horsemanship.

Picnics were always near a waterfall. There was an inexhaustible supply of waterfalls in the English countryside; and before some sweetly purling brook tumbling over a height of fifteen feet, our friends would unfailingly ask, 'How does it compare with your Niagara?'

At Alnwick Castle, home of the Duke of Northumberland, archery was a popular diversion. I had a rosewood bow with blue velvet over the part held in the draw. It was a pretty sport, with feathered arrows, and large white targets striped with red set against the green of the park. We played much croquet, too, and in the late afternoons women's wide skirts swept daintily over the lawns after bright-colored balls. Men had a mean advantage in croquet. They would bend at an angle of fifty degrees to give the ball an effective whack. Women's figures, all properly whale-boned, had more a Leaning Tower of Pisa slant, and naturally with their superior flexibility the men scored.

The May-Day garden party at Alnwick Castle was an elaborate fête. Villagers did a Maypole dance and we all tripped the polka on the lawn. Under an oak tree a village maiden milked her cow for the syllabub we drank. This was warm milk mixed with wine or cider and highly thought of as a beverage.

We danced the redowa a great deal that year, and quadrilles, of course, with 'Salute your partners' and 'Grand right and left.' But the polka was a favorite with every one because elderly gentlemen could polka nicely if the waltz baffled them, and young people put a dash and verve into it impossible in other dances.

I am aware now that in this year of grace, while I was carelessly going to balls in London and dancing on English lawns, Carlyle was writing masterpieces in Cheyne Row, and gathering material for his 'Frederick the Great.' D'Israeli sauntered across the literary scene as he did through the life at Court. The Brownings, having eloped and lived for a time in Italy, came back to London for a visit. Thackeray was dining with his friends, the Brookfields, and gave a party for Charlotte Brontë when she came from her North Country home to see the Great Exhibition. In Devonshire Terrace, where we sometimes passed, Dickens was writing 'Bleak House.'

It was the year the new poet laureate, young Alfred Tennyson, brought his bride to London to live, and Herbert Spencer published 'Social Statics,' which his friend, Miss Marian Evans, later known as George Eliot, praised highly. I might have seen them together at a performance of 'Merry Wives of Windsor' in Drury Lane, but, alas, I did not. I was all unaware of their existence. Of all these things I had then no knowledge.

For, as a matter of dreadful fact, reading was not fashionable in the eighteen-fifties, and the literary world was quite distinct and far removed from the *beau monde*.

Young ladies were not encouraged to be bookish. There were female freaks called 'blue-stockings' who were given to study and much reading, and no one wanted to be classed with these. I can think of no modern term so filled with polite opprobrium as 'blue-stocking.' A girl who liked 'heavy' books kept her failing very secret. We were not unintelligent, merely retarded. And of course there were brilliant women in society and many well-read men. I am speaking of the eighteen-fifty *jeune fille*.

When the season in London was over, many of the fashionable set who owned estates in Ireland would cross for the Dublin season which came later. No country in Europe had then a gayer court than that at the Irish Capital, and in Ireland I had the happiest time of my stay abroad, and met the most charming people. The Irish are so lovable and friendly, so generous in their hospitality.

With my aunt we took a house in Merrion Square after a short stay at the Gresham Hotel in Sackville Street, and Dublin proved a city of delight for me. My first dinner-party was at Beaumont, the home of Mr. Arthur Guinness, head of the brewing firm, an old gentleman of courtly manner who was greatly revered. A daughter, Lady Waller, presided over her father's home which had been hers since her mother's death, and she was hostess at the dinner-party of which I recall gold plate and an épergne of gold in the center of the table.

The charities of the Guinness family have always been generous, and a number of years later, Mr. Guinness's two grandsons were elevated to the peerage for their benefactions, as Lord Ardilaun and Lord Iveagh. His son, their father, was Mr. Benjamin Guinness, then Lord Mayor of Dublin, and we dined with him at Mansion House on several occasions.

Another son, Mr. Arthur Lee Guinness, had the most enchanting home I have ever known, Stillorgan Park, a short drive from the city, where we passed delightful weekends. The long, low house covered with ivy was set in a park with lovely gardens and a winding avenue that ended in a circular gravel space at the front entrance. One stepped into a restful, beautiful court with broad stairways sweeping upward on either side, and in the center a fountain fringed with growing plants. Always in the afternoon a blind harper, with white beard and flowing white hair, sat over at one side of the court and sang old melodies while he played an Irish harp.

To the right of the court a small reception-room led to the grand salon paneled in carved oak, with a great fireplace half-circled by many comfortable seats. A Chinese room on the opposite side of the court was hung with embroidered silks and filled with beautiful things — carved teak, ivories, and bronze gods. This was used for a ballroom and from it opened the conservatory filled with flowers.

Mr. Arthur Lee Guinness was a bachelor, and his cousin, Mrs. O'Gready, presided over his home. She was very fat and merry and could dance a marvelous jig. With her brother she would dance for us, stepping lightly for all her weight, her wide black satin skirt held a little high on either side. Mrs. O'Gready always wore black satin, décolleté in the evening, and high-necked for day wear, and her own hair was covered by a spirited yellow wig. Every one adored Mrs. O'Gready.

There was an informal program for week-end parties at Stillorgan. We arrived about four on Saturday afternoon, driving out from Dublin, and then dressed for the six-o'clock dinner. This was served in the Chinese room, since the dining-room was too small for many guests, and a score of others, beside the week-end visitors, would be present to remain for music afterward and a late supper. Sundays we all went to church. Luncheon followed, then drives, strolls about the grounds, or letter-writing. We wrote many letters before the days of telephones and telegraph.

Sunday evenings at Stillorgan we spent about the great fireplace in the salon and every one contributed to the entertainment. The men told anecdotes, and we sang familiar tunes with some one at the piano. Recitations were popular, and I knew a few poems by heart to recite when it was my turn.

Among guests at these house-parties I remember the Duke of Leinster and his son, Lord Otho Fitzgerald, then A.D.C. to the Viceroy. Lord Otho's dancing impressed him on my memory. He could reverse in the waltz, a rare accomplishment for a Britisher. One simply went on whirling in a spiral and no help for it, once committed to a waltz in an English ballroom. But the first night we danced at Stillorgan, Lord Otho asked, 'Do you reverse?'

'Oh, do you?' I countered, and we stepped out with our innovation. I have no idea why, but it was considered a little bold to reverse in the waltz, and we were applauded for our daring.

At Stillorgan, also, were Lord Cosmo Russell, and the Earl of Clarendon, Lord Lieutenant of Ireland, with his Countess; and Lord Gough, the hero of India, with Lady Gough. He was now retired after putting down the Sikh rebellion of '49 in India, and was living at the Castle of Lough Cutra in Western Galway, lately presented to him by the Government for his services. It was a beautiful place with one original detail in the decorations. Walls of the great hall were covered with brown leather adorned with graceful, curving hieroglyphics in gold and rich colors. These resolved themselves into Spencerian script, on examination, and spelled the names of Lord Gough's many victories.

He was a striking-looking man, this old soldier, with white hair and mustache, sun-bronzed skin, and a military bearing. As a young lieutenant he had served under Wellington in the Peninsular War, fighting the French forces of Joseph Bonaparte, in Spain.

The Iron Duke, himself, we met at the home of Lord Hawarden, and I recall so clearly the gentle smile back of his formidable beak of a nose. He was a very old man then. Waterloo was thirty-six years past, and he died in the following year. But he was erect and soldierly, with his white hair and remarkable profile.

He placed a kind old hand on my shoulder and said his

daughter-in-law, the Marchioness of Douro, had spoken of us. It was she who had arranged for our presentation at Court in London. Every one honored the Duke of Wellington, and paid him the greatest deference, and my schoolgirlish pride was thrilled to be chatting, thus casually, with the conqueror of Napoleon. I felt so vividly in touch with history, too, and do now when I remember the Iron Duke's hand on my shoulder.

Lord Hawarden was one of the Queen's lords-in-waiting, and house-parties at his castle were formal affairs. Dinner at eight-thirty was ceremonious to the nth degree, with much gold plate, many courses, and a manservant standing behind every second guest. The first night, the Earl of Carlisle took me in. As Lord Morpeth he had traveled in the United States and so discovered that streets of our cities were not terrible with tomahawks. People often asked us if we were not afraid to live in America — afraid, that is, of the Indians.

At night at Lord Hawarden's I thought of ghosts. If any ghosts there were, they must have haunted the great shadowy rooms of this castle. My bedroom was vastly proportioned. When I sought it that first night with my lighted candle from the hall, I found two other candles burning on the dresser. By their wavering light I undressed and climbed into the great bed with its heavy draperies. But I took one candle with me, and not until I was safely under the covers did I blow it out, to lay it on the counterpane beside me. During the night the heavy silver stick rolled off onto the polished floor with a crash and clatter. In the morning, guests quartered in neighboring rooms all spoke of it; wondered what could have happened about two in the morning when they were wakened by the sound of something heavy falling. I wondered with them, and never confessed.

Every evening in his rounds of the drawing-room after dinner, the Duke of Wellington stopped to speak with me. He would pass among the guests, the center of a little group, escorted as royalty would be. He seemed to inspire great devotion. Lady Douro, his daughter-in-law and one of the Queen's ladies-of-honor, was like a daughter to him in her care and solicitude.

Ladies had but a brief hour in these old evenings. As soon as dinner was ended, we retired to the drawing-room while men enjoyed their port or liqueurs with goodfellowship in the dining-room. We sat and yawned until they joined us. An interlude of music and conversation, then it was time for ladies to retire. Docile creatures that we were, we took our candles and went to bed while the gentlemen finished their evening with cards, billiards, and talk.

A 'Drawing-Room' at the Irish Court was very different from one at St. James's Palace. Every one enjoyed it. The Earl of St. Germains was Viceroy then, a delightful man, not in the least forbidding. He was short and stout with a bald head and a jolly, red face, and he teetered when he walked. Lady St. Germains had all the family hauteur. She was tall and thin and had that look of passive indifference then worn by many English women: a

'We are not amused' expression which may have been borrowed from the Queen.

When I made my curtsy to Lord St. Germains, he took my hand and leaned down to kiss me in fatherly fashion on the cheek. After presentations, we all adjourned to St. Patrick's Hall and had a wonderful time. A long table, the length of the hall on one side, was loaded with refreshments and there was a general spirited informality that made it a lovely party.

On a Command Night at the Theater Royal in Dublin, we saw Miss Glyn in 'Antony and Cleopatra'; an excellent actress of the stilted, declamatory school. Fanny Kemble was a greater artist whom we heard in a reading of 'Hamlet.' It was under the patronage of Lord Clarendon, and Lord Clarendon was late. The reading could not begin until he was in his box, ready to listen. Moments passed. Presently Miss Kemble swept onto the stage and seated herself at the small table, front, to do her waiting there. She tapped the floor with her foot, and beat an impatient tattoo on the table with her fingers, until the tardy Lord Lieutenant and his friends finally arrived. Then in the gloomy manner of one who has suffered unjust indignity, she began her reading. After a few lines the childish exhibition of impatience was forgotten. Her lovely voice and diction and the dramatic fire that burned back of all her expression held us in a spell. The Prince of Denmark lived, for me, at Elsinore on the bare stage of a Dublin theater where a woman in flaring silk gown sat alone.

During our stay in Dublin, my father's friend, ex-

President Van Buren, was a visitor at the Vice-Regal Lodge. He dined with us several times and we talked of home. It was good to see the homage paid him. All the troops in garrison were turned out for a grand review in his honor. Lord St. Germains and Mr. Van Buren got on famously together. Both had a jolly sense of humor, and in appearance, Mr. Van Buren was not unlike the Viceroy, plump and portly.

The regular weekly review of troops was always a party for me. Our carriage with many others would be drawn up at the parade ground and the Viceroy on horseback would review the regiments. Once the Earl of Cardigan, whom we had met in London, led the 'March Past' and waved a slight salute to me which pleased my youthful vanity immensely. His brigade was the smartest in the garrison and he took the greatest pride in it, himself buying many of the glittering accessories of the men's uniforms. It was a pride very gloriously justified, for three years after that summer in Dublin, Lord Cardigan led his men in the famous 'Charge of the Light Brigade' celebrated in Tennyson's poem. When we heard of it, I was glad to have seen this gallant soldier leading his 'Six Hundred' down a field of peace.

The young officers we knew in Dublin would ride up to our carriage at review and station themselves near us on their mounts. I had been laughing and chatting with several one day, when the most tragic and extraordinary happening silenced all present.

In the 'Gallop Past' one of the horses of a gun carriage

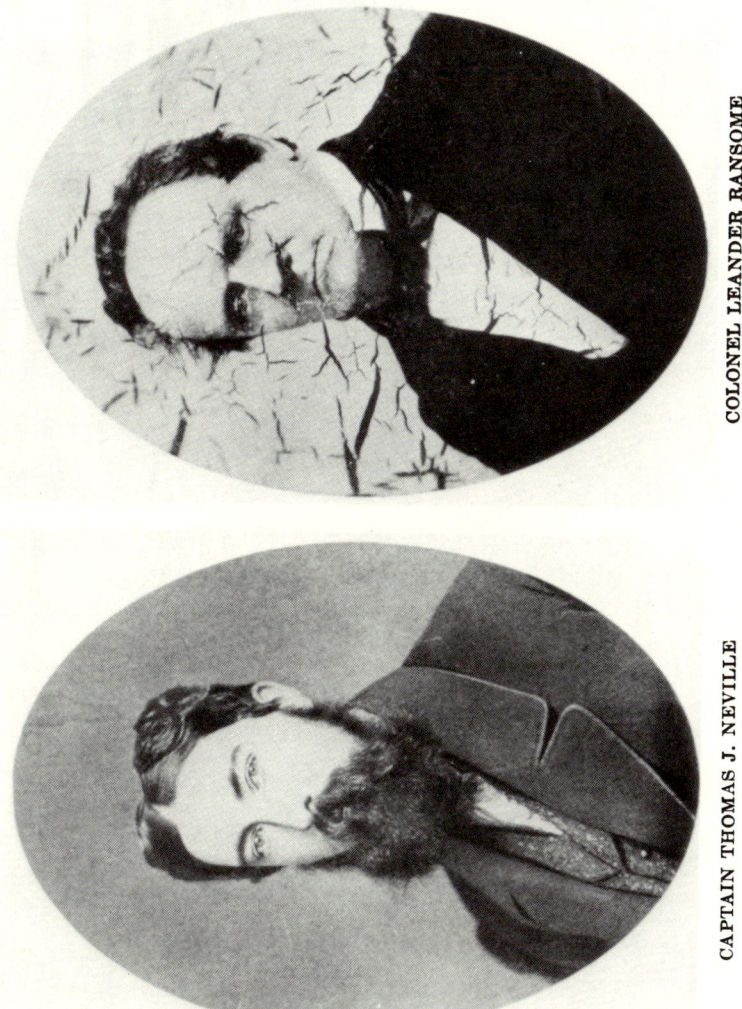

CAPTAIN THOMAS J. NEVILLE

COLONEL LEANDER RANSOME

fell, throwing its rider under the wheels, which passed over him. But he jumped to his feet, picked up the sword which had been knocked from his hand, and then fell full length on the ground.

The surgeon of the Hussars was near our carriage, and an officer on horseback dashed up, calling to him, 'Wilkin, Wilkin, at the left!' Dr. Wilkin galloped away toward the man on the ground. When he rose from beside the still figure, we knew that the man was dead.

The next day he called to see us and told us the soldier was so crushed, it seemed he must have been instantly killed. Yet he had risen to his feet and recovered his sword. We thought that to do this had been the message flashed from his brain when he lost his sword and just before the wheels were upon him; and the broken body had automatically obeyed. It was a strange thing to have seen.

With interruptions of visits to the Continent and England, our stay in Ireland lengthened, and before we left Dublin my marriage to Captain Thomas J. Neville, of the famous 'Buffs' Regiment, Her Majesty's Service, had taken place. I was a bride at sixteen. For our wedding-trip we made a carriage tour of the lovely land of County Wicklow. But for all the happiness I had found abroad I was not sorry when Captain Neville resigned from the Army and we turned toward America, my own country.

Most of my old Manhattan memories are centered in the New York Hotel, where we stopped on our return to America. It was on the west side of Broadway, covering the block between Washington Place and Waverly, and was then a fashionable hostelry much favored by Southerners. Mr. Hiram Cranston, the proprietor, catered to them, and the cuisine was noted for its Southern dishes. Potatoes and Irish potatoes were both on the menu, the former being the sweet variety, the only potatoes recognized in the South. White or Irish potatoes were there considered coarse food in a class with cabbage or turnips, gustatory indelicacies of that sort.

The dining-room of the New York held three prodigiously long tables, and meals were served at stated hours on 'the American plan.' We all dined in six parallel rows at six o'clock. I liked our table near the door, where we could see the diners enter. A handsomely gowned woman would be led the length of the room by a prideful head waiter, her skirts billowing about her and her progress like that of an ocean liner following a pilot boat. Family groups moved down the room in loose formation to be caught in a long line along one side of a table.

The entrance of Sir Roderick Cameron and his lady was always interesting. Sometimes he wore his kilts, and they had a little fling as he walked. Lady Cameron, who was an American, followed him with a sort of Amazon stride, her hands clasped low in front of her with falls of lace at the wrists of her sleeves.

Beckwourth, the explorer, lately returned from the Pacific Coast, sat near us and always ordered 'apple pie' for dessert. Near us also sat Ole Bull, a rugged old man still playing his violin at concerts. Frequently a waiter would appear unexpectedly with a bottle of champagne to fill our glasses and murmur as he did so, 'Compliments of Mr. So-and-So.' One looked across the room to smile at Mr. So-and-So and lift the glass in thanks. This was long a custom of public dining in America.

Peacock Alley, many years later in the Waldorf-Astoria, followed an innovation at the New York. A wide corridor extended the length of the old hotel on the parlor floor. There guests would promenade after dinner to greet friends and watch the passing show. The brothers Tucker one always met. They were handsome young gallants from Virginia who for some reason of family pride called themselves respectively Carroll Tucker and Tucker Carroll, but it was understood that Mr. Tucker Carroll was born Tucker.

Among celebrities one saw P. T. Barnum, still radiating his pride in having been Jenny Lind's manager. He had acquired something of the manner of an *impresario*, all, all flourishes. Jenny Lind stopped at the New York Hotel, but before we arrived had sailed for England with her new husband, Otto Goldschmidt, and I never heard her sing. There were stories that Barnum was in love with her, but I think they were 'publicity,' although it is true the Swedish Nightingale had a devastating charm. The Italian baritone of her concert troupe, Signor Belletti, has spent days in bed in his room at the New York, we were told, ill over his hopeless attachment for her. When she married her accompanist, he could sing with her no more, and returned to Italy. It is pleasant to know that in later years Signor Belletti recovered and was frequently a guest at the Goldschmidt home in London.

Washington Irving, then living at Riverdale, was sometimes the center of a group. He was punctilious in deportment and in dress, and had a touch of romance about him even then, in the twilight of his days. Every one had heard of his lost love, beautiful Matilda Hoffman, who had died long years before while they were betrothed. She was the daughter of a distinguished lawyer, Josiah Ogden Hoffman, in whose office Irving read law as a young man. Afterward, in San Francisco, we knew her relatives of a later generation, Judge Ogden Hoffman and his brother, Southard. Judge Hoffman never married, but his brother's daughter, May Hoffman, was one of the belles of San Francisco society with, doubtless, some of the graces of the lovely Matilda.

One shining night in New York I saw Rachel play 'Camille.' In London we had heard much of her and of her rival, Ristori, the Italian tragedienne who had lately made a conquest of Paris. Ristori I was not to see until her youth was past, but Rachel was still young, in all her illumined beauty when she came to New York to play at the Metropolitan Theater. She had crossed with her company on our old Pacific with Captain Nye, and we heard that a death on board during the voyage had greatly shaken her. She might have felt death touch her, too, in passing, for she was never again to play in France, and was already ill when she reached America. After the first performance of 'La Dame aux Camellias,' she wavered and would have fainted on the stage when she bowed to the applause, except that some one caught her.

RACHEL

I saw her also as Adrienne Lecouvreur, with her dark hair powdered and her dark eyes preternaturally brilliant in the white frame. It was one of her last performances. She went from New York to Philadelphia and there closed her engagement to sail for the West Indies in a vain search for health; and she returned to Europe to die. The greatest of all actresses, they said of her then. She was only thirty-seven when she died.

Once, years afterward in San Francisco, I asked Raphael Weill if he had seen Rachel in his youth in France; and he said but once as a boy, when he sat high in a gallery and she chanted the 'Marseillaise' at some celebration. She made a drama of the hymn, tragic and inspired, which none who heard her could ever forget. He remembered, as I did, the illumination of her beauty.

Broadway was a haphazard-looking street in the eighteen-fifties. Buildings were any height from one story to five and were set unevenly on the line of the sidewalk. Some of them far back with garden space in front were old residences converted to business uses. The white marble store of A. T. Stewart at Chambers Street was one of the finer structures. I remember the laces there, among them the rose-point *barbes* which Mother wore, caught with a brooch, like a jabot, at the neck of her gown. They really were flaring lace *barbes*, or beards, in effect. But they were not for youth. Point lace and diamonds were for older women.

A gold locket on a slender gold chain served often for my necklace with party gowns even after I was married.

Young girls wore only pearls for jewels; never an emerald or a ruby, and not on any account a diamond until the betrothal ring. For lace, Valenciennes was considered suitable; and in this sartorial review I may state that young women never wore black except for mourning, while older ladies, those past forty, wore only subdued colors and very often black, with their gray and lavender. Bottle green and garnet or plum color were permissible also before fifty. Once when I was a small girl, my grandfather brought for my mother from New York a black silk cloak lined with red. She was no more than twenty-seven years old at the time, but the red lining shocked her. It was too bright for a married woman! Of the myriad changes I've seen in the long years of my life, those of fashion sometimes seem stranger than all others.

It was long undecided whether we were to live in Washington or the West. Finally, my father decided on San Francisco, and there was much preparing for the long trip to join him. We were going to World's End and farewells of our friends were elaborate. My father's old friend, Judge Salmon P. Chase, came from Washington to wish us *bon voyage* and incidentally to save Mother from an absurd embarrassment. Some one with a low sense of humor had told us that food on the Panama steamers was unfit to eat: advised us to take a crate of chickens with all sorts of provender to be served on the voyage. So with many boxes, the chickens were ordered for delivery at the dock. Happily, Mother spoke of her foresight to Judge Chase, who was moved to bewildering mirth. 'My dear Mrs. Ransome,' he said, 'don't, on any account, take a crate of chickens! Meals on the Panama steamers are as good as those on the Collins liners. Your chickens would be the joke of the voyage' — and he roared again.

So the chickens remained at the market when we sailed on the George Law, May 21, 1856, for Panama *en route* to California. A little Irish maid we had brought from Dublin went with us, and altogether we were quite a party — my mother, my sister, and brother, with my husband and myself. Though we did not know it then, it was the week of excitement over the shooting of James King of William in San Francisco, and execution of his slayer by the Vigilance Committee, one of California's historic tragedies, which we heard of first at Acapulco when our steamer stopped there on the Pacific voyage north from Panama.

Captain Herndon, of the George Law, was an Annapolis man, and with all the gallantry of a navy officer gave us the daytime use of his cabin when we sailed into hot weather. Dr. Tenison and the first officer, Mr. Van Rensselaer, also helped to make this part of the voyage a happy memory.

At Kingston, Jamaica, we stopped to coal, and had time to drive out to the barracks where British officers commanded native soldiers. The black men in Her Majesty's uniform were, to me, irresistibly *opéra bouffe*, with the natty caps on their woolly heads. That evening we watched Negro women loading coal. Tubs of the glinting black pieces were carried on their heads in the light of flaring torches, and they sang as they worked, keeping up a rhythmic stamping of their bare feet. For background to this scene, weird and barbaric, a company of Negroes on shore danced a queer fandango, waving torches as they danced. Long after I had gone to bed, I heard the singing and the rhythmic tramp of feet.

The George Law carried 576 passengers bound for California, but of these only a few were in the first cabin. Dr. and Mrs. McNulty were fellow voyagers as were Major and Mrs. Mackall and their large family, going to the new army post at the Presidio of San Francisco. Dr. Hayne and his wife, the actress, Julia Dean Hayne, were on board, lately married; Señor and Señora Berreda were on their way to Chile, where he was to serve as Minister from Spain, and we parted with them at Panama. Long afterward Señora Berreda and her daughters came to live in San Francisco, where one of the daughters married Dr. Harry Sherman and another became Mrs. Willis Polk. But neither of these lovely girls was on the George Law. They were yet to be born.

Aspinwall on May 31. There we left the George Law at an unholy hour — half-past six in the morning — to find breakfast at the Howard House. A sad meal, gastronomically speaking, and we passed a sad morning waiting in the messy little town for our train. Two train-loads of passengers preceded us, but finally we climbed into the toy cars and at half-past twelve started across the Isthmus as the George Law fired a farewell salute. We were bound for Panama City on the west side of the Isthmus, there to embark on the steamer Golden Gate for San Francisco. It was a day of heavy heat. Natives all innocent of raiment stood in the doorways of their huts to watch us pass. The train wound through green country, the thick foliage of tropic forests brushing our windows.

The railway was a recent innovation. Travelers formerly crossed the Isthmus in mule trains, a long line making its way over narrow roads. We heard of bandits, and of children kidnaped and held for ransom by the natives. Two years earlier, in '54, Mrs. James Pelham, of Kentucky, crossed with her little daughters, Sally and Acanthus, to join Dr. Pelham in San Francisco; with them, two Negro servants, the children's nurse and this woman's son. Servants were few in California, and often Southern families would bring one or two slaves who were given their freedom and wages in the new country.

That year the railroad was completed to a point called Summit, about eleven miles from the city of Panama, and this distance was covered on mule-back. Sally Pelham rode with her nurse toward the end of the long procession, the boy following. Somewhere between Summit and Panama City the Negroes were stolen or enticed away by agents of a South American peonage system, who were always on the lookout for slaves from the States; and the little girl was taken with them to be held for ransom. Not until the ship's company reached Panama were they missed.

Only a few weeks before, a white child had been kidnaped from the mule train, and at Panama a native presented himself with an offer to 'find' her for five hundred dollars. Distracted parents paid the money and the child was safely returned. Without waiting for native volunteers, however, fellow travelers of Mrs. Pelham organized a search party and turned back to look for her little girl.

The steamer waited down the bay through long hours. Two shots, fired ten seconds apart, on shore, were to announce that the search was successful, and at dusk they sounded. The rescuers returned with the child unharmed. They had come upon her sitting in the doorway of a native hut, while the Negroes and their guards were gloriously inebriated within; too happily indifferent to interpose when she was gathered up and rushed away by the rescue party. Leaders of the band were absent, probably gone to Panama to plan overtures for ransom.

Bandits had often attacked the mule trains, but the railway baffled them. Presumably it was necessary to adjust methods to this new mode of travel and they were still studying the problem. So we reached the west shore safely. There the little steamer Tobega waited to convey us to the Golden Gate, anchored four miles down the bay in deep water. But the Tobega was soon crowded, and some of us preferred to make the trip on the baggage barge towed behind her. Seated comfortably on trunks, we watched the beauty of the harbor in the late afternoon light.

The water was a sheet of glass on which lay little islands covered with rich green foliage; here and there a white-sailed boat. We passed a small war sloop, the St. Mary, and the men of our company who had pistols were inspired to fire a salute. Cheers from the St. Mary's sailors, and

SALLY PELHAM
Who was kidnapped in crossing the
Isthmus of Panama in 1854

waving caps, answered it. Loaded pistols were here carried casually, it appeared. I felt the touch of the West.

The Golden Gate was a large boat, but so overcrowded that we were all desperately uncomfortable. Steamers from New Orleans, St. Thomas, and South American ports had all brought consignments of passengers to be stowed somewhere. There were two thousand souls on board, and so many children! — four hundred and fifty in the first cabin alone. Beds were made up anywhere at night — even on tables of the salon. No one had his fixed place at meals, but took the nearest seat, and this particular informality nearly caused a tragedy.

One night at dinner Dr. Hayne dropped into an empty chair at the head of a table. At once the purser dashed up and seized him by the shoulder. 'Here, you!' he roared, 'that's the captain's place.'

Dr. Hayne explained that he had not known this; had merely taken the first available seat. But the purser's fury consumed him. 'You lie!' he shouted.

There was a sudden, dead silence in the room. Dr. Hayne was a fiery Southerner. Slowly he picked up a knife from the table, his face white with anger. The purser stood transfixed. Mrs. Hayne rose and caught her husband's arm, pleading, 'Doctor! Doctor!'

In the tense pause that followed, Dr. Hayne discovered, as we all did, that the purser was intoxicated. The knife was flung back on the table and Dr. Hayne turned and walked out of the room. Some one led the purser away, and dinner proceeded.

A genuine tragedy a few days afterward shocked us all. One of the sailors who had disobeyed orders was confined in the boiler room for punishment and through some terrible oversight was left there too long. He was dying when they released him, and lived only a few moments, having literally been baked to death. Indignation against the ship's officers was very bitter and sailors were almost in a state of mutiny. The man was buried that evening and we all went on deck for the service. Trouble from the crew seemed imminent. But men passengers made an armed guard around the Captain while he read the burial service and the sailors looked on, silently hostile. When the body slid over the ship's side and splashed into the black waters below, the tension was broken and the men went peaceably back to their tasks.

The Gate's commander was an impervious soul. Nothing disturbed the equanimity of Captain Lapidge. He would promenade the deck wearing white kid gloves and smoking a long cigar, picking his way among the children as though they were inanimate obstructions, and in the same detached manner he officiated at the funeral of a little child who died during the voyage.

Two deaths and the profoundly moving burial at sea depressed us all, and I was so grateful for the happy, irrepressible wit of Rufus Lockwood. He was one of the young lights of the law in San Francisco, returning after a visit 'back East,' and he was frequently my partner at the endless games of whist and cribbage we played to pass the time. When we would all relieve our feelings over discomforts of the voyage, he would say solemnly, 'If ever I go to sea again, I hope to drown.'

He did go to sea again a few years later, and was drowned, one of those who went down on the Central America — our old George Law — when she foundered off Cape Hatteras. He had asked one of the officers if the ship was doomed. Assured that it was, he went to his stateroom and locked himself in, and so met death alone. Some of the passengers who took to the lifeboats were saved.

There is a happier story of him. In San Francisco it happened some trivial matter weighed on his mind, and one evening he walked out to Meiggs's Wharf to think it over. A friend who called to see him was told where he had gone, followed him, and tactfully suggested that, if he were brooding over money troubles, there was plenty of cash at his disposal on a loan. Lockwood laughed, drew a handful of gold twenty-dollar pieces from his pocket, and began to skate the coins over the water as boys do stones. 'I can keep that up as long as you can,' he said.

Eugene Delessert, a brother of Edouard Delessert, French explorer, was one of our fellow passengers. These two young Parisians, touched with *Wanderlust*, were nephews of Benjamin Delessert, financier and philanthropist of the Napoleonic era in France. They had come to America in the eighteen-forties and journeyed through Canada and British Columbia, sailing down the coast to California, where our friend had lived for several years. Early in the eighteen-fifties he had gone back to France and published his 'Voyages on Two Oceans,' and was now returning for a second visit to San Francisco, where we enjoyed his friendship until he once more departed for his beloved France, to remain. He had been a member of the first Vigilance Committee in San Francisco, and when at Acapulco we found California newspapers with accounts of the James King of William tragedy, he told us much of this organization which defied law to enforce it.

The Vigilantes were organized in '49 to suppress the Hounds, a band of lawless ruffians whose idea of an evening's pleasure was to terrorize peaceful citizens. They raided the Chileño quarter at the foot of Telegraph Hill, one night, killing and burning. The next day law-abiding men of the city met and formed a committee to deal with them. The Hounds were driven from the community, hundreds of crooked gamblers and cut-throats departing hastily for Mexico or down the coast anywhere.

Two years later, the Committee met again in the rooms at 215 Sacramento Street, in the small building known as Fort Gunnybags until it was burned in the fire of 1906; so named because the Vigilantes fortified themselves there with bags of sand. At the sessions of '51, four men were tried and condemned for murder by the Committee. Now again in 1856, it had been called together to see justice done for the shooting of King. Court trials were too often travesties, with packed juries.

James King of William, newspaper editor and one of the honored men of the community, had been shot down in Montgomery Street by James Casey, ex-convict, then serving as city supervisor, whose record King had pub-

ARRIVAL OF CASEY AND CORA AT THE VIGILANCE COMMITTEE ROOMS

A MEETING OF THE VIGILANCE COMMITTEE ON PORTSMOUTH SQUARE, 1856

THE LYNCHING OF CASEY AND CORA

lished. Public excitement was intense, and three thousand men answered the call of William T. Coleman for volunteer Vigilantes. They were backed by bankers of the city. Opposed to them were Law and Order men, organized several years before when the Vigilantes, essentially an emergency organization, threatened to function too long. Opposition in this case, however, seems to have been passive.

Casey was taken from the jail on Broadway to Fort Gunnybags on Sunday morning following the shooting. With him was taken Charles Cora, gambler, who killed Colonel William H. Richardson and was in jail awaiting trial. The prisoners' removal was profoundly dramatic and was watched in silence by thousands of citizens gathered on the roofs and on the slopes of Telegraph Hill. General William T. Sherman, with his Civil War fame still in the future, stood a spectator on the roof of the International Hotel. He was then employed in a San Francisco bank, and serving as an officer of the State Militia. With him that morning were Governor Johnson and Mayor Van Ness, and these three watched in silence the march of the Vigilantes. The Governor and the Mayor had made formal futile pleas that the law be allowed to take its course, and now stood aside.

A company of Vigilantes marched up Sacramento Street, turned into Kearney and drew up before the jail on Broadway. William T. Coleman and his aide Truet were driven up in a carriage, and, while their men stood at attention, mounted the iron stairway to the rather high entrance of the jail. The sheriff refused to admit them. They gave him five minutes. At the end of that time, he surrendered and the doors were opened. Coleman and Truet entered. When they emerged with the prisoners, a cheer started, but Coleman stilled it with a wave of his hand and in silence they were driven to Fort Gunnybags.

There the men were tried and sentenced to death; and were hanged ignominiously from a second-story window for every one to see. A beam from the roof served for gallows.

Much of all this we learned after we reached San Francisco, where Belle Cora, the gambler's widow, still enjoyed her notoriety. She was a woman of the gambling-halls who had taken Cora's name long before, and he married her an hour before his execution, in the room from which he stepped out the window to be hanged. A tragic business, although there seems to have been little sympathy for the bride. She wore mourning for months and promenaded Montgomery Street, where I saw her in her weeds.

CHAPTER II

On a windy day in June we sailed through the Golden Gate, every one on deck for the first glimpse of California. The Pacific trade wind whipped the waters, and the hills on either side were bare and brown. We had looked forward to green country after so many days at sea, not realizing that this was the dry season and that fresh greenery would come in fall and winter months to remain until summer again. Sand hills of San Francisco rolled away on our right, Telegraph Hill in bold relief at the turn of the bay shore line. Alcatraz rose high out of the water straight ahead, a rocky island fortress like a menace. It has since been graded many feet, and seems less ferociously on guard, although I thought this the most forbidding place I had ever seen. Not until the ship rounded the promontory of Telegraph Hill and I saw the long wharf extended out over the shallows, with animated people waving to welcome us, did I forget my disappointment in the thrill of arrival.

The coming of a steamer from Panama meant a holiday in San Francisco. The day a vessel was due there was a pervading expectancy. All eyes turned constantly to the lookout on Telegraph Hill, where a flag was run up as soon as she was sighted outside the Heads. As the ship sailed between the headlands to enter the bay, a gun was fired to announce her and the population trooped down to the wharf. That morning the wharf was crowded, and we finally saw my father frantically waving his hat as hundreds of others were doing in impersonal welcome. In a few moments he was on board and in a few more we were on shore.

It was an exciting scene, full of life and good-nature. Men and women stood or rushed about, called greetings or brandished papers with New York news. Some of the crowd followed bags of mail to the post-office. Ramshackle conveyances gathered passengers to drive them through unpaved streets into the city, straggling up Jackson, Commercial, Sacramento Streets — to the hills beyond — twenty dollars for a 'steamer load.' Crude as it all was, there was something vital and strong in this queer little city, and we liked it at once.

In a crazy hack — a four-wheeler driven by Mike Brannagan, afterward one of the town's notorious characters — we went to the International Hotel in Jackson Street. Bare white walls and black horsehair-covered furniture might have been discouraging, but after long weeks in ships' cabins, anything stationary seemed attractive.

That night at dinner we saw some of our fellow boarders. Meals at the International were on 'the American plan,' and not at all bad. Long tables were each adorned with a center line of pies, the line broken by an occasional jelly cake in a high glass dish with glass cover. Facing me sat a stout elderly woman in a low-necked red velvet dress with a diamond necklace and fingers literally covered with rings set with every variety of precious stone. It was the

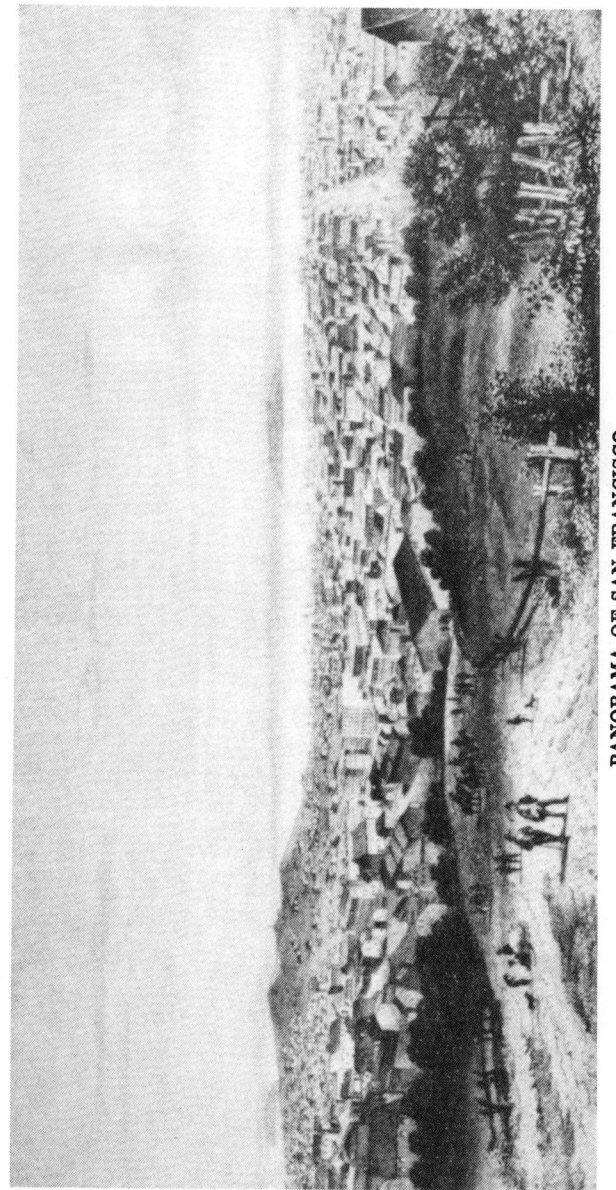

PANORAMA OF SAN FRANCISCO

custom for gamblers to invest their winnings in diamonds rather than hoard them in a bank. Diamonds could be seen, while bank savings were a total loss so far as display was concerned. The lady had been lucky — or perhaps it was her husband.

Next to the red velvet lady, a tall young man tilted back and forth in his chair while he waited for dinner to appear. The wait was long. Presently his chair came down with a snap and he reached across the table to take a slab of pie. Then he tilted back again and ate pie from his fingers until roast beef arrived. Who could have guessed that in time he would be a very courtly diplomat, the American Minister to Japan? He was the young John F. Swift.

General Sherman's West Point manners were a contrast. He was living somewhere in 'rooms' and dining at the International occasionally with his friend, Captain Folsom, who had been a classmate at the Point — a way of living followed by many men, so that the *table d'hôte* was quite a center of the city's life. General Sherman was then manager of the San Francisco branch of a St. Louis bank, having resigned from the Army, although he was an officer of the National Guard. He told us that Mrs. Sherman and their son had recently gone home to Ohio after several years of San Francisco. They had lived in Green Street, not very comfortably, and he had built a house on Rincon Hill shortly before her departure. But she longed for her old home and he had sent her back in charge of his friend, William Aspinwall, of New York, returning from a trip to the Coast. Not long afterward, General Sherman, convinced that San Francisco had no great business future, closed his bank and joined his family in the East. Commodore Sloat bought the Rincon Hill house.

Long afterward in Monterey, we saw 'Sherman's rose tree,' and the ancient señorita said to have been his sweetheart when as a young lieutenant he had been stationed at the Monterey army post, in '47 and '48. The señorita was reticent and very old when we met her, but the rose tree still bloomed. According to the legend, she and the young officer had planted it together.

The day after our arrival, we explored downtown streets with Mr. Delessert for guide. I was keen to see Fort Gunnybags, with all its tragic associations and the implacable power it held over the city. For years after we came to San Francisco, the mere existence of the Vigilance Committee put the fear of law and retribution into the hearts of miscreants, or would-be miscreants thus transformed into orderly citizens; or abandoned to their ways, seeking more friendly fields.

Gunnybags was just a step from the International, and we turned in the little side doorway to climb a narrow flight of stairs. The judicial chamber looked like a country courthouse. On one wall hung a long blue satin banner lettered in gold — a gift to the Vigilance Committee from 'Ladies of Trinity Church' for its efforts toward 'the protection of life and property of citizens and residents of the city of San Francisco.' Strange evidence of the Vigilantes' high place in public regard.

On Kearney Street facing the Plaza, now Portsmouth

Square, 'El Dorado' fascinated me. It was the most famous of the gambling-halls, a four-story brick building with an iron balcony across the front and 'El Dorado' in tall letters of gold. The upper stories were rooms occupied by miners and gamblers and women of the halls. The lower floor held the gilded splendor of the gambling-palace, where fortunes were won and lost at roulette, poker, and monte.

Before its doors and along Kearney Street in front of the adjoining Hall of Justice — once the Jenny Lind Theater — lounged gamblers in their distinguishing attire. A gambler in those days invariably wore a drooping mustache, wide felt hat, and Prince Albert coat, open to show a cable of gold stretched across a gorgeous waistcoat, to serve for watch-chain. Diamond shirt-studs flashed above the waistcoat of velvet or brocade, and usually a large solitaire was worn on the right hand in a perpetual state of display.

In the eighties it happened that we knew Bill Briggs, successful professional gambler of that later time who came to Shasta Springs for summer visits. Conservative guests avoided him, but others found him an engaging person, devoted to his small son and talking of everything but cards. His profession he left at home, and nothing could persuade him into a game while he sojourned among us. But he wore his mustache and wide-awake hat and the largest solitaire diamond I have ever seen in a ring. When he died, he left a fortune to the little son, then at a military school, and a reputation for square dealing.

While the taste of the gamblers was for diamonds, that

of miners ran to enormous gold watches, the larger the better. They carried them attached to the conventional gold cables stretched across the waistcoat when arrayed in the urban splendor of boiled shirts for the Kearney Street parade; otherwise, carefully encased in chamois skin bags in the trousers pockets. Tucker, the jeweler, had a card in his window in Clay Street which read, 'One pound watches for sale here.' Undoubtedly they weighed all of that.

Shops were the happiest surprise. Low frame buildings were filled with lovely silks and laces from Paris and the smartest of bonnets. San Francisco shops have always been remarkable for the taste and richness of their wares and San Francisco women have always dressed well.

Mr. Delessert's mind was full of historical facts. Crossing the Plaza, he led us to the northwest corner, where in 1846 Commodore Sloat had raised the American flag before the house of the Spanish *comandante* — being under the impression that the United States was then at war with Mexico. The colorful pagoda of the Chinese telephone exchange stands there now, but when Mr. Delessert led us to the spot there were only ruins of the old adobe house built in 1776. It had been destroyed by one of the many fires which swept over the flimsy little city in the early years when water was scarce and the trade winds whipped the flames to their will. However, we regarded the ruins, and then turned down Washington Street past a line of Chinese shops, restaurants, and saloons, to Kearney and so northward to Broadway to see the new brick jail. A narrow iron stairway curved upward from the street to its high entrance where a few weeks before William T. Coleman had stood demanding delivery to the Vigilantes of the prisoners, Casey and Cora.

Just east of the jail in the lee of Telegraph Hill was the Chileño quarter. This had been Yerba Buena, the original settlement founded by Anza, the Spanish explorer who marched north from Arizona with his colonists in 1776. With him came the three priests, Father Junípero Serra, Father Crespi, and Father Palou, who established missions along the way. Father Palou lived longest at Mission Dolores, then across the sand dunes from Yerba Buena and now in a residence district of the city.

Yerba Buena, named for a 'good herb' — sweet mint, it was, which grew on the hillside — had been on the shore of a little cove of the bay, already in '56 filled in and built over. We thought it might have been about at Jackson and Montgomery Streets that Richard Dana, doing his 'Two Years Before the Mast,' stepped ashore in 1838 and met William Richardson, the first American resident of the place which was to be called San Francisco; the same Richardson lately shot to death by Cora, the gambler, who was hanged for his crime by the Vigilantes.

It was an alpine climb to the crest of Russian Hill, named for visitors who came down from Alaska early in the century and established a settlement at Fort Ross, north of San Francisco Bay, where the Russian River still flows. But at sunset the climb up the Hill from Broadway was worth while. Flimsy wooden staircases made it possible, and once on the crest the view was magnificent. One looked far across the dunes to the Golden Gate with sand and waters reflecting the red-gold light. At Fort Point, jutting out into the waters of the Gate, the flag flew over the Presidio, a little settlement founded by Anza and now the United States Army post. Officers' cottages faced the parade ground, at the head of which a low whitewashed adobe building gleamed — the old house of the *comandante* converted into an officers' club. Sand hills rolled away, beyond. I think it was in the eighteen-seventies that the Presidio hills were planted with their forests of eucalyptus and pines.

South across sand dunes was the white building of Mission Dolores — the church of St. Francis d'Assisi in the little Spanish village of Dolores.

Picturesque and interesting it all was, but we saw none of the perilous Wild West that Jack and I, at least, had anticipated. Back in 1850, San Francisco had been called 'the wickedest city in the world.' In my belief this was an unmerited distinction. Singapore, Shanghai, and Port Said surpassed it in downright evil, but lawless it surely had been before the Vigilantes. They had done their house-cleaning well, however, and only once did we see a flash of the old Dangerous Dan spirit.

It was on an evening soon after our arrival. We were sitting in our rooms when the sound of commotion in the street below startled us and we rushed to windows with the thought of two-gun men abroad terrorizing the town.

Nothing of that sort, however. We saw only excited citizens haranguing each other. Then we saw that one had fallen. They were carrying him into a doorway. He must be wounded, not dead, or they would have left him where he lay.

Father went downstairs to learn details and found his friend, Dr. R. P. Ashe, in the thick of the excitement. Judge Terry had stabbed a man, had been arrested by the Vigilantes, and taken to Fort Gunnybags. If the man died, he would be hanged — a judge of the Supreme Court! When we heard this, my wildest dream of the West seemed justified.

We had met Judge and Mrs. David Terry at the hotel, and for all his judicial eminence he seemed a stormy man, one who had for me a disquieting presence, with his tall, ungainly figure and restless eyes under shaggy brows. Before his California days he had been a 'dangerous man' in Texas. Mrs. Terry was a gentle little Southern woman and for her we felt deep sympathy in this crisis.

The day following, Dr. Ashe, then United States Navy agent, called and told us what had happened. He and Judge Terry, both members of the Law and Order Association opposed to the Vigilantes, had been sitting in his office when a man sought by the Vigilance Committee rushed in to demand protection. With him they started down Jackson Street toward the Armory of the National Guard where he could be safely held until the law considered his case. In front of the Hotel they met Hopkins, sheriff of the Vigilantes, with some of his men. Hopkins stepped forward and there was some altercation over the fugitive. Terry drew his gun. Hopkins seized it. Dr. Ashe cried 'Don't shoot' which Terry mistook for 'I'm shot' and believing Dr. Ashe had been attacked drew his knife and slashed. Hopkins fell and his men took the Judge into custody. If Hopkins should die, he would be hanged without a doubt. Here were elements of the wildest possible West. The whole town was keyed to a bewildered sense of outrage, yet never against the Vigilantes. In a few days the strain was broken. To the profound relief of the community and to Judge Terry, one safely assumes, Hopkins was out of danger and the prisoner at Fort Gunnybags was released. Poor little Mrs. Terry was nearly wrecked by the ordeal. She died a few years later, but Judge Terry pursued a long and stormy way to his own violent end.

The street scene was endlessly diverting and the city enchanted us from the first. In spite of shanties and unpaved streets, plank sidewalks and swirling dust, and a general look of having been hurriedly thrown together, it was metropolitan. Nothing small-town about it, but a touch of Old-World sophistication, and that charm I cannot describe, a prevailing gayety of spirit, youth in everything.

Street crowds were a collection of types in assorted costumes. Richly gowned women in velvet cloaks or black lace shawls of Broadway fashion; well-dressed men in light trousers and Prince Albert coats who might have stepped out of the Astor House; miners like stage characters; Mexicans with scarlet sashes, striped serapes slung over the shoulder; Spanish women in long, flaring skirts or cotton print, thickly pleated; and in Washington Street, where a row of Chinese shops faced the Plaza, meek-looking Orientals in blue blouses padded back and forth in their soft slippers, their queues swinging behind them. Gentlemen were wearing shovel beards a great deal, and wide felt hats which they swept off with a flourish to greet a lady. I might have forgotten what the well-dressed man was wearing in 1856 if I had not lately read a letter written that year by my father's friend, Judge Shafter, to his wife in Vermont. She was sailing with her children to join him in San Francisco; he informs her that he will be at the head of the pier when the steamer arrives, 'clad in light pants, buff vest, and snuff-colored frock coat with a broad-brimmed white sombrero.'[1]

Foreign-looking sailors who swaggered up from the wharves added their color to the scene, and there were many uniforms worn by officers from the military post at the Presidio, or the navy station on Mare Island, and from visiting battleships in the harbor. I have always regretted that I did not see the young Pierre Loti when he came to San Francisco as junior officer on a French warship arrived from Tahiti. He visited the Chinese Theater in Washington Street and there had a gorgeous inspiration of which he has somewhere written.

A long bench in front of him held a row of solemn Chinamen absorbed in the drama while their queues hung behind

[1] *Life, Diary, and Letters of Oscar Lovel Shafter.* Privately printed.

them. Loti's idea was to tie the queues together, two and two, and then slip out in the darkness. He may have done so; there is no evidence to the contrary. The thought of it has always evoked for me a subsequent scene of indescribable chaos.

We went, one day, down to Long Wharf, now in '56 part of the filled-in land which extended the city's water-front eastward from Montgomery Street. It was strange to see old ships built into the city streets; derelicts that had been left where they lay in the mud flats when the land was filled in, waves and lapping waters forever lost to them. The old Niantic of many voyages, perilous and historic, was a thriving hotel until fire destroyed it. Others were saloons and restaurants. I remember a sign hung from the prow of one: 'Coffee and doughnuts, $1.00. A square meal, $1.50. A regular gorge, $2.50.'

Probably the proprietor was some gay-hearted youth restauranting temporarily. We afterward knew a banker who had sold blackberries in the streets of Sacramento in '51. He had arrived with another adventurous youth from a New England college, and their first business venture was the blackberries picked from bushes growing wild along the Sacramento River. Newspaper cornucopias filled sold for a dollar apiece.

Nearly all the blithe young men we met had like adventures to relate. One had come out from Harvard in '49 to practice law, and had encountered periods of financial stress. In one of these he decided to sell his wardrobe which included an evening suit. Things went at top prices.

VIEW FROM STOCKTON STREET IN 1856

Customers called in numbers. But no one wanted the 'claw-hammer.' It was left on his hands, so he wore it himself; disposed of all the other things and serenely went about his daily affairs in the sleek formality of black broadcloth, cut swallow-tail.

So quickly had the tent city grown, that in '56 the population was about seventy thousand and there were stable, handsome buildings here and there in the business district. The Parrott Block had lately been built at the corner of Montgomery and California Streets, where it stood in a solid, eternal sort of way, through the earthquake and fire of 1906. It was torn down only a few years ago to make way for a skyscraper, and if the men who demolish buildings have any sentiment, this was surely sad work. It was for so long a landmark, and into its building had gone so much of the dauntless spirit of the pioneers. The most accessible granite quarry in 1852 was in China, so John Parrott, the banker, sent to China for the gray granite of which his building was constructed. It was there cut into square blocks, each block marked with a Chinese character to designate its place in the structure, and so came across the Pacific. With it came Chinese laborers to put the building together, and a popular pastime of '52 was to stand and watch the coolies in their native garb and bare feet, silently matching blocks.

When it came time to return calls, Mother and I started out in Mike Brannagan's hack. It was proper then to spend not less than ten minutes with each hostess, and no ten minutes could have been so totally unproductive of anything but ennui. We sat on black haircloth and talked of the weather; of Dr. Scott's sermon on Sunday, or new silks at Belloc Frères'. Black haircloth was the prevailing fabric for parlor upholstery; red plush had not yet arrived. It was slippery stuff that kept one sliding and readjusting in a restless manner most inimical to poise. I'm sure it was a black haircloth chair in which the old man in one of Dickens's novels sat; the one of whom some one was always saying, 'Do pull Father up.'

Parlors of the period were ghastly places, anyway. No room could have been less suited to human habitation or use. I knew one — rather elegant it was — that had a black velvet carpet, patterned with deathly gray roses; black horsehair furniture, and a black-walnut center table with wax flowers under a glass globe. Perfect setting for the family funerals; and I believe on these melancholy occasions alone the 1860 parlor came into its own — really shone. I could fancy it waiting in grim static patience for its day.

Who that ever knew them could forget the what-nots? — graduated sets of shelves made to fit in corners, the top shelf just large enough to support proudly a polished sea-shell. And center-table books with heavy gilt-edge pages and steel engravings. They were placed at careful angles not to be disturbed. 'Wreath of Immortelles' was a favorite title, the 'immortelles' being sentimental selections of prose and verse suitable for the center table, not at all for reading.

These things persisted, I think, until the eighties in America, and their passing is one of many marks of progress I have seen in my life. It is always dangerously controversial to compare morals and ethics of the generations. Those of the eighteen-hundreds may have been better than those of today; they may possibly have been worse. But on the advancement of the race in matters of dress, common-sense, and things like what-nots, there is simply no argument.

We used Mike Brannagan's hack a great deal because the 'going' was bad for pedestrians and there were no street-cars. A bus-line that extended across Stockton Street from North Beach, down Kearney and Third Streets, eventually to South Park, was much patronized. The fare was twenty-five cents for one block or the whole distance. We had very few dimes to make change in those days, no nickels, and never a penny. I remember little silver five-cent pieces that were curios, not taken seriously at all: half-dimes, they were called. No one paid the slightest attention to nickels for years after they appeared; and it was in 1912, I think, that a Market Street department store placed pennies in circulation in California, with a campaign of marking prices and giving coppers in change, that was unpopular for months.

A quarter or less was always thrown off on a bill. 'Never mind the bits,' a tradesman would say cheerfully: a 'bit' was an eighth part of a dollar. Twenty-five cents was always 'two bits' as fifty cents was 'four bits,' and seventy-five, 'six bits,' in everyday parlance.

When street-cars arrived the fare was ten cents. It is a matter of transportation history that San Francisco had the first cable cars, invented by one of her citizens, A. S. Halladie. The old Clay Street line from a turn-table at Kearney Street to one at Van Ness Avenue was built in the seventies. There was then the most engaging little line of balloon horse-cars out Pacific Avenue from Van Ness to Fillmore Street, much of the way through a waste of sand with blue lupine bushes, now all built over with beautiful homes. The cars were perfectly round, small, with mushroom roofs. Inside, a single seat extended all the way round. The fare was ten cents, children five, and infants free. No conductor; instead, a coin box at the window to a little platform where the driver stood. He would tie his reins about the brake and let the horse jog along while he made change.

But in the fifties we had only the bus-lines. One followed the Mission Road to Mission Dolores in the shadow of Twin Peaks. The old adobe church where Father Junípero Serra said mass in 1777 still stands, but the most enchanting and mournful little cemetery, planted with weeping willows, has been partly removed. There we found graves of some of the Spanish dons of a past century. Don Luis Arguello, Spanish Governor of California, was buried there; and his not distant neighbor, lately arrived, was James Casey, hanged by the Vigilantes.

Mission Dolores had seen a strange wedding in 1852 when Lola Montez, famous in London and Paris for her beauty, a king's favorite who had been called the 'Uncrowned Queen of Bavaria,' was married there to Pat Hull, San Francisco newspaper editor, late of Ohio. They met on the voyage to California when Lola, discouraged by London failures after her downfall in the Bavarian Revolution, with King Ludwig's favor lost, had left Europe in a sort of flight. She had danced in New York and then in New Orleans with indifferent success, and was in flight again from unhappiness, planning a tour of the world when she encountered the jovial Pat Hull whose keen mind and careless, easy ways appealed to her tired spirit. They were married soon after reaching San Francisco, but of course it couldn't last. Two years later, the restless lady sailed for Australia, leaving her husband — he was her third — to his editorial consolations.

We heard much light gossip of her; there had been no scandals in her San Francisco days. Every one who had seen her spoke of her startling beauty; a perfect figure, smooth brown hair, magnolia skin, and large gray eyes filled with expression. She would promenade Montgomery Street in a short black velvet jacket over a flaring skirt of silk, a broad hat with black lace falling over the brim. Word would go down the street, 'Lola Montez,' and every one stared in the most discreet manner possible. It was known that she had once struck her riding-whip across the face of a man too bold in his admiration.

Living in Stockton Street as Mrs. Hull, playing cards with Pat Hull's friends and seeing an occasional stray figure from her old world may have amused her for a while. She danced, too, for a brief season in the theater. But presently it all must have seemed insupportably dull, remembering her palace in Munich and the adulation of kings and princes; men like Liszt, Théophile Gautier, and Dumas who were her friends, and all the luxury of other days. At any rate, she suddenly packed her trunks one day, to sail away for Australia, and Pat Hull rarely spoke of her afterward.

Lola had a vivacious mind. I have still a rusty little book, 'The Arts of Beauty or Secrets of a Lady's Toilet. By Madame Lola Montez,' which reflects her wit. It was published in 1856, in the last unhappy period of her life. By that time Lola's opinion of men had fallen very low, or so one must assume reading 'Hints to Gentlemen on the Art of Fascination' with which her opus ends.

The beauty secrets are graciously revealed, but each of the fifty rules for gentlemen who would be successful gallants glitters with sarcasm like cut steel. Rule twenty is a sample:

Dance with all the might of your body and all the fire of your soul in order that you may shake all melancholy out of your liver; and you need not restrain yourself with the apprehension that any lady will have the least fear that the violence of your movements will ever shake anything out of your brains.

Less brilliant than Lola Montez, but still a flashing figure in the San Francisco scene, was Adah Isaacs Menken, who came from New Orleans to play 'Mazeppa' at Maguire's Opera House and was the toast of the town in the sixties. An indifferent actress, she had a lovely face, with masses of red-gold hair, and the figure of a Greek dancer. With her beauty she had, too, a melancholy charm alluring as music. I think it was a natural mood and not in the least induced by tribulation, but when she went to London, it so affected the young Swinburne that he wrote his poem, 'Our Lady of Sorrows' for her.

'Mazeppa' was melodrama with a grand climax that revealed the actress in a ride of death. In scant array she lay strapped to the back of a white horse which raced across the stage and up a zigzag mountain-path against the back-drop. Her gorgeous hair swept out behind her, and she was a magnificent picture. Audiences went wild over her, and thrilled young ladies who rarely met people of the theater would ask more privileged men friends, 'What is she like off the stage?'

She was a gentle young adventuress, it appeared, given to writing poetry. In London she published 'Infelicia,' a thin book of fragile verses Swinburne had praised. San Francisco friends were amazed when she married a pugilist, Johnny Heenan from Benicia, to whom poetry must have been forever a closed book, although he had his own distinction as 'the Benicia Boy of the Ring.' He went to England with Menken and returned without her.

In Paris, Menken was noted as an equestrienne. There she won the friendship of Dumas and his circle, ever cordial to beauty; and she died there while she was still young. On her gravestone in Père la Chaise is carved an appealing line, 'Thou Knowest.'

The white horse, named Mazeppa, Adah Menken left to one of our bachelor friends when she departed California. He rode it daily to his office in Sansome Street until one day it disappeared — stolen from the hitching-post. It was traced to a ship that had sailed for Australia that morning, and there was nothing to be done about it after that.

Hitching-posts were usually safe places to leave valuable possessions. There was a careless, common honesty in early days, after law-breakers were suppressed by the Vigilantes; an accepted standard of fair play in everything. A shooting affray would be preceded by a call, 'Defend yourself!' from the aggressor. The bitterness of feeling against Charles Cora, who was hanged with Casey by the Vigilantes, was due in part to the fact that Colonel Richardson was unarmed when attacked. Cora had approached him in Sansome Street with the cry, 'Defend yourself!' Colonel Richardson drew back and answered, 'I am not armed. Would you shoot an unarmed man?' And Cora had shot him down.

But of hitching-posts: It is recorded that a man carrying a bag of gold dust, valued at several thousand dollars, met a friend in Montgomery Street and was invited to enter a saloon for refreshment. 'Leave your bag outside,' the friend suggested. So the man placed his bag on the square top of a hitching-post and went in and had a drink. When he came back for the bag, there it rested on the post with a sheet of paper over it, and on this a silver dollar with the written words, 'To help along.'

Sunday was a sort of fête day, with shops all open and gambling-halls going merrily; a general air of festivity. Theaters gave matinée and evening performances; but these and the fashionable street promenade of week-days were on Sundays given over to the unfashionable element — miners, gamblers, and ladies of the dance-halls.

This promenade, where on other days one met friends and loitered through the shops, extended from Sutter Street along Montgomery to Clay, up Clay to Kearney Street and across the Plaza to Washington, and so up to Stockton Street, where were the city's most attractive homes. I remember the small château with cupola and mansard roof built by Captain Roberts at Stockton and Washington Streets, with high iron fence about the garden, where iron dogs stood guard. He was a retired sea captain, the father of Theodore Roberts, afterward famous as an actor and star of the Hollywood firmament. I recall very well the sympathy felt for the Roberts family when young Theodore 'went on the stage.' It wasn't exactly a disgrace, but it was very sad.

Along this route were the shops of Belloc Frères, the Ville de Paris, and at Sacramento and Kearney Streets, Davidson and Lane's, where Raphael Weill, a handsome black-eyed French boy whom every one liked, was clerk. In time he owned Davidson and Lane's and later founded the White House, which was then the 'A. T. Stewart's' of San Francisco, and became a sort of social rendezvous on shopping mornings when it stood at Post and Kearney Streets. His career as a merchant was unique, I think. He became a patron of the arts, a connoisseur and an epicure whose dinners, given in the Red Room of the Bohemian Club, were a gastronomic education. During a long life in San Francisco, he was host to many of the celebrities who came that way. When they were dined by the Bohemian Club, he arranged the menu. There was a breakfast for Bernhardt back in the lithe, slender days when 'An empty cab drew up at the curb and Sarah Bernhardt stepped out of it'; a dinner for Coquelin the Elder, who brought beautiful Jane Hading from Paris to play Molière in Mission Street. Wines for this event were imported from France weeks before the guest of honor reached California. Dinners for Modjeska and her husband, Count Bozenta; for Paderewski, for Ysaye — this followed by a reception for the violinist in the old club at Post Street and Grant Avenue, when Horace Platt, the club's president, made a speech and said he was sorry that there wasn't a chair for every one in the crowded rooms, but that there were, nevertheless, three cheers for every one, which was accounted a happy specimen of Horace Platt's well-known wit. Anyway, carefully translated, it made Ysaye relax his heavy features into a smile.

All of these bring to mind another Red Room dinner of a much later time for which Raphael Weill directed the menu, when Melba was guest of honor and young Joe Thompson, Kathleen's brother, made a memorable speech. He had lately been appointed a member of the jinks, or entertainment committee of the club, with the duty of arranging programs and persuading talented members to perform, and in his speech told of difficulties he encountered. He said that while men who could sing were all willing to render solos, he found that none was willing to

RAPHAEL WEILL AS CHEF OF THE BOHEMIAN CLUB
From a painting in the Club by Joe Strong

sing in the chorus as an inglorious member of the *ensemble*. Collecting a chorus was desperate work. He'd reached a point, he said, where meeting strangers he'd discover himself appraising their 'jinks' possibilities. 'So,' he concluded, 'when I met our charming guest of honor this evening [here he bowed at Madame Melba, acknowledging a lovely lady] when I met Madame Melba this evening, my first thought was, "Can she sing? If so, will she consent to sing in the chorus?"'

The post-office, at Washington and Stockton Streets in the fifties was the turning-point for promenaders. It was in the former residence of W. D. M. Howard, where Colonel Geary, as postmaster, had introduced order and efficiency. Before his day, an engaging informality had prevailed in the handling of mail. One postmaster, who found it too confining to sit at a window, would fill his hat with letters and shut up shop. Then, as he met the addressees in his walks abroad, he would remove his hat and deliver the mail.

Our Eastern post was, of course, several weeks coming to us by way of Panama, so we thrilled to important events of the world nearly a month late. In 1860, this time was shortened by the Pony Express, with a proper increase of postage to five dollars a letter. The ride from Sacramento to St. Joseph, Missouri, two thousand miles, was covered in nine days. Business men could send letters to associates in 'St. Joe,' who would telegraph messages to the East for them, and they were the principal patrons of the service.

The day the first Pony mail started East was an exciting one in Sacramento, and my father, with many other San Francisco men, went up to the Capital to see the service inaugurated. At a given hour the slim young rider — his name was Henry Roff — swung into his saddle, in front of the express office, and at a signal was off like a shot while cannon boomed a parting salute and the citizenry cheered. They were courageous knights, these young riders of the Pony Express, who went unarmed to save weight for their horses — game little mustangs that would sometimes drop from exhaustion when the run of ten miles, at an unbroken gallop, was ended.

It has often been told how the riders would call their coming when they approached a station, where horses were changed. The fresh mount would be rushed out to stand ready at the side of the road and, without breaking speed, a rider would swing from one horse to the other and dash on. I have seen the mail start from the Sacramento office. The bags were slung across the saddle and the spirited, intelligent horse stood ready to go like a shot the instant his rider's foot touched the stirrup. Irresistibly thrilling, to see the sudden dash down the street and know that the mail thus starting went with unbroken speed across two thousand miles of wilderness.

One of the popular Sunday resorts of San Francisco was Russ Gardens on the Mission Road; never fashionable, but the setting for all national celebrations. National groups were clannish. At the Irish picnic on St. Patrick's

Day, for example, only sons and daughters of Erin were gathered. Caledonian picnics, and German picnics, French celebrations on Bastile Day, and Spanish *fiestas* were given there, and the races never mixed. But on Fourth of July they were all represented to hear the Declaration of Independence read and enjoy the spectacle of fireworks in the evening. Admission Day, to commemorate California's entrance to the Union as a State, in 1850, found them all loyal Californians at a grand celebration in Russ Gardens. Henry Russ made a fortune out of the resort and built the Russ House at Bush and Montgomery Streets, long the favorite hotel of miners and ranchers.

Farther out on Mission Road was 'The Willows.' Here there was a zoo, with bear pit and a pond of clamorous sea lions among the attractions. The gardens were rather pretty with lawns and flowers and a little winding stream fringed with willows, which was to be their destruction. In the winter of '61 there were extraordinarily heavy rains, and they flooded the little winding stream until it washed away the gardens, and they were never rebuilt. But before this catastrophe, 'The Willows' on Sunday afternoons was crowded with a cosmopolitan collection of visitors, most of whom had attended church that morning.

For, in spite of Sunday festivities, San Francisco was never a godless city. There were always churches. People worshiped in consecrated tents before buildings were erected. But the godless element was naturally most conspicuous, and a certain *insouciant* flourish to the ungodliness lent it grace. Not unnaturally, writers of romance have gone to the gilded palaces of sin, so called, for drama and color in the West, rather than to a lecture on Seneca at the First Unitarian Church, for example. Yet Thomas Starr King gave weekly lectures at the church on the old philosophers and they were attended by large and attentive audiences. Much of their success was due to the young clergyman's magnetic personality, but the fact remains that many San Francisco citizens passed evenings with Socrates and Goethe, while others made history and fiction in the gilded palaces. There was a certain happy leavening influence of each element upon the other.

Dr. King was a fascinating speaker, a young Boston clergyman who in the three short years of his residence placed the stamp of his eager young personality on California history. In '60 and '61, when there was talk of California's secession from the Union, he traveled through the State making speeches of loyalty to the Government; and his impassioned patriotism won the day for the Union in San Francisco when civil war was declared. He it was who organized the California branch of the Sanitary Committee which contributed over a million dollars of the five millions subscribed by the country. Bret Harte was one of his devoted friends.

The little iron church of Trinity and the village meeting house effect of Grace Church dated back to '49. The 'Iron Church' in Pine Street above Montgomery had actually been built of sheet-iron when lumber was scarce and bricks worth their weight in silver. When new Trinity was built at Post and Powell Streets, Bishop Kip desired to introduce there a vested choir, as proper in the largest Episcopal Church in the State. It lasted just one Sunday, for the following morning an irreverent press referred to 'Kip's Melodeon and Performing Boys,' and the name caught. The melodeon was abandoned until long afterward a vested choir was successfully established in St. Luke's.

We were members of Grace Church, and followed it from the meeting-house to the brick cathedral on the steep California Street declivity of Nob Hill, where standing above it one looked through open arches of the belfry to the bay and Contra Costa Hills far beyond. Below it on California Street was 'old St. Mary's,' with its tall steeple, standing at the gateway to Chinatown, one of the surviving landmarks of the old city.

At the southern base of Nob Hill rose another tall steeple, that of the First Congregational Church, where Dr. Stone preached for many years. Both Dr. and Mrs. Stone were important figures in the San Francisco scene, and the church was for long a significant influence. Mrs. Stone was a lady of interesting ancestry, descended from Dr. Bertody, distinguished Persian physician of the eighteenth-century who was summoned to France by Louis XV. He married in Paris and founded a family which in time migrated to America. Mrs. Stone and her sons were all distinguished-looking, with the faint print of the Orient in their finely featured faces.

We found, as others did, countless discomforts in the

new city, but no one brooded over them. San Franciscans have always had a gift for taking life lightly, whatever it brings. I don't mean frivolously, but with an unaffected lightness of spirit, as they took the disaster of earthquake and fire in 1906. In the fifties we laughed at amusing makeshifts for what were everyday comforts 'back East.'

There were the board-paved streets that developed wicked slivers, fatal to flounces. Once in Sacramento Street, my skirt caught on one and yards of lace were ripped from the dust ruffle. I had to tear it off and leave it there.

There was the limited water supply. Baths in hotels were twenty-five cents apiece extra on the bill, and for a large family this could amount to an imposing sum. In these early days most of the city's water was brought across the bay from Sausalito in boats built for the purpose, and was sold at three dollars a barrel in the streets. The water-cart man called at houses to replenish barrels as the ice-man calls with ice.

For illumination, there were only candles and oil lamps in the residence district. But in hotels we found gas, and in the theaters were gas footlights with shields like a row of scallops across the stage. An actress watched her skirts when she took a call, and there had been terrifying accidents when flaring tarlatan drifted into the lights.

And we knew the dread of fire. Already there had been what the newspapers called disastrous conflagrations when blocks of tent houses and wood shanties had burned away and the whole city had been menaced; so that the sound of the fire-bell filled people with alarm. It was rung from a tower of the City Hall on the Plaza, where the fire lookout was stationed. A man in the tower watched night and day, and whenever a suspicious cloud of smoke or flash of flame appeared, he guessed the locality and tapped out on his bell the number of the ward. Each ward had an engine-house and a volunteer company of firemen, who ran from their homes or business to answer the calls. Most of the young men of the city belonged to some company and always 'ran with the machine.' Every citizen knew the ward numbers and could locate the fire when the taps sounded.

The history of the San Francisco fire department is filled with romance and adventure, and no one could speak of it without recalling Lily Hitchcock. She was the daughter of a retired army officer, a flashing, brilliant girl, who for some favor or service was made honorary member of one company. She always wore her badge, proudly pinned to her ball gowns, as it was to her street dress, and she never failed to answer a call for her company, if she had to leave a dance to do it. Lily Hitchcock married Howard Coit, caller of the Stock Exchange in the sixties, and afterward went to Paris to live. Her name is still honored in San Francisco's fire department.

But not the dread of fire nor the high cost of bathing seriously affected our spirits, and we enjoyed life tremendously. There were many parties and we went often to the theater.

Sometimes we walked down to the docks, where ships

from all over the world brought strange cargoes and strange crews. I never counted clipper ships that lay at anchor like so many great birds resting with folded wings while busy little tugboats, ferry-boats, and schooners fussed about them, but Richard Henry Dana is authority for the statement that in '59 there were more than could be counted in the harbor of Liverpool or of London.

Dana's book, 'Two Years Before the Mast,' was still a best seller when he made a last visit to California that year, and in later editions he included a chapter, 'Twenty-Four Years After,'[1] with a vivid picture of the city as it then appeared:

When I looked from my windows over the city of San Francisco, with its storehouses, towers and steeples, its courthouse, theaters and hospitals; its daily journals; its well-filled learned professions; its fortresses and lighthouses; its wharves and harbor with their thousand-ton clipper ships more in number than London or Liverpool sheltered that day;... when I looked across the bay and beheld a beautiful town on the fertile, wooded shores of the Contra Costa, and capacious freighters and passenger carriers to all parts of the great bay and its tributaries with lines of their smoke on the horizon — when I saw all these things and reflected on what I once was and saw here and what now surrounded me, I could scarcely keep my hold on reality at all....

Of Grace Church on an August Sunday of 1859, he wrote:

The congregation at the Bishop's church (Bishop Kip) was precisely like one you would meet in New York, Philadelphia or Boston. To be sure the identity of the service makes one feel at once at home, but the people were alike, nearly all of the English

---

[1] *Two Years Before the Mast.* Houghton Mifflin Company.

race though from all parts of the Union. The latest French bonnets were at the head of the chief pews....

One of the bonnets was mine.

Interesting travelers arrived on every steamer — the whole world's attention seemed turned to California — and in the harbor were usually anchored several foreign warships, just calling. Officers of British ships were often our guests. Some of them my husband had known when he served in 'The Buffs,' and others were glad to meet a one-time British officer in this strange, remote place. Lady Franklin, widow of the explorer, Sir John Franklin, arrived unexpectedly, one day on the little British war sloop Plumper, from British Columbia. She had been in Victoria awaiting news from a ship sent to Arctic waters in the hope of finding trace of her husband, lost years before seeking the 'Northwest Passage.' Poor Lady Franklin! She spent a fortune and years of her life sending ships to the frozen North, before all the searching was finally rewarded and the lost expedition was traced. This time there had been only disappointment, and it was no wonder she cared little about meeting people or accepting social courtesies. The Plumper had been ordered to bring her to San Francisco, where she took the Panama steamer on her long journey back to England. She had not made herself popular on the Plumper, but she was old and tired. Still, after meeting her, to encounter a detached manner and uninterested glance from beneath the quilted black satin hood she wore in place of a bonnet, I could understand the little middie who confessed to me she had so many airs he'd 'chewed up her India rubber for her!' — the soft rubber eraser from her writing-table. A peculiarly satisfying performance, I fancy, with much outraged feeling worked off on the rubber.

Lady Franklin's niece was with her, acting as her secretary. I've forgotten her name, but she was far more gracious than her aunt, and I wondered, of the rubber, if it could have been this really pleasant person who was inconvenienced by its loss, and not Lady Franklin at all.

Maguire's Opera House was the leading theater, and there we saw Mrs. John Wood in 'Love's Disguises.' She was a handsome woman and a clever comédienne with a following of devoted admirers, among whom was Judge John S. Hager. He would watch her performance from a second-tier stage box, and, when she was in range, drop a white japonica flower at her feet. In the next scene Mrs. Wood would appear with the flower in her hair, and the audience enjoyed this lightly romantic episode, not at all unusual in the theater then.

Eventually Mrs. Wood decided to divorce Mr. Wood, who was a member of her company. She charged him with intemperance and the suit was heard in Judge Hager's court. To the profound surprise of every one concerned, he decided it against her, and the japonica flowers fell at her feet no more. In 1915, I was startled to read of Mrs. Wood's death in England. For so long I had thought of her as a figure of the dead past, not among the living.

Our friend Mrs. Hayne played in 'The Hunchback' at

the Metropolitan Theater, and at once became a favorite in San Francisco, as she had been in New York. She had made her New York début as Julia in 'The Hunchback' at the old Bowery Theater early in the fifties and critics predicted a brilliant future. But she married Dr. Hayne and sailed away for the gold country. I remember her lovely hair, rich golden brown and parted smoothly in the middle, drawn down over her ears. It would never stay properly sleek and flat; there was always a fluff of life about it. She died soon after the Civil War while she was still young and vividly charming, and left a little daughter, who grew up to marry one of the Langhornes of Virginia.

Lotta we saw when she returned from New York, a captivating little creature, *méchante enfant* in all her parts, and not to be resisted. I liked her best as the Marchioness in the rag-tag dress of a London slavey, high buttoned shoes without a button on them. She had an inimitable way of slithering about in them, and kept the house in a ripple of mirth with her comedy. One rarely heard of her outside the theater. She lived almost in seclusion with her mother, Mrs. Crabtree.

Lotta's Fountain, her gift to the city which stands at the intersection of Market and Kearney Streets, recalls her to a present generation of Californians. It is a recklessly ornate monument of black iron which astonishes the sophisticated visitor. But if it isn't art, it has a certain grace of sentiment and tradition. Interesting events have had their setting at Lotta's Fountain.

One memorable night Tetrazzini sang there — on

Christmas Eve, 1910. The converging streets were black with people and the windows of near-by buildings were all filled. Those who heard her said her silver voice seemed to rise to the stars through the still night; and the utter silence of the great crowd in the dark streets was curiously thrilling. The singing was Tetrazzini's Christmas gift to the city which had first welcomed her to America.

Living at the International Hotel had prolonged itself because of the difficulty of finding a suitable house. Father deferred building a home while so much of his time was passed on surveying expeditions, and we finally decided to move over to the more homelike Oriental Hotel in Market Street where Bush and Battery meet.

The Government land surveys sometimes took my father as far south as Los Angeles, and at one time he owned a ranch covering much of the land on which Hollywood is now built. His service to the State was recognized by the California Society of Engineers so recently as October 24, 1926, when they formally gave the name of Ransome's Point to one of the spurs of Mount Diablo. It is part of the State Park on this peak of the Coast Range of which in 1851 my father established the basic and meridian lines. On these lines the surveys of most of California and all of Nevada are founded.

We were in England then, and he wrote to us of the Mount Diablo expedition in a letter now preserved in the Bancroft Library of the University of California. He described the panorama of rivers, mountains, and bay that

LOTTA

THE MOUNT DIABLO EXPEDITION 71

stretched before him when he stood on what is now Ransome's Point and looked far westward to the Golden Gate and San Francisco hills. The empty plains below, he noted, had 'the appearance of being susceptible to a high state of cultivation.' They are now the rich farm lands of the San Joaquin and Sacramento Valleys which send their products to the world's markets.

From the bay to Mount Diablo there has been built a broad highway and the state road winds around the mountain to its crest. One may drive there and back for a day's outing from the city. But in '51 the now thickly populated eastern shore of the bay was thinly settled; a little town at Oakland, the Gonzales Ranch, a few other Spanish ranches, then a wilderness to the settlement of Benicia at the far eastern end of the bay, where the United States had established a military station. My father's surveying party made the trip to Benicia by boat, and at Benicia Barracks, Major Allen furnished horses, mules, and equipment for the expedition. A little river boat took the explorers eight miles up a creek toward the base of the mountain. A third of the way to the summit, they made their camp and the rest of the distance was covered on foot, the men carrying their instruments. Herds of elk and antelope crossed their way. Wild country it was, where, with all his prophetic vision, my father could not foresee golf links and a country club.

Father was the son of a soldier of the Revolution, and was born in Connecticut in the year 1800. He was tall and very distinguished-looking, and had the fineness of character that seemed bred in that generation of Americans. I remember so many of his friends who were from New England and the South, Judge McMillen Shafter, Judge McAllister, William T. Coleman, and a dozen others, all tall, fine-looking men with a certain nobility of spirit.

When my father died in San Francisco in 1874, his friend Judge Noah Swayne, of Washington, the friend also of Lincoln and of Grant, wrote to my mother:

Take him altogether, he was the noblest human being that ever came within the circle of my personal knowledge. The magnitude and power of his mind were equal to those of his body. He was disinterested and generous to a fault. His whole heart seemed to be without a bad fiber, and his whole nature without a blemish.

This, of course, is in the fluorescent style of the time; but it is true that my father was one of the men who, with far vision and without self-interest, laid foundations for California's empire.

The Oriental was very much of a social center because of its ballroom where dances were given. It stood on Market Street at the foot of Bush, opposite and a little below St. Patrick's Church and Orphan Asylum, which were removed to make way for the Palace Hotel. Directly across the street, in a sand lot now covered by a skyscraper, Peter Donahue manufactured boilers with incessant din.

The Oriental was a two-story frame building with long

galleries across the front. Partitions between rooms were of cloth covered with paper which necessitated the carrying-on of any intimate conversation in whispers. But in spite of these slight disadvantages, we were happy there, and found what was known as the élite of the city sharing the discomforts. In the dining-room, one long table was reserved for men who took their meals there and lodged elsewhere.

At its head sat William T. Coleman, chief of the Vigilance Committee and usually on his right sat Isaac Bluxome, the Secretary, known as 'Sec'ty 33,' which he signed to all the Committee's documents. With them occasionally was Dr. Beverly Cole, physician of the Vigilantes, a good-looking young man with courtly manners. His daughter in after years married Major McClung, of the Army, who met a curiously tragic death. It was early in the present century when Mrs. Howard Coit, then living in Paris, came home for a visit. She had been Lily Hitchcock, the most dashing belle San Francisco ever knew, with her gay spirits and spectacular independence. Major McClung, an old admirer and friend, was calling on her in her rooms at the Palace, when suddenly and unannounced the door of her sitting-room opened and there entered a highly excited young man, son of an old Rincon Hill family known to them both. Mrs. Coit rose in surprise. While she stood staring, the young man drew a gun and, with incoherent words about some business deal, shot Major McClung to death in his chair.

Not long ago the tragic end of William T. Coleman's

son recalled to me the Vigilantes. Robert Coleman and George DeLong, of New York, were killed by bandits in the Balkans in 1924 while on a motor tour of the country. Robert Coleman had inherited his father's good looks. The latter had been the handsomest man in his class at the University of St. Louis back in the forties as the son was at Yale in the eighteen-nineties, although neither, I'm sure, coveted the distinction.

One delightful lady at the Oriental unconsciously afforded us much entertainment, discreetly concealed. She was Mrs. Greenough, of Washington, who had come West to visit her daughter, the wife of Captain Treadwell Moore, of the Presidio. Mrs. Greenough had known Washington society for many years, and would talk of events back in Dolly Madison's reign, and other remote periods, until we wondered how old on earth she must be! She looked fifty, or seventy. Her age became a matter of wide speculation and bets were made on it but they remained unsettled. Mrs. Greenough persistently evaded determining statements and she departed for Washington with her age an unrevealed secret.

Not long afterward she was called as a witness in the Limanteur Land Case and returned to San Francisco to testify. 'She will have to tell her age, now,' we grimly gloated.

The day she was questioned, her amiably curious friends filled the courtroom — all tense with expectancy when she took the stand. 'How old are you, Mrs. Greenough?' counsel asked. Every one leaned a little forward.

DR. R. BEVERLEY COLE
Physician of the Vigilance Committee

WILLIAM T. COLEMAN
Of the Vigilance Committee

Mrs. Greenough looked placidly about her, and then with dignified finality answered, 'Of sufficient age to testify.' The bets were never paid.

Mrs. Moore, who had been Florence Greenough, was a gay, pretty woman who often asked us to dances at the post. She was a close friend of Mrs. Hall McAllister, leader of San Francisco society in the sixties and seventies, as her brother-in-law, Ward McAllister, was in New York's fashionable set. But with a difference. All of the San Francisco McAllisters were blessed with a sense of humor.

After he came to live in San Francisco, Ward McAllister, Jr., once told me that, if he walked down Kearney Street with a young lady, her social position was thereby assured; and he was quite simple and sincere about it. Ward, Jr., took his title of 'the Crown Prince' a bit seriously when we bestowed it in a spirit of friendly fun, but he was a sweet and amiable soul with none of the arrogance that made his father an implacable arbiter. The arbiter himself had adorned the bar of San Francisco for a year or two, but before our advent had returned to what the Western press liked to refer to as 'the effete East.'

Judge and Mrs. McAllister had brought their family from Georgia in the earliest fifties, and except the son Ward, they all lived in a spacious mansion in Stockton Street. There were Harriet, the daughter, and three sons; Hall with his wife, Cutler with his wife, and the Reverend Marion McAllister, who never married and became pastor of the Church of the Advent out in the Mission District.

They gave the merriest parties in the Stockton Street house. At Christmas and New Year's it was filled with young people. The large old-fashioned parlors were lit with many candles, and Cutler McAllister led the merry-making. We played 'Blindman's Buff,' danced 'Old Dan Tucker,' and the Virginia Reel. One evening we had charades, with 'The Seasons' represented by men of the party. Hall McAllister was Spring with a wreath of artificial flowers on his head and a scarf draped over his black broadcloth. Judge Hager in a toga, carrying a feather fan, was Summer. Autumn was presented by Arthur Goddefroy, who carried a pumpkin, and Cutler McAllister in an overcoat was Winter. Lieutenant McPherson, of the Presidio, wore a cotton-wool beard to suggest Father Time, and Billy Botts was the New Year with infant's cap and bib, carrying a rattle. Innocuous entertainment, possibly, but hardly more so, I should say, than one-stepping through an evening in the modern manner.

We often raced through 'Fox-and-Geese' at these parties, and sometimes Mrs. Hall McAllister sang for us. She had a lovely voice, and was altogether one of the most fascinating women San Francisco society has known.

Harriet McAllister went to New York early in the sixties and there married her cousin, Sam Francis. When the Prince of Wales visited America, she danced with him at a ball and wrote letters about it to the family; of how she found the Prince really very much of a gentleman, as though the McAllisters had their own standards.

Ward McAllister, Jr., was a great beau, but he never married, developing, instead, into one of the perennial bachelors of the Pacific Union Club, where he made his home. Of these late years I remember an incident, entirely trivial but delectably characteristic.

When he had become a famous figure of finance, Senator William A. Clark, of Montana, visited San Francisco and was a guest at the club. The whole country was talking of the Copper King, but Mr. McAllister, it appeared, had never heard of him — or so he wished to imply — and it amused him to tell it as much as it did me to hear it.

'I was in the lounge the other afternoon [he related], when one of the servants whispered, "That's Senator Clark, sir, over there." "Don't know him," I answered. There he sat [giving a lightly scornful side glance], but *I* didn't know him.'

Poor Ward McAllister had a sad experience in the 1906 disaster. A stroke of paralysis had rendered him speechless and he was a patient in the McNutt Hospital. When the fire began to sweep northward from the Mission District, where it started, patients were hurriedly removed, and by the time his relatives could reach it, the hospital was deserted; no one left to tell them his whereabouts.

It happened, in the confusion of the morning, that strangers took charge of him and he could not tell them his name or for whom to send. So, with other patients, he was taken to Fort Mason, from where nurses accompanied them by boat to the Navy Hospital at Mare Island. It was days before his troubled family found him.

One always heard laughter where Cutler McAllister passed, but his wit was the light, inconsequential sort that passes with the moment. He had amusing names for most of his friends. Sylvester Mowery, of New York, who had been in Arizona before he came to California, was always 'Sylvester the Magnificent, Prince of Arizona.'

He delighted to tell of an incident at the Pacific Club the first 'gentlemen's club' of San Francisco, which took itself a bit seriously. Most of the important men of the community belonged to it and the club-rooms in Commercial Street were fairly luxurious. They had formerly been Steve Whipple's gambling-hall, fitted up with what was then considered a degree of gilded splendor. One evening, when dignified members were grouped in the lounge, a miner in blue shirt and high boots entered and looked about, slightly bewildered. One of the servants went over to him and told him he had strayed into a private club.

'A private club, eh?' he answered. 'Well, this used to be Steve Whipple's place and I see the same old crowd around.'

The Pacific Club soon moved from Steve Whipple's old quarters to rooms in the Parrott Block, and there a tragic accident occurred. The rooms were over those occupied by the offices of Wells-Fargo and Company's Express. One day at the noon hour, when the club dining-room was filled, a package of nitro-glycerine exploded in

MRS. HALL MCALLISTER

HALL MCALLISTER

the express office beneath, wrecking the club's dining-room and killing several of the members.

Eventually the Pacific Club combined with the Union Club, and the Pacific Union, housed in the huge brownstone palace built by the bonanza king, James Flood, on Nob Hill, is now the millionaires' club of San Francisco.

The Bohemian Club was not founded until the seventies, by actors, artists, and writers who met in rooms over the California Market and arranged entertainments for themselves and their friends which they called 'High Jinks' in the slang of the day. 'Captain Jinks of the Horse Marines' was a popular song, and I fancy the word was derived from that. However, it has gained greatly in dignity, and the Bohemian Club's Midsummer Jinks, in the Cazadero redwood forest, are famed pageants of rare beauty and high art.

CHAPTER III

The grand social events of a season of the fifties were the Apollo Balls. These were subscription parties given in Apollo Hall in Pacific Street, since then part of the notorious Barbary Coast, and even then a far from select neighborhood. But in it was the only hall spacious enough for a large ball, so to Pacific Street we flocked in hacks and buses, or on foot across the Plaza. Apollo Hall was a bare loft with unfinished rafters which were hung with bunting for our dances. Wooden benches were the only seats, but they supported the wealth and fashion of San Francisco, and many handsome gowns.

At one of the Apollos, Lucy Gwin made a memorable début. She was the spirited daughter of Senator William Gwin, one of the promoters of the Pony Express. In time she became the very stately dowager, Mrs. Evan Coleman. We were all assembled that evening when music sounded for the first dance, a redowa. Suddenly a couple swooped down the room, in the dance, turned and rushed back again at a breakneck speed. It was Lucy Gwin making her début, assisted by Billy Botts. He was a small man, and Lucy Gwin towered above him, while her crinolines nearly hid him from view. But he kept the pace, and emerged triumphant. He was the best 'fancy dancer' in society, and his speed in the redowa was terrific. He would race with high steps down the length of a room, pause for the turn with one foot pointed, and then race back again. Usually his partner was a mere accessory to the performance.

This irrepressible William, son of Governor Botts of Virginia, was a clerk in the Custom House, where so many young Southerners of limited means were employed that it was known as the 'Virginia Poor House.' Harry Wise, whose 'Uncle Henry' was another one-time Governor of Virginia, was one of them. His brother Tully was law partner of John C. Calhoun's son, and these three were among popular bachelors of the Apollo, who, all considered, were a cosmopolitan band.

Romano Bernardo Sanches was a dark young Spaniard from Florida. Robert Johnson was a son of the Swedish Consul. Henri Tricou was French; Emil Justh, a Hungarian. Alfred Goddefroy, a German, was the partner of a young Englishman, Willy Sillem, in a lumber shipping business. After the eccentric Henry Meiggs, builder of Meiggs's Wharf, exiled himself to Chile, Willy Sillem sailed down after him to collect a bill due the firm and returned, not only with the money but with a bride, the niece of Henry Meiggs.

A great beau was Charley Fairfax, of Virginia, 'the Baron' to all his friends, since he actually was heir to the title in England, although the family had lived for generations in America. He was a clerk in the Supreme Court at Sacramento, but commuted to San Francisco weekly or oftener, and was one of the early members of the Pacific Club, where his wit and good-fellowship made him a favorite.

One of my father's favorite stories was of an encounter with the Baron at the Club one afternoon just before the Civil War. Father's title of Colonel, I may explain, was one of those synthetic military titles so often bestowed in the South, probably because, with his tall, soldierly figure and gallant manners, he suggested a Virginia Colonel. At any rate, he was 'Colonel' until his death, and the appellation sometimes misled acquaintances to mistake him for a Southerner. On the afternoon in question, he found himself one of a group of Southern gentlemen, including Charley Fairfax, who fell into discussion of differences between the North and South. The Baron delivered a scathing denunciation of the North and Northerners while Father listened with detached amusement. In a pause the speaker turned to Father. 'You are from the South, of course,' Colonel, he said, to reassure himself.

Father considered. 'Why, yes,' he answered finally, and excoriations continued. But once more, vaguely uncertain, the Baron paused. 'By the way, what part of the South are you from, Colonel?' he inquired.

'Why, I'm from the southern part of Connecticut,' Father replied mildly, and the meeting adjourned without formality.

Our Beau Brummel was George T. Marye, who came out from Oxford with the dress and ways of Mayfair, and always wore gloves on the street, pale lemon-color kid, with clothes that could have come only from Bond Street. Sunday mornings he made an impressive progress down the aisle of Trinity Church to his pew, faultlessly attired, his

CHARLES, LORD FAIRFAX

JAMES R. KEENE

pot hat held a little high in a gloved hand. He was very well liked, and so, in later times, was his son, George T. Marye, Jr., who was Ambassador to Russia before the Great War.

Judge A. C. Monson, who came out from New York for several long visits, was another glass of masculine fashion. He wore his hair, as did my husband, in the English effect of a part extending from the forehead to the nape of the neck. The hair was brushed forward from the back, and down on either side in front, to meet in a ridge above the ears. 'Dundrearys' were the usual accompaniment of this effect. They were the extraordinary development of side-burns into long, flowing side-whiskers, which took their name from E. A. Sothern's rôle of Lord Dundreary in an English comedy. Judge Monson never pronounced the letter 'R.' He said he couldn't, but the fops of London were then deliberately ignoring it for some reason I never knew, and I fancy Judge Monson merely emulated them when he spoke of 'Wushing about Pawis while he was abwoad.'

Of the Apollo beaux who founded families still prominent in California were Edward Pringle, of South Carolina, William and Pepe Barron, Pelham Ames, of Boston, William T. Wallace, and J. B. Crockett; and little Joe Thompson, 'Spanish Joe,' whose high ambition it was to be mistaken for a Spaniard. He studied Spanish assiduously until he had mastered language and mannerisms, and spoke English with an accent.

As early as these years of the eighteen-fifties there were

children of Spanish-American marriages, and the son of an American father married to a Spanish señorita would be called 'Don' in the Spanish manner. Such hybrid effects in nomenclature as Don Abel Stearns, Don Daniel Gibb, Don Abel Guy, and Don José Thompson were not unusual. But by the time a scion of the Ashe family married a granddaughter of Don Bolado, the custom had long been discontinued.

The prettiest woman at the Apollo dances was young Mrs. Baldwin, wife of Captain Charles Baldwin, of the Navy. She had the wax-doll prettiness so much admired then, with golden hair worn in short curls all over her head. Mrs. Thomas Holt was a beauty of the same type, who as Addie Smith had been a belle in Washington, sharing laurels with her friend, Addie Cutts, who married the 'Little Giant,' Stephen A. Douglas.

In the same set were the A. P. Crittendens, at whose home in Taylor Street we sometimes dined with no presentiment that our host would one day be the victim of a sensational murder. He was of the Kentucky Crittendens, a lawyer and at the time of his death one of the leaders of the California bar. I've forgotten preliminary details to the murder. Possibly Mr. Crittenden had met Mrs. Fair, the lady who killed him, over some legal business. She chose an effective moment to end their friendship. Mrs. Crittenden had been visiting in Washington and her husband had crossed the bay to meet her at the railroad terminus in Oakland. Laura D. Fair (no connection of

Senator Fair) crossed on the same ferry-boat, saw him greet Mrs. Crittenden, and followed them to the deck of the boat returning to San Francisco. While they sat talking together on the open deck, she suddenly stepped before them and shot Mr. Crittenden dead. News of the murder was called through the streets, and not since the Broderick-Terry duel back in '59 had the city been so stirred. It was in 1870. The trial was a *cause célèbre* which seemed to be all the more shocking when Laura D. Fair was sentenced to be hanged. However, a new trial was granted, and this time she was acquitted on the ground of temporary insanity. I think no one was sorry, although none felt sympathy for Mrs. Fair, who was neither very young nor very beautiful as a really successful murderess should be. But the thought of hanging a woman was too dreadful. I believe it had never been done in California.

In the mountains above Napa Valley were hot sulphur springs long known to the Spanish Californians. Early in the fifties an enterprising American built a hotel near them and gave it the name of the fashionable old Virginia resort, White Sulphur Springs. It was the resort of San Francisco's fashionables for many years.

To escape the summer trade winds and blowing dust of the city, we went to the Springs for a visit late in our first San Francisco summer. A charming place, but a truly dreadful day's journey to attain. We traveled by land and water from 9 A.M. to 7 P.M., seated upright on hard seats all of the way. The Benicia boat first took us up the bay to

Mare Island, where we changed to a little river boat for the trip up the Napa River; a yellow, winding stream between flat banks. At the straggling little town of Napa, we found a four-horse stage-coach to convey us to the Springs. It was a long, hot, dusty ride that ended in a flourish in front of a cool, white hotel, where ladies in crisp cool muslins and gentlemen in fresh linen watched our arrival. We were too tired to care.

The hotel was a low, white building with long piazzas, set among tall trees in a wooded gorge of the mountains. A little stream with fern-covered banks flowed through the gorge, spanned by rustic bridges. Here and there were white spring-houses, arbors built over the springs and covered with vines. Shady paths wound over the mountain-side, and if one followed them to a summit, the valley lay below, spreading to the bay and distant hills. It was wild, beautiful country and gave me a glimpse of California's beauty that the city's sand hills had not suggested.

The second evening after our arrival, we were among crisp, cool spectators when dusty travelers alighted from the stage. Among them was a dapper little gentleman who turned to assist a dainty little lady following him: Captain David Farragut, of Mare Island, with Mrs. Farragut, we were told. They were a delightful little couple, devoted to one another. We became friends at once, and exchanged many visits with them until Captain Farragut was ordered East two years later. He had been sent from Washington in 1854 to establish the Navy Yard at Mare Island in San Francisco Bay.

ADMIRAL DAVID GLASGOW FARRAGUT

In spite of his small, slight figure, Captain Farragut had 'presence.' Already he had lived adventurous years sailing the seven seas, and his face was weather-browned, with the look of a man who has seen many things. As a boy of eleven, he had fought in a battle of the War of 1812, midshipman on the Essex when she was engaged by a British ship off the coast of Chile; I have heard him tell of his baptism of blood — a genuine baptism. When fighting began on the Essex, he stood waiting for orders at the foot of a companionway. Suddenly a wounded man toppled down the stairs, his blood pouring over the horrified boy. Farragut staggered away, he said, ready to faint, but pulled himself together and got on deck; and presently, with men falling on every side, he became indifferent to blood and death and fought like a veteran.

In the evenings at White Sulphur, we danced in the rustic ballroom, and it was always a joy to watch Captain Farragut. He was a most meticulous dancer. Holding some tall and stately belle at arms' length, he would rhythmically rise and fall on his toes with each slow step, while they revolved in the old-fashioned waltz.

Senator and Mrs. Gwin, with dashing Miss Lucy, were there; Senator — soon to be Governor — John B. Weller with Mrs. Weller; Mr. and Mrs. Joseph Haven; and with the Farraguts and ourselves made a congenial group. We drove one day across the valley to Calistoga Hot Springs where a low, whitewashed hotel accommodated a few guests; accommodated also a rattlesnake the day we lunched there. We were enjoying fried chicken, country style, when we noticed the proprietor at the door of the dining-room, whispering to a waitress. Presently she came over to us. 'Don't be scared, folks,' she said, 'but there's a rattlesnake got in the house and they can't find it. You only got to watch out for it.' Very promptly we adjourned dinner, preferring to forgo fried chicken consumed on guard, and retired from the premises.

Often on our stage trips through the mountain country a rattlesnake would scurry across the road ahead of us. Stage-drivers said they were curious, and liked to see us go by. If one shook his rattle in the undergrowth, the stage-horses would shy and tremble with instinctive dread, for the sound itself was light and pleasant.

Soon after the White Sulphur visit, we went to Mare Island to visit the Farraguts. They had a charming home. Mrs. Farragut was a Virginian with the Southern woman's gift of hospitality. She had been Virginia Royall, of Norfolk. The Captain's first wife had likewise been a Norfolk girl, a Miss Marchant, who died after years of invalidism. Mrs. Farragut told me that before she met the Captain, she had heard stories of his devotion to the invalid wife and thought he must be the kindest man alive. They were a singularly happy married couple.

We were often visitors at the Yard after that. It was becoming a most attractive place, with lawns and flower parterres and the pretty cottage homes of the officers. Usually we made the trip up the bay on the United States surveying ship Active, which was placed at the service of navy officers. Captain Alden, afterward Admiral Alden, was in command, and lived on board with his quaint little wife, who fitted nicely into her compact home. They were generous hosts, especially so on one happy trip when San Francisco guests went to Mare Island for the wedding of Miss Alice Turner to Dr. Brown, surgeon on the Active. The bride was a daughter of Mr. and Mrs. Daniel Turner. He was civil engineer at the Yard and long our friend.

The wedding-supper on this occasion was unusually elaborate, a gastronomic diversion of scalloped oysters, glazed hams, hot quail on toast, and many other delicacies. Mrs. Inge had lent her famous colored cook, who went from San Francisco to prepare it.

Wedding-guests remained overnight at various homes in the Yard, and, returning on the Active the next day, we were a merry party, quite ready to fall in with Joseph Haven's nonsense. Going up from the city, Captain Alden had entertained us at a feast of a luncheon. Returning, the Lucullan feast was repeated, with champagne for every one in unstinted measure. We were overwhelmed with all this amiable hospitality, and discussing it on deck Joseph Haven said, in a sort of reversed appreciation, 'Let's call an indignation meeting and protest!'

Some one found Bishop Kip who had officiated at the wedding, and placed him in the chair. He thought the meeting was called to pass a straight vote of thanks to Captain Alden. 'Fancy my feelings,' he said later, 'when I found myself presiding at a farce!'

Joseph Haven made a speech advising passengers to demand the return of their passage-money (there was none, of course), in view of the treatment they had received, food not fit to eat and nothing to drink! Moreover, first-cabin passengers had been obliged to mingle with the steerage on deck.

This referred to Mrs. Inge's colored cook returning to the city. Unluckily, she heard the speech and at this point burst into tears and lamentations. The farce abruptly terminated, and Joseph Haven explained for an hour to the injured lady that it was a joke and that we all had for her a most profound respect as the Number One cook of San Francisco; and Bishop Kip assured her that Joseph Haven spoke the truth before her grief was pacified. What a lot of nonsense to remember so long!

Once at Mare Island the *entente cordiale* was seriously strained, when H. M. S. Satellite called to permit Captain Prevost to pay his respects to Captain Farragut — at least it was strained in the mind of one young Britisher. The Satellite had brought members of the Boundary Commission from British Columbia to meet a Panama steamer at San Francisco. While she was in port, Captain Prevost desired to call on the commandant at the Navy Yard and asked us to go with him as guests on his ship.

When we reached Mare Island, an American officer stood on the wharf to welcome us, and we made the landing in small boats. A swift tide was running, dashing us with spray, and with the thought that British seamen might not understand our bay currents, the American started to call a few suggestions to the rowers. Up jumped a little middie in Her Majesty's uniform, in charge of the small craft. 'I command this boat, sir!' he barked. The American stared a moment, then, controlling a grin, he turned and walked away, and Great Britain landed her envoys without further American interference.

Distance has never discouraged Californians. In the mere matter of mileage they are probably the greatest travelers on earth. Children were sent across the continent to school and came home for holidays, and in the old days of a week to cross from coast to coast, business men would step on an overland train to attend a conference in Wall Street as lightly as a New-Yorker might have journeyed from Long Island. In the not distant future they will probably commute by airship.

We traveled less, of course, before the railroads came to California, but distance never dimmed our vivid interest in events of the world. When news of them reached us, our celebrations, a month late, were spirited and enthusiastic.

We were three weeks from any source of news of the presidential election in 1856 and the time of waiting to know results was highly exciting. Both parties celebrated with equal conviction of victory, certain, after election day, that its candidate was now President-elect of the United States. Buchanan, with Breckinridge for Vice-President, was a favorite in the Southern contingent, and General Frémont, Republican nominee, had strong support. Torch light processions of 'Buck-and-Breck' men alternated with those of Frémont supporters, and, of course, in the sporting spirit of the time, many and large were the bets made.

We were enthusiastic and vigorous about politics in those days. Men discussed them with high voices and excited gestures. Women expounded the opinions of husbands and fathers. For our political convictions, like our religion, were inherited (I am speaking of women), although the daughter of a Democrat married to a Republican would discard her father's politics to assume those of her husband — usually; not always. I have known strong-minded women to remain staunch Democrats through years of happy marriage to a Republican. But the children were raised Republicans.

It is true women did not vote. It did not occur to us to desire to vote. We never thought of women's rights, assuming, I suppose, that we had them. But we were keenly interested in elections, cheered for our candidates at torchlight parades, and did much informal electioneering. It is possible that we were effective in a way; hardly probable.

Men whose offices were on the line of march of torchlight processions gave parties for them. Politics were mixed at these affairs, and no ill-will. Often a gay crowd gathered in Dr. Ashe's office at Washington and Kearny Streets on Buck-and-Breck nights, to cheer the marchers and drink toasts in champagne.

On the day a Panama steamer was due with news of election results, business was fairly at a standstill, but no steamer arrived. The next day people went about with eyes fixed on Telegraph Hill for first sight of the signal flag. None appeared. That night Mr. and Mrs. J. W. Wallack opened a season at Maguire's Opera House in 'The Merchant of Venice.' It was to have been a brilliant *première* for Shylock, Wallack's great rôle, but, although the audience was gayly caparisoned and boxes overflowed with fashion, our attention was divided. Ears were alert for the sound of a shot from Telegraph Hill — the night signal of a steamer sighted. In the middle of the fifth act, it came. Without a second's hesitation, men dived for their hats and rushed out of the theater. Women rose and gathered their wraps. On the stage the actors stared at us, and then the curtain was rung down as the feminine division of the audience filed out after the men. In evening gowns and lace scarfs we made our way across Montgomery Street. Hacks and conveyances had all dashed down to the dock. The streets were filled with excited crowds gathering at newspaper offices or on their way to the wharf for first news.

At the Oriental, men had all disappeared, and women guests were gathered in the long parlor, elated and excited. As soon as the names of Buchanan and Breckinridge were shouted from the steamer's deck, couriers raced back through the streets to spread the news, and we had heard it by the time our men returned. Buck-and-Brecks spent the rest of the night celebrating. My father had voted for his old friend, General Frémont, at whose ranch in Mariposa, beyond Stockton, he had often been a guest, but true as he was to friendship and his party, I believe he had doubts of Frémont's talent for the presidency. A great soldier, he had not been brilliant as a statesman during a broken term in the Senate.

It would be too bad to give the impression that women were a mere flock of butterflies, in my youth. We were not. But since our place was in the home, we did what we could to make it attractive. Besides the pleasant duty of playing hostess, there were many tedious domestic details involved in this avocation, an extraordinary amount of sewing, for one thing. We hemmed ruffles, embroidered flounces, monogrammed household linen with thick stuffed letters, and, unless there were several servants, accomplished the family mending. Stiletto embroidery was popular, and I pierced and embroidered yards of sheer muslin for summer gowns.

But it was for no particular gift or triumph with the needle that I was asked to be judge of fancy work at the first Mechanics' Fair, in 1857. I felt important and very 'advanced' when I accepted the honor, and gravely considered the merits of lace bibs, patchwork quilts, and satin glove-cases, for medal or honorable mention.

There was great excitement over this fair. To house it, a low frame building in the form of a Maltese cross was built on Montgomery Street, where the Lick House afterward stood, the entrance midway between Post and Sutter Streets. The fair was held under the auspices of the new Mechanics' Institute, but needlework, an art gallery, and farm products were included among the exhibits. The noise of quartz mills filled the place. In Machinery Hall they pounded and ground gold and silver quartz while you watched them, the ore washed out of sluice-boxes before your eyes. Given the quartz, it was all beautifully simple and fascinated spectators watched it for hours on end.

The art gallery became a favorite evening rendezvous. After dinner we would throw on our lace or Paisley shawls and walk up from the Oriental to meet friends at the fair and watch the passing pageant from settees in the art room. Of the pictures in this first exhibition, I remember only an enormous canvas depicting the royal family of Hawaii on horseback, all of the figures, including the horses, of course, life-size. As a work of art its proportions made a profound impression, which is quite the fact and not at all an attempt at satire.

The Mechanics' Fair was repeated annually for many years in the newer Larkin Street Pavilion, and during its six weeks' season the city was filled with visitors from all over the State, and from Oregon and Nevada. Many of them made long stage-coach journeys to see the newest improvements in mine and farm machinery, as well as the latest fashions. The art gallery really looked up in later years when Virgil Williams, the friend of Robert Louis Stevenson in San Francisco, and a talented painter, interested himself in it with several other authentic artists. Toby Rosenthal's 'Constance de Beverly' was a sensation one year. He was a San Francisco boy who had achieved the Salon in Paris with his 'Elaine' — 'The dead rowed by the dumb' of Tennyson's poem. Occasionally private galleries of Nob Hill lent their treasures. There was a Bouguereau period, and we saw Millet's 'The Sower,' which was owned by the Crocker family; is still, I believe. It escaped the 1906 fire when the Crocker home was burned. There were only servants in the house, but they saved many things. The butler put 'The Sower' under his arm and walked many blocks to the home of one of his family's friends beyond the fire zone, where he left it for safe-keeping and it was returned when the excitement was over.

Our local stars were William Keith and Thomas Hill. Keith's landscapes found wider fame, and many are now owned by galleries in the Eastern States and abroad. Thomas Hill painted Yosemite from every point of vantage and was considered a great artist in that day. When Queen Victoria's daughter, Princess Louise, with her husband, the Marquis of Lorne, visited San Francisco in the eighties, she spent a morning in his studio. He told me of her interest in his California landscapes and her modesty over her own talent, which was really marked. In Santa Barbara, monks of the Old Mission opened their walled garden to her and she painted its ancient beauty.

The fashionable portrait-painter of the eighteen sixties was W. S. Jewett, who 'did' many of San Francisco's beautiful women, painting them under difficulties. For he was very deaf and, if one were sitting and wished to communicate with him, it was necessary to break the pose and use pantomime.

Which reminds me of another amiable gentleman, Mr. Carolan, who grew very deaf in his old age. A friend who had known him many years before in Sacramento, where they had been neighbors, found herself, one day, sitting next to him in a Pacific Avenue car. They exchanged greetings. 'Where are you living now?' she asked. After a louder repetition of the question, he told her, 'In Scott Street near Pacific.'

'How strange that we should be neighbors again!' she exclaimed. 'I live on Pacific Avenue near Scott.' The old gentleman musingly nodded assent.

'Life is curious, isn't it?' she went on. 'It must be forty years ago that we were neighbors in Sacramento, and after so many changes, here we are neighbors again. How strange it is!'

Her old friend, bowed over the head of his gold-topped cane, kept nodding agreement. 'Yes, yes, indeed,' he answered her last remark.

There was a short pause. Presently the old gentleman looked up with a sudden access of interest. 'Where are you living now?' he asked.

Naturally there was much talk of gold, of new strikes near Grass Valley or Shasta, a new lode in this or that mine, and the ravages of hydraulic mining along the rivers; but less, really, than might be supposed. In San Francisco, men financed prospecting trips and speculated wildly in mining shares after the Stock Exchange opened, but the gold-seekers made headquarters at Sacramento. They came to San Francisco with 'dust' for the Mint or to spend a stake, but Sacramento, the terminus of the Overland Stage Line and of stage lines to the mining country, was their metropolis. An exhilarant little city it was, built up around old Sutter's Fort in a bend of the Sacramento River. There had been a devastating flood which the irrepressible pioneers turned into a sort of water carnival, floating merrily about the streets in rowboats until the waters subsided; and the cholera epidemic had been a tragic visitation. But in spite of setbacks, Sacramento flourished, and at least two of the great fortunes of California were founded there, one in a grocery store and the other in the bank established by D. O. Mills and his brother Edgar. Except for their life and activity, downtown streets were unimpressive, but in the residence district were pretty cottages and a few 'mansions.' In one of these lived the Sanger family with a sparkling, black-eyed daughter Harriet who became Mrs. George M. Pullman, of Chicago, and whose daughter was to marry the young son of a neighbor of the Sangers in Sacramento. In another mansion on July 28, 1859, Mary Anderson was born.

We were occasional visitors at the capital, and for me it was thrilling to see the Overland Stage start on its long trip to St. Joseph — never called that, but always 'St. Joe': like the sailing of an ocean liner, repeated many times, but each time with its own flourish and excitement. The six-horse coach would roll down from the stables to be drawn up before the stage office. Passengers would be packed inside, luggage at the back and on top. Perched high beside the driver would be a favored traveler, and higher still, behind the driver, Wells-Fargo's shot-gun messenger took his place. Seemingly a careless, light-hearted youth,

MRS. GEORGE PULLMAN

he was picked for his courage and character to guard the treasure-box which carried papers and gold to the value of many thousands of dollars. The treasure-box would be brought out last thing from the office and stowed with the mail-bag in the 'boot' beneath the driver's feet. The stage agent would wave his hand; the driver would gather up the long reins twisted about the brake, and at a word, or touch of the whip-lash on a wheeler's flank, the horses pranced a little, then swung into their pace down the street, and so out to the road, the coach with a festive air rolling behind them.

I have sat in the coveted place beside the driver when eight horses drew us over the mountains, and their long, swinging curves down winding grades were thrilling and beautiful to watch. One lost all sense of danger, and there was always danger with the most skillful of drivers. A curve taken too widely, or a stumbling horse, and the coach toppled over, down the mountain-side. Such accidents were not rare, and hold-ups were far from uncommon occurrences. My father, who traveled much through the State, had several adventures with 'road agents.'

Usually the Wells-Fargo treasure would be all these bandits demanded. They would step out on a moonlit road with masked faces and lifted guns, to halt the stage. One would stand at the team's head covering the driver and express messenger while another covered passengers, sitting very tight inside. 'Throw out the box!' they would order. If there were no women passengers, the express messenger drew and fired, for answer, while the driver whipped up his horses, and the coach and treasure escaped in a fusillade of shots, not infrequently effective. Father was once lined up with other passengers at the side of the road and his pockets rifled. But ladies were spared. This was the chivalrous rule of highwaymen in the eighteen-fifties — a chivalry occasionally extended to men.

'I wish you boys would leave me fifty dollars,' a victim once pleaded.

'How much have you got?' the highwayman asked.

'Two hundred and fifty in gold.'

'Well, keep a hundred,' said the generous gentleman of the road. So the man counted his gold pieces and handed over one hundred and fifty dollars with grateful thanks.

The Placerville Road was the main highway over the Sierra Nevada Mountains. From Sacramento to Carson and Virginia City in Nevada, it was a busy thoroughfare, and the pride of two States. For a stretch of many miles it was sprinkled daily by watering-carts replenished from tanks along the way. The surveys on which it was built had been made with difficulty and danger. Although they could not have escaped beauty, surveyors seemed to have designedly drawn the line through a panorama of enchanting vistas. The road curved among mountains to follow the edge of some cliff with a sheer drop of a thousand feet to a still lake set in the depths of forests. Donner Lake, like a fallen silver shield, far below recalled always with its name the lost Donner party snow-bound on its shore through a terrible winter of starvation and death. From snow-covered crests one looked down on green valleys over lower peaks and ranges mounting like waves, dark with pines. During the sixties, when newly discovered lodes made Virginia City an important center, the richest traffic in the world, I believe, passed over the Placerville Road. Silver from Nevada and California's gold representing many millions were transported over it to the Mint in San Francisco.

Jack and I made a trip through the mining country one summer, starting out on the Placerville Road from the stage office in Sacramento with all the flourish I had so often watched. Stage-coach traveling was full of fascination for me, and the country was magnificent, forest-covered mountains, rushing rivers, and quiet valleys with long miles of solitude; and the funny one-street mining towns where life centered in the general merchandise store by day and the hotel bar at night. We stopped over in towns when accommodations were good, but mining-camp hotels were primitive places with only the bar a perfectly well-developed detail. Meals, however, were usually excellent, and there was one touch that delighted me. While we ate at a long table in the bare dining-room, the proprietor would stand behind us waving over our heads a sort of mop made of long strips of paper on the end of a stick — to shoo the flies away. I felt like Cleopatra on her barge when it gently swayed above my head.

Angel's Camp, Red Bluff, Redding, Oroville, Nevada City, and Grass Valley were all busy towns filled with life and excitement, where beyond the inevitable 'Main Street' were scattered pretty homes.

Shasta was a thriving little metropolis two hundred miles to the north of San Francisco, where the long main street boasted some of California's first skyscrapers — brick buildings four stories high; and where shops kept scales to weigh the gold dust used for currency. The plaza was a meeting-place for miners of the country, and long pack-trains of mules were constantly arriving and departing to camps in the north, or to Yreka, another 'metropolis' far up toward the Oregon line. On the hillsides were many attractive homes, cottages with 'Hamburg embroidery' in wood, edging the eaves, and one, the Shurtleff home, that had 'come around the Horn' in sections from New York. Near it was the Daingerfield house, where the Judge's daughter married James R. Keene, afterward the 'Bear of Wall Street.' Joaquin Miller mined near Shasta, ''Twixt Redding and sweet Shasta town,' as he later phrased it in a poem. In the eighteen-sixties no one could have thought that the railroad would pass it by and leave Shasta to fade into a ghost city of the West.

Marysville was like older places. The Convent of Notre Dame, built there in the early fifties, with picturesque, galleried buildings and a walled garden overflowing with flowers, gave it a touch of the Old World. It was one of the first 'select' girls' schools in California and pupils were of all creeds. Two of those I knew were the mothers of Sibyl Sanderson and Kathleen Thompson Norris.

Sibyl Sanderson's name brings a picture of the sparkling

girl I knew in her youth when she sometimes sang for her mother's friends in a voice like high, clear bells of a carillon. Her mother, Jenny Ormsby, had married Judge Sanderson, and they lived in a big white house with a cupola on Holladay's Hill at Sacramento and Laguna Streets. Sibyl was a belle in her teens, and even then shocked the family friends with her light disdain of conventions. We were still in the Victorian period when conventions were profoundly respected. Once she startled a dinner-party by announcing that she wanted to know life from its heights to its depths. Young girls were not supposed to know there were depths. She did find the heights when Paris acclaimed her and Massenet wrote his music for her. 'Thaïs' and 'Manon' were hers, and no other prima donna could sing the high notes of 'Esclarmonde.' She died while she was still young and lovely, leaving many of her costumes and stage jewels to Mary Garden, then starting her career.

Only once I heard Sibyl Sanderson sing after she found fame abroad. It was in 1903, when she came to San Francisco with the Metropolitan Grand Opera Company under Maurice Grau. The old Grand Opera House in Mission Street was *en fête*, and filled to the doors, for her début as Manon, and for some reason it all fell sadly flat. San Francisco was disappointed. I think it may have been that the Wagner mood, which had just descended heavily on the city, made French music, with Sibyl's exquisite art, seem trivial to an audience more or less musically unsophisticated. She had lost, too, some of the sparkle of her personality. Not long afterward she retired, a hopeless invalid, to her villa at Cannes, where she died. But this was many years after our visit to Marysville where her mother went to school.

The Marysville Convent eventually merged with Notre Dame in San José, near the Jesuit College of Santa Clara, where pupils were likewise of mixed creeds. But something of the 'genteel tradition,' that blight on American life in the eighteen-hundreds, had come around the Horn, and we soon had any number of 'select academies' of learning. Across the bay from San Francisco was 'The Alameda Collegiate Institute for Young Ladies and Gentlemen.'

From Marysville and Shasta the stage line extended northward to Oregon. During the eighteen-eighties we followed it many times in the 'coach-and-six' to Sisson's at the foot of Mount Shasta, where an old farmhouse had become an inn famed for the hunting. Two days and a night we drove through the High Sierra, much of the way along the course of the Upper Sacramento. Here it was a rushing mountain stream that dashed between cliffs or fragrant, ferny banks thick with wild azalea. The sibilant rush of its waters could be heard long before we reached it in the mountain silence. Everywhere was the wild, inspiriting beauty that still lives in Yosemite.

Pitt River was slow and deep and smooth, with dark forests on either side. A long barge ferried the stage across. Charon and the Styx always came to my mind when we reached Pitt River. It was always at dusk.

Often at night we heard the call of panthers, high and poignant like a woman's cry. At Upper Soda Springs near

Sisson's, where 'Uncle Dick' Campbell had built a hotel like a boat — long and narrow with double-deck piazzas — the skin of one of these wild-cats was nailed on a wall. One spring morning, Uncle Dick had heard his little grandson scream, and rushed out to see him caught in a panther's claws, not thirty feet from the house. I saw the scars of the teeth on the small boy's throat that summer.

There still remained to stage-coach travel in the eighties the piquant hazard of an encounter with Black Bart, poet and knight of the road, a bandit of distinguished courtesy who worked always alone and in moonlight, wearing a narrow black mask across his face. He was politeness itself to passengers whose pockets he never rifled. The Wells-Fargo treasure-box was all he asked. If it was thrown out without protest, the whole affair passed off pleasantly enough for every one. Black Bart was his *nom de plume*, signed to poems pinned to trees along the roadside — gay verses of defiance after some successful robbery, occasionally a warning that he would pass that way again.

On moonlit nights, while the coach rolled over mountain roads of the High Sierras, the driver might turn to remark casually, 'A good night for Black Bart'; or, 'Right at that turn ahead Black Bart held the stage up last spring.' One peered into the shadows of the pines, half-hoping to see the figure of a man step out into the moonlight with uplifted gun. But I never saw Black Bart, although I have seen some of his poems, and have heard the story of his capture in San Francisco after a long, elusive career. Once too often he raided the Wells-Fargo treasure and dropped a handkerchief near the road with the broken, discarded box. On it was a laundry mark. This the Wells-Fargo detective, James Hume, traced to a San Francisco laundry, and so to its owner, a quiet, scholarly gentleman who lived in a San Francisco boarding-house. He was interested in mines, the landlady said, and often went on trips into the mountains.

Hume waited for him in his room one day and, when he returned, asked Mr. Bolton, which was the gentleman's name, if he would accompany him to a downtown office to discuss a mining deal. Mr. Bolton may have had his misgivings, but he went very readily with the stranger to discuss the deal. When they reached the entrance of the Wells-Fargo Building in Sansome Street, he stopped for an instant, but made no comment and turned in with his guide. They went to the office of one of the company's executives, and there on a table lay an axe and a broken treasure-box with its top crushed in. Mr. Bolton saw them, but gave no sign, waiting uncertainly at the door.

Hume crossed to the table and picked up a handkerchief, the one found with the box. 'Yours, I believe, Mr. Bolton,' he said.

A few seconds of silence, then Bolton made a slight gesture of surrender. 'I guess it's all up,' he answered.

'I guess it is,' the detective agreed pleasantly, and thus a notorious bandit was captured with all the quiet courtesy to which his victims were accustomed.

South of Sisson's where the first view of Castle Crags is like a sudden vision of the Alps the stage crossed Portuguese Flat and passengers invariably heard the story of the unfortunate Portuguese killed and eaten by a bear. Only his bones were found under a tree on the mesa.

'This Portuguese had been tracked home by a bear,' the driver would relate. 'She was on his heels before he could get to the house and his gun was empty. He ran and climbed that tree, and she clumb up after him. They found the branches all broken and scraped and figured she'd got him in the tree. Found his bones and his gun there at the foot of it. Yes ma'am, I knew him. Used to throw a paper out to him once a week. One day noticed them piled up at the road-side and told the folks at Slate Creek.'

It was the favorite story of Johnny Curtis, premier driver on the route, and left me always with a picture of the brief, terrible battle in a tree. Since then I've been told that bears do not climb trees after their quarry, but having treed it, wait grimly on the ground below for the inevitable, final scene. Either way the fate of the Portuguese was frightful enough.

The Sisson family had crossed the plains in a covered wagon and stopped there in Siskiyou County on the road to Oregon. Mr. Sisson was a mild little man who wore a black patch over one eye and had lost the fingers of one hand. He could tell exciting stories of Indian fights on the plains, when he would.

Many times this mild little man, who looked like a professor in some fresh-water college, had made the difficult ascent of Shasta, looming like a vast white dream-mountain above the valley. For he was an intrepid guide and hunter who knew the California mountains as few other men ever did. I was glad, when the railroad came, that they gave his name to the now thriving town of Sisson.

Covered wagons still passed on the Oregon road — immigrant wagons we called them. They overflowed with tow-headed children whose hair, bleached white by the sun, looked whiter against their sun-browned faces. Long freight trains passed constantly, eight hooded wagons linked in a single train, sometimes, the train drawn by ten or twelve mules. One driver would be seated on the first wagon and another midway the length of the mule team. They came from Sacramento laden with farm implements, household furniture, and supplies of all kinds for settlers in the north.

Three times a week the stage arrived from 'down below,' with mail and dusty passengers who dined at Sisson's and freshened up before going on their way again. The stage stations served marvelous meals; rainbow trout, venison, and a delectable assortment of wild berries — white raspberries, thimbleberries, tiny wild strawberries, and huckleberries which the Indians brought in and poured from huge, cone-shaped baskets into milk-pans aligned on the piazza. The squaws stood with the heavy filled baskets on their backs, slung from a head-strap which passed across the forehead, while their men bargained. They were of the Modoc tribe and seemed to have a congenital distaste for work. Occasionally the men fished and brought baskets of trout and McCloud River salmon to the inn, but principally they sat and smoked the pipe of peace at their camp a few miles down the road.

At that, they were just as energetic as the Washoes or any other Indians I knew in Northern California. None of them belonged to noble tribes of red men. The Washoes were of Nevada, but in the summer season they straggled up about Lake Tahoe, where, in the nineties, Old Annie had a summer wigwam near the Tallac House. Summer visitors from the old hotel would walk through the pine woods to Annie's camp and bargain for her baskets. One day callers found her seated before the wigwam mourning with tears and lamentations.

'What is it, Annie? What is the trouble?' they asked.

'My son-in-law,' she wailed.

'But what has happened to him?'

'Get hung today. Reno jail,' Annie sobbed.

'Oh, poor Annie! Your poor daughter!' sympathized the visitors. 'What did he do?'

Annie calmed herself. 'Him kill my daughter,' she said simply as one stating a mere preliminary detail of tragedy.

Finer types of the South, that we called Spanish Indians, were descended from those who came with Anza and Junípero Serra from Arizona. Some of these were among colonists of New Helvetia, that lost country of California, of brief and tragic history.

General John Sutter, founder of New Helvetia, was a Swiss who came adventuring through the Golden Gate in 1839. To reach California, he had sailed with fine determination from British Columbia to the Sandwich Islands, on a trading vessel, then back again across the Pacific on another. From the Spanish Governor at Monterey he received a grant of land on Yerba Buena peninsula (San Francisco), and one in the country where Sacramento now stands. There he built Sutter's Fort and founded New Helvetia. The old adobe fort has lately been restored on its original site in a city park of Sacramento. For colonists Sutter imported Kanakas from Hawaii, Chinese coolies, and Indians from the South, who with a number of Spaniards formed a heterogeneous population that, curiously enough, lived amicably and prospered. Farms, factories, and mills were built, and the Swiss adventurer was made Alcalde of the region which he extended far to the north — so far that General Vallejo in Sonoma suggested to his friend, the Alcalde in Monterey, that this stranger was becoming a menace. But whatever menace there was soon passed, for the discovery of gold at Sutter's Mill, in '48, ended Sutter's reign. Just before it, he had sent to Switzerland for his family. While they were voyaging across two oceans to the home he had built for them, James Marshall, a wheelwright at the mill, found the famous piece of gold quartz that changed California's history. News of the discovery spread until the gold rush swept like a tidal wave over New Helvetia. Colonists and laborers were caught in the rush, farms and factories were deserted. The land was gashed and torn by gold-hunters and orchards were destroyed. Sutter's family arrived to scenes of desolation. It all has the cumulative quality of Greek tragedy. Sutter's wife died at the end of her long journey. A son was killed defending his property against invaders, and misfortune followed misfortune. The Alcalde, whose governorship was gone in the new American régime, sat among the ruins of New Helvetia.

Early in the fifties my father knew the General when he came to San Francisco from his ranch to file suit against the Government for land lost in the confusion of old Mexican grants in a new State. The intrepid adventurer who had built an empire of a sort and lost it, all in ten years' time, had become a broken, bewildered old man looking helplessly at the city covering acres he once had owned.

For years the Sutter case dragged through the courts while the General lived on a pension from the State. Finally he went to Washington to petition Congress for indemnity, and he died there, forgotten and forlorn. Sutter Street in San Francisco is named for him, and Sutter County, which was part of New Helvetia.

The Sutter case, among others, brought Edwin M. Stanton to San Francisco. He came from Washington in 1857 to act as United States counsel in lawsuits over Mexican land grants, and my father's knowledge of California land surveys threw them much together. Often he dined with us; a difficult guest, since he appeared to hold that women, like children, should be seen and not heard. Taciturn and grim he was, although finely intellectual. Father admired him greatly. Mother and I thought he might have been disappointed in love. Possibly he walked in the shadow of grave and tragic events to come. He was Lincoln's War

Secretary and stood at the President's bedside when he died. It was this cold, ungracious man, who, looking at the dead President through a rush of tears, said the poignantly final words, 'Now he belongs to history.'

More gracious and gallant guests were some of the Spanish *caballeros*, Don Pio Pico, last of the Spanish Governors, Don Pablo de la Guerra, and others at whose *ranchos* my father had been entertained. The De la Guerras were all delightful — an old Spanish family which had come with land grants from Spain in the eighteenth century and lived like feudal barons in the South. The original De la Guerra *hacienda* still stands in Santa Barbara, in the heart of the city which covers part of the old De la Guerra domain. Members of the family still live in the low adobe house built around a *patio* with homes for several households in it. Beauty is their inheritance and descendants of the De la Guerras are among the loveliest of California women. Of one of them Gertrude Atherton wrote that she was like a slender, beautiful flagon of old Spain, filled with California wine.

Don Pablo, who was a member of the legislature in Sacramento for several years, was courtly and handsome, as were all of the Spanish dons. General Vallejo, for whom the town of Vallejo was named, was old and impoverished when I met him, but with still flashing dark eyes and a princely courtesy with his gesture of hospitality as he sat on the piazza of his old house in Sonoma surveying broad acres that were no longer his.

Colonel and Mrs. Jack Hays were friends in these early

years who came from their home in Oakland to dine with us. He had been Sheriff of San Francisco in the first Vigilantes days, and in youth was a noted Texas Ranger. With his alert, wiry little figure and piercing eyes, he looked then, in his quiet middle age, quite capable of swinging into a saddle and dashing into danger. Colonel Hays had built a home in Oakland and owned many acres in the growing town across the bay. They never ceased trying to persuade us to come there to live.

'I'll tell you, Mrs. Ransome,' said the Colonel to my mother one day, 'I'll give you a block of land in Oakland if you'll build a house on it.'

'Where?' Mother asked, laughing. 'Out in the tule marshes?'

'No, ma'am. Right in the city of Oakland. I'll give you a block on Broadway.' There were then attractive homes on this new thoroughfare, but Mother remained untempted. Years afterward, we could amuse ourselves computing the fortune blithely resigned with a block on Oakland's Broadway.

Colonel Hays's sister had married Major R. P. Hammond, of the Army, one of the young West Point officers sent out to California in the early fifties, and they had a little son, born in San Francisco, who was named for his uncle, John Hays Hammond.

It must have been at the Hays home that we met Colonel Andrew Williams, and his wife, who was the mother of Bret Harte by a former marriage. They had a charming home. The Colonel was then Mayor of Oakland, a courtly gentleman of the old school from New York, who, with the still dashing ex-Texas Ranger, Colonel Hays, formed an example of contrasts we constantly encountered in this new society, vital and refreshing. Men of many sorts met on a common ground of character, intelligence, and the zest for adventure; and in common they seemed always to have that delightful, irreverent sense of humor which was as distinctively Californian as the quiet, repressive brand is of New England.

Young Francis Bret Harte was adventuring in Northern California then. We did not meet him until years later, when he was a famous author and, with his wife and children, was our neighbor in San Rafael. But this belongs to a later chapter.

In spite of the fact that we preferred our fantastic city across the bay, Oakland was a pretty place even then, with spacious houses and gardens overflowing with flowers. In the eighteen-sixties, many beautiful homes were built in the neighborhood of Lake Merritt. I remember the Kirkham mansion, *en fête* for the wedding of Major Kirkham's daughter, Leila, to David Boyle Blair, an Englishman, who afterward inherited a title and made her Lady Yarde-Buller.

When, on the afternoon of the wedding, we drove into the grounds and a turn in the avenue brought us to the house set among palms, we found the veranda filled with guests.

'Why is this? Is the wedding to be out of doors?' we asked.

'Oh, no,' they answered, 'but it's so dark inside you can't see your hand before your face.'

They had all trooped out the long French windows into daylight to identify each other. However, we all trooped indoors before the wedding march sounded, to be greeted by the punctilious Major in a dim twilight. It was the first daytime entertainment given in the latest New York manner of darkened rooms, with artificial light, and really rather startling in this land of glaring sunlight which made the darkness seem very thick for all the flaming gas-jets in crystal chandeliers. What with the shrouded rooms, masses of flowers everywhere, and the heavy fragrance of orange blossoms, there was an inevitable suggestion of obsequies. But it was a happy wedding, nevertheless.

CHAPTER IV

CITY and state elections were especially exciting when our friends ran for office, and we electioneered for them in the feminine manner of the day, with discreet suggestions to tradesmen that Mr. Selby or Mr. Otis would make a far better mayor than his opponent. I was among enthusiasts thus electioneering for Senator Weller when he ran for Governor in '57, and was one of those who planned to make the inaugural ball at Sacramento an unusually grand affair. Vain plans they proved. It was, spectacularly at least, a dismal failure. Guests danced in their wraps, all their brave array hidden beneath evening cloaks and top-coats. It was in January, '58, one of the rare cold Januarys of those old winters, and the ballroom in a Sacramento theater, with stage extended over orchestra and parquet, had no provision whatever for heating. We shivered through the Grand March, and then there was a rush for dressing-rooms to retrieve wraps. Lumpy-looking dolmans and long fur-lined capes revolved heavily on the crowded floor. Still, it had a certain terpsichorean significance, this chilly ball, since it served to introduce the Lancers to California.

This innovation we planned on the steamer going up from San Francisco — the New World it was, which left the city at 4 P.M. and was due at Sacramento at midnight, taking a contingent of San Francisco guests for

CONSTANCE NEVILLE ABOUT 1860
Daughter of the author; afterwards Mrs. Stephen Rickard

the ball the following night. Soon after we turned from the bay into the Sacramento River, the New World struck a sandbar known as the Hog's Back, and there we were stranded until tides turned in the morning. No staterooms for sleep. To pass the time we danced on deck.

In London I had danced the Lancers, a spirited improvement on the old quadrille, and Peter Naylor had learned it in New York. We evolved the idea of teaching others in our party, and introducing the new dance at the Inaugural Ball. So while Billy Botts whistled 'Money Musk' and called figures, we balanced to the right, swung our partners, and all chassez-ed on the deck of the New World, in the Sacramento River. That night in Sacramento, when we formed a hollow square and went through the maneuvers, we stopped the ball.

One of the applauding spectators was Colonel Joe Hooker with whom I danced several times. A handsome man he was, who looked like Lord Cardigan, tall and soldierly. But heroic figures alone do not make great soldiers, and conversely, as Farragut, Grant, and Sherman among so many others, have proved. Colonel Hooker's score in the Civil War, beside theirs, was very low, something like zero, I think. In the fifties he lived on a ranch beyond Sacramento, where he entertained at elaborate *fiestas* in the Spanish manner. Wild parties, some of them were, although distinguished visitors in California were often his guests, as they were at General Frémont's ranch, 'La Mariposa,' beyond Stockton, where Mrs. Frémont and her little girl lived in the fifties. But here the hospitality was quiet and charming.

A great world event occurred in this year of 1858, the laying of the Atlantic cable. When the first message flashed under the sea between America and England, the people of two continents thrilled to the miracle. We thrilled nearly a month late, of course, but San Francisco at once declared a holiday, and Judge Shafter said, 'It is doubtless the greatest news the globe has heard since it was announced that "To Castile and Aragon, Columbus has given a new world."' That was the way we felt about it.

The Panama steamer Sonora brought the news. We had heard that summer of failures when the cable parted under the ocean, and knew that a third attempt to lay it would be made in August. As the Sonora drew near her dock one day in September, some one shouted from the deck, 'The Atlantic cable is laid!' and soon the whole city knew it. With awe we read the pious words which had opened the service on August 17, 1858: 'Europe and America are united by telegraph. Glory to God in the Highest; on earth, peace and good will toward men.' Since then the human race has grown more accustomed to miracles. Few people stop to glorify God for one, or even to remark the human courage and patient concentration of men who accomplish it.

We celebrated with flying flags, streamers of colored bunting, and a grand parade in which military companies, civic dignitaries, firemen, mercantile organizations, and all the foreign consuls participated.

We were in the gay company that viewed the procession from the windows of the French Consulate in Stockton Street, where we were guests of Madame Gautier, wife of the Consul. When it was over, gentlemen of the party who had been passing in review joined us, and we drank toasts to President Buchanan, to Queen Victoria, to the Atlantic cable, and the countries of all the consuls.

In a notebook of 1859 is listed for March 3, 'Launching of the Toucey at Mare Island.' The Toucey, soon to be rechristened the Saginaw, was the first ship built at the Navy Yard, and her launching was a great occasion. Excursion boats went from San Francisco with flying flags, bands, and festive crowds dancing all the way up the bay. We were guests of Captain Alden on the Active. Soon after this he was ordered East and departed with his quaint little wife, but Captain Richard Cuyler who succeeded him was an equally indefatigable host, forever arranging parties. The Army and Navy contributed generously to the gayety of our city — a sparkling froth that covered much important and distinguished service.

Captain and Mrs. Farragut had gone to Washington, and Captain Cunningham, new commandant at the Yard, was our host at the launching. His little daughter, Mollie, christened the Toucey, and after a collation at the Cunningham house, we danced in the sailmakers' loft — long used for hops at Mare Island — until a signal gun announced that boats were ready to depart; and the gay fleet sailed down the bay. Collations were feasts of cold delicacies, baked hams, roast fowl, and such things, with sweets and champagne. Any such spread was called a collation, whether served at noon or midnight.

That summer, Edgar Mills decided to tour the world, and fired two of his friends with a like ambition. Joseph Donahoe and John Y. Hallock arranged to go with him. The three musketeers took passage on the clipper ship Storm King bound for the Orient, and planned a party which facilitated the enthusiastic farewells of their friends — enthusiastic over the great adventure of a world tour.

On the day of their departure, they chartered the little steamer Surprise and invited a happy company to a champagne lunch on board. We steamed about the bay while the Storm King lay at anchor off Fort Point, and toward sundown we drew near her. She sent a small boat over to us and Edgar Mills and his friends left in a confusion of cheers, waving hats and handkerchiefs. As the Storm King sailed majestically through the Golden Gate with her canvas spread, the sunset gun on Alcatraz sounded a last farewell. I seem to recall that they all came home from Honolulu, but it may have been only one of them.

Excursions on the bay were popular for years — water frolics the Southerners called them: the bay was so inviting with its island hills and many inlets, and there was so little driving then on the peninsula. The Swiss Consul, Monsieur Berton, gave a party on a revenue cutter and introduced the novelty of fishing for rock cod; and Colonel and Mrs. Swords, who lived at the Oriental, commandeered the Active for another water frolic. He was chief quartermaster of the Department of the Pacific, where I always thought his name was wasted. A Colonel Swords should have been an officer of cavalry.

In a later time Albert Bierstadt, the painter, revived the water frolic for a party in honor of the visiting Duke of Manchester. We stopped at Lime Point that day to inspect the lighthouse and the Duke climbed the fragile stairway up the cliff, arriving breathless, but still affable, at the top.

Among invitation cards yellow with age, I still have one to a ball at the Presidio in 1859. It was given to mark the tenth anniversary of the establishment of the United States Army Post on the old Spanish reservation, and was a handsome affair — we referred to 'handsome affairs' in 'genteel' society, then. The Officers' Club at the post was the ballroom, a low adobe building facing the parade ground, which had been built by the Spanish *comandante* in 1776, with walls so thick that window-frames made broad, comfortable seats; still do, no doubt, since the old building still stands. It was bright with flags, glittering uniforms, and lovely gowns, and the flowers that bloomed in profusion in Presidio gardens.

The Plaza was festive that night, for there we gathered in all our finery to take omnibuses for the long drive over sand dunes to the post. We arrived at the Plaza in nondescript hacks or on foot, to pile into waiting army carry-alls, with our flaring skirts, fans, and bouquets, all to the vast entertainment of loiterers along Kearney Street.

The invitation reads:

> The pleasure of Captain and Mrs. Thomas J. Neville's
> company is requested at the
> Presidio of San Francisco
> on Monday evening, May 2nd, 1859
> at nine o'clock
>
> Major E. D. Keyes   Lieut. H. G. Gibson   Lieut. G. W. Custis Lee
> Lieut. J. B. McPherson   Surgeon C. C. Keeney   Lieut. G. H. Elliott
> Lafayette Hammond, Esq.
>
> N.B. Omnibuses will leave the Plaza for the Barracks at 8½ and at 9 P.M.

Of our hosts, Lieutenant Custis Lee was a son of General Robert E. Lee, of Virginia, and was then aide to General Clarke, Commandant of the Department of California. Lieutenant Gibson was everybody's favorite. He was known as 'Little Gibson' and his blithe good-nature was unfailing. Afterward he was prominent in official life at Washington, and he died there in 1924, in his ninety-seventh year. When I heard of his death, I wished we might have met in recent years to recall these long-ago times.

Lieutenant McPherson became Brigadier-General of Volunteers in the Civil War and was killed in the Battle of the Wilderness. He was full of fun and almost as popular as 'Little Gibson.' Lafayette Hammond was one of our South Park beaux, a Virginian, tall, and dark as a Spaniard. He was a close friend of Custis Lee, and was included among the hosts to welcome guests who might be strangers to the officers. Mrs. C. C. Keeney received with them, and 'every one' was there.

The clans gathered from Stockton Street, South Park, and Rincon Hill for the Mount Vernon Ball on June 1 of that gay year. It was the first entertainment of the sort given in the new country, a brilliant, semi-public affair, at which boxes were filled with the city's wealth and beauty, and the Grand March was a pageant of fashion. Mrs. William Blanding was Vice-Regent of the Mount Vernon Association in San Francisco. Her husband was a lawyer, one of the South Carolina Blandings, which I fancy gave him equal rank with Pinckneys and Izards; and she had a very becoming hauteur. Her aides were Mrs. Louis McLean, of the Baltimore McLeans; Mrs. Harrison Randolph, of Virginia; Mrs. Vandewater, and Miss Sarah Haight.

Possibly I should explain that we were interested in purchasing Mount Vernon from the first President's nephew, John Washington, to make it a national shrine. The Mount Vernon Association of American women, with chapters in all large cities of the country, was formed for this purpose. Our ball was a contributory detail in raising the necessary funds. We voted down Apollo Hall for this grand event, and decided on the American Theater, where the stage was built out over orchestra and parquet for a dancing-floor. The sartorial display that evening was long discussed.

With us were Mr. and Mrs. Hart and their daughter, Mrs. Carnegie, who had come from Australia to build an English country house out near Mission Dolores. Mrs. Carnegie was a pretty young widow who soon married Captain Stevenson, a gallant and distinguished gentleman who had brought the first regiment of United States Volunteers around the Horn. To the end of his very long life he wore his captain's cap covered with black oilcloth above the visor, a high black satin stock and long-tailed coat. For sixty years he was a quaint, revered figure in the San Francisco Pageant.

The Stevensons went to live on Nob Hill, where they gave innumerable parties that added to the gayety of a gay and carefree period. But I remember a dark day of these sunlit years when the city was plunged into grief. It was the 13th of September, 1859, when news that Senator Broderick had been fatally shot in a duel with Judge Terry spread a heavy wave of depression. It came without warning. The meeting had been secretly arranged, climax to a bitter political quarrel over Broderick's reëlection to the Senate. William M. Gwin was his opponent and Terry was Gwin's fiery protagonist — the same tempestuous Terry who had stabbed the man Hopkins in Commercial Street.

The two men met on the lonely shore of Lake Merced, beyond the city's limits, in the early morning gray with fog. Broderick, forced against his will and judgment into the encounter, was ill. He went from a sick-bed to the rendezvous. Terry's shot passed through his lungs. His own shot went wild, deliberately so aimed, many people believed. Duels and killings were not in his philosophy.

They drove him to the home of friends at Fort Mason — a long, rough drive from one end of the peninsula to the other. There he lingered several days. During this time hourly bulletins of his condition were brought into the city by couriers on horseback. Broderick was loved throughout California. His sincerity, with his gift for political leadership, and his zeal for the State's best interests, had won a devoted following. There is no question he had his eyes fixed on high places and reason to believe he would have reached them. It seemed too tragic that it should all needlessly end in the stupid insanity of a duel.

When his death was announced, tears coursed down the faces of men in the streets. They stood about bulletin boards of the newspaper offices in stricken silence, and no one had the heart for business that day. I remember how on the day of his funeral blinds were closed everywhere and buildings were draped in black. In the Plaza, Colonel Baker delivered the funeral oration to thirty thousand people gathered there and in the windows of neighboring buildings. Many followed the cortège to Lone Mountain Cemetery.

Terry had waited in seclusion for news of Broderick's death. When it came, he fled, but was followed and arrested near the Nevada border, to be brought back for trial. His acquittal left him under a cloud which never lifted and finally obscured him. We heard of his going to Texas to fight for the Confederacy in the Civil War, but his return was unmarked. People had fairly forgotten him when in the eighteen eighties he stepped back into the limelight as counsel for the notorious Sarah Althea Hill in a *cause célèbre*. The lady sued to establish a contract marriage with Senator Sharon, and lost her case. Judge Stephen J. Field decided it against her, and Terry became Field's avowed enemy, an enmity that was to bring about his own death.

The trial was full of sensational details. One I recall was the introduction of a love charm given to Sarah Althea by Mammy Pleasants — or Pleasaunce as it had been in New Orleans. She was one of our figures of mystery, a shrewd old Negress who had made a fortune in mining stocks and gained a neat profit on the side from the sale of love charms to enterprising young ladies desiring the favor of wealthy gentlemen. But her reticence concerning her affairs was complete. She was the despair of cross-examiners.

One saw her picturesque and solitary figure passing through streets of the financial district. She had been born in slavery, but she walked like a duchess, tall and slim. In all the years I saw her, she never varied the style of her costume, a long, full-skirted gown, with kerchief crossed over her bosom and a wide black hat tied over her head, such a costume as she might have worn in New Orleans when she was given her freedom before the war.

Promoting romance and gambling in stocks were mere avocations — Mammy Pleasants was by vocation a housekeeper, and lived at the home of Judge Bell, a huge old house out on Octavia Street surrounded by neglected gardens and veiled in mystery, as baffling as her own.

Not long after the close of the Hill *versus* Sharon case, the marriage of Judge Terry and his defeated client was announced, to the astonishment of all his friends. The couple went to live in retirement on their ranch near Fresno and it was said, incredibly, to be a happy marriage.

Only once more this brilliant, violent man flashed into the limelight to die spectacularly with his boots on. The final scene was in a restaurant at Lathrop, an eating station on the railroad north of Los Angeles. Judge Field, then one of the Supreme Court in Washington, was making one of his accustomed trips through California with the armed bodyguard who always accompanied him in the territory of his old enemy. They had boarded the train at Los Angeles, unaware that Judge and Mrs. Terry were also passengers. At Lathrop, all passengers alighted to dine, and in the restaurant the two met. Judge Field was already seated when Terry and his wife entered and passed him to go to the far end of the room. There Terry turned to walk back to Field's table, where he stood and glared in silence for a moment, then struck his hand across Field's face. In an instant he fell, shot to death by the guard. Mrs. Terry's lamentations filled the room, and she was taken away a screaming maniac. She died in a hospital for the insane.

Some of the clash and storm of Judge Terry's life seemed to enter the lives of those near him. His law partner, D. W. Perley, was involved in a melodramatic romance that stirred public interest early in the sixties and was remembered of him for years. Its heroine was a young girl named Josie Mansfield, whose mother kept a boarding-house in Sutter Street — the same Josie Mansfield over whom Ed Stokes shot Colonel Jim Fisk in New York in '72. The Perley romance was her début as a heart-breaker. She was very young then, and the attentions of Mr. Perley, who was old enough to be her grandfather, were resented by a stepfather who played the rôle of irate parent. In the middle of melodramatic complications, the heroine eloped with an actor and went to New York, so the curtain was rung down. But when news of the assassination of Fisk, Jay Gould's partner, startled the country, and the opulently beautiful Miss Mansfield took her place in the limelight, the Perley affair was recalled in all its details in San Francisco which took a proprietary interest in the New York tragedy. I remember photographs of Miss Mansfield and the jaunty Colonel Fisk displayed for sale in a Kearney Street window, and have no doubt they found purchasers to acquire and cherish them.

Stokes came to San Francisco after he had served a term in Sing Sing, and for a time in the late seventies was often seen driving his fast trotters on the Cliff House road; but socially he was more or less of an outlaw, although he was still handsome and distinguished-looking; perfectly tailored after the Sing Sing stripes as he had been before them.

Lone Mountain, where Senator Broderick was buried, and where so many figures of his generation rest, is a lovely place; a cemetery of sloping lawns, roses, and flowering acacia trees, from where, standing near Senator Latham's bronze tomb, one may look eastward over the city's hills, or westward to the Golden Gate. It was a long drive over sand hills from the Plaza in '59, but the cemetery, since called Laurel Hill, lies now in the heart of the residence district. Castilian roses and nasturtiums cover the tree-trunks, pansies and violets bloom in the grass, and tapestries of flowers overhang low stone walls. It has sometimes been a gently melancholy pleasure for me to wander through it and read the epitaphs and names familiar to me long ago.

A granite slab is 'In memory of the first inhabitant of this Silent City, John Orr, interred June 10th, 1854.' I knew his son, who married Mary Shafter.

But the rarest of all San Francisco epitaphs is carved on a granite pyramid in Cypress Lawn, whither it was removed from the old Masonic Cemetery on McAllister Street. The pyramid marks the grave of Hugh Whittell, once a prominent citizen of San Francisco, who composed his epitaph before his death and saw it carved on the stone. I have wished that Hugh Whittell had written the story of his adventures in detail. On his gravestone they are thus recounted:

Hugh Whittell

In the five divisions of the world I've been;
The cities of Peking and Constantinople I have seen.
On the first railway I rode before others were made,
Saw the first telegraph operate, so useful to trade.
In the first steamship, the Atlantic I crossed;
Suffered six shipwrecks where lives were lost.
In the first steamer to California I did sail,
And went to China by the first Pacific Mail.
After many endeavors my affairs to fix,
In a short time I'll occupy less than two by six.

On the opposite side of the pyramid is carved;

As you that chance this grave to see,
If you can read English, may learn of me.
I traveled, read and studied, mankind to know,
And what most interested them here below;

> The present or the future state. Love of Power,
> Envy, fear or hate occupied each wakeful hour.
> All would teach, but few would understand.
> The greater part knew little of either God or Man.
> 'Love one another,' was a good maxim, all agreed.
> Learn, labor, and wait, if you would succeed.

A year or two before the Broderick-Terry duel, there had been a fatal affair of honor, so called, which ended in tragedy for victor as well as victim. The first was a young Southerner, George Penn Johnson, who reluctantly met a politician named Ferguson in a duel arranged by Ferguson's political enemies. Johnson was a happy soul whose wit I had often enjoyed at dinner-parties, a journalist by profession. It was through his newspaper affiliations that he was dragged into the affair. Neither duelist desired to fight, but there was this honor business. Neither could do the common-sense thing and withdraw without sacrificing honor. So they met and Ferguson fell. Johnson's life thereafter was of little use to him. He became a recluse, morose and embittered, and slowly drank himself to death.

With the Broderick-Terry affair, dueling ceased to be an honorable method of settling differences in California.

The city grew with astonishing rapidity. New buildings were constantly going up in downtown districts and new residences on the hills — attractive, stable-looking structures to replace the shanties which had served their time. Men of wealth built luxurious homes. In Folsom Street at the foot of Rincon Hill, the Milton Latham house was a

NELLIE GORDON
Upon whose life-story *A Daughter of the Vine* was based

mansion set in a broad sweep of lawns with marble statuary gleaming against the shrubbery. A black-and-white flagged marble walk led from high iron gates to the house. Near it John Parrott, the banker, had an imposing home, and on Rincon Hill were many charming houses built in the old style with long French windows opening to galleries; and each with its flower-filled garden.

The Thomas Selby house was among them, and as early as '57 was a center of hospitality. In its pretty little ballroom built out in a wing at one side, we danced at our first ball in San Francisco given for a recent bride and bridegroom, Mr. and Mrs. Hayne.

Mrs. Selby was a fragile little lady, but indefatigably hospitable. While her husband was Mayor of the city, she entertained constantly, and afterward at their Menlo Park home a happy hospitality prevailed. This easy grace of hospitality was a characteristic of the old San Francisco set that the bonanza kings never acquired. Their palaces were opened for splendid balls and state occasions, but too often the great rooms were empty.

In the early sixties, South Park had become an attractive neighborhood, laid out like an English 'Crescent,' with a long strip of parkway on which the houses faced. It was planned by George Gordon, an enterprising Englishman who owned the first sugar refinery in San Francisco. Mrs. Gordon and pretty Miss Nellie were conspicuous in the social scene and George Gordon himself was just generally conspicuous. He had that British sense of a gentleman's duty to offer constructive criticism of public affairs which inspires so many letters to the London 'Times,' and was forever rushing into print about something.

·The Gordons built a country home, Mayfield Grange, near Menlo Park, and for a time gave house-parties there in the English manner, serving cold joints for breakfast, to the great astonishment of some of the local gentry. But George Gordon died, and then Miss Nellie; and Mrs. Gordon sold Mayfield Grange to Senator Stanford. It became part of his estate at Palo Alto on which the buildings of Stanford University stand.

One of the most hospitable of South Park homes was that of Senator and Mrs. Gwin, where two daughters and a young son brought the gayety of youth. Mrs. Gwin's oyster suppers were famous and her Christmas eggnog parties. Commodore and Mrs. Watkins were neighbors. He was the urbane commodore of Pacific Mail steamers, and she was a dear soul who wore clusters of corkscrew curls over her ears through changing fashions, until her death; as Mrs. Foard wore her hoopskirts well into the twentieth century. A Market Street dealer who catered to theatrical trade supplied them when others failed.

Mrs. Foard, of the Baltimore Foards, lived at the Oriental with her daughter Julia, who was one of the beauties of the old set. She married Joe Tilden, of Boston, famed as San Francisco's first epicure. I remember how lovely Julia Foard was as bridesmaid for Augusta Hooper at her wedding to Pelham Ames, of Boston. Joe Tilden was best man and their engagement was soon announced.

The Hoopers of South Park were an interesting family,

all gifted musically. They had come from Honolulu, where Mr. and Mrs. Hooper had been missionaries in the zeal of their youth, and on musical evenings at their home they often sang old hymns. Gussie, the daughter, played the piano, her brother Edward, the flute, and William Little, a half-brother, the cornet. At Gussie's marriage to Pelham Ames, one of the wedding presents from Boston was a treasured family heirloom, a decanter of old wine, the stopper broken cleanly across the top, which had once been set before George Washington. It had been in the cellar of Fisher Ames, member of Congress from Massachusetts under the first President, and had been placed upon the table at a dinner-party given at the Ames home in Washington's honor. When the butler prepared to pour the wine, the glass stopper proved stubborn, and in his efforts to remove it, it was broken. The host ordered another decanter, and the discarded bottle of Madeira was preserved as souvenir of the dinner, to be handed down through the generations. It met a tragic end, eventually. I must flash forward to the Pelham Ames home in Pacific Avenue, where it stood on a shelf in the dining-room, to record the disaster.

At a dinner-party a few years ago, one of the daughters of the household told the story of the decanter to assembled guests, and finished effectively, indicating the shelf, 'There is the wine that was set before Washington.' Every one looked up, of course, but there was only an empty shelf. The bottle was not in its accustomed place. Mrs. Ames summoned the Japanese butler and made inquiries.

He was puzzled. No wine had he seen. Then a great light: 'Oh, yes! Vinegar! Bottle top broken, so I break to get vinegar. Vinegar not good. I throw all away.'

Joe Tilden was a *bon viveur* of unusual epicurean distinction. He liked to invade the kitchen of the Bohemian Club, don the chef's cap and concoct marvelous dishes for his friends' delectation. Raphael Weill was his successor, and some of their recipes are still honored and used by San Francisco chefs. After his death, a collection of Joe Tilden's recipes was published — the only gentleman's cook-book ever printed, I believe. There was a rare salad of artichoke hearts, and the flavors still linger of Virginia ham boiled in champagne, and iced watermelon filled with claret — triumphs of a gastronomic period now sadly past.

In those days there were feasts at the Friedlander and Bowie homes in South Park, the like of which will probably never again regale the human race. For gourmets as I knew them are extinct in this age of counted calories. We never thought of our silhouettes in the dietary dark ages of which I write, but lingered for hours over dinner, discussing a menu of seventeen courses. Mrs. Bowie once told me that if she sat down at half-past six and rose from the table before midnight, she considered the dinner a failure; either rushed in the serving, or not enough to eat. She was the wife of Dr. Alexander Bowie, a retired navy surgeon, and their South Park home was a social center for long years. Mrs. Friedlander, whose dinners rivaled the Bowies', was from South Carolina, the wife of Isaac Friedlander, who aspired to be the Grain King of California. He

MRS. JOSEPH TILDEN
(Julia Foard)

JOSEPH TILDEN
Epicure and *bon viveur*

was a clever, cultured Jew from Hamburg, of whom his wife always insisted with dignity that Isaac was a Hebrew, not a Jew; so perhaps he was.

Half-past six was the fashionable hour for dinners, which began with oysters on the half-shell, went through soup, fish, entrées (note the plural), salad, game, roast, 'Roman punch,' and desserts to liqueurs. Wines would be sherry, sauterne, claret, and champagne, with sometimes port at the end. Naturally a dinner of this sort, all served in courses, was an affair of several hours.

A curious relic of this gastronomic period is the menu for a dinner we gave to some English visitors, of which I append a copy:

Oysters on the half-shell

Julien Soup
Shrimp Salad
Baked sole — Potatoes
Ris de Veau
Filet de Boeuf
Roman Punch
Roast Turkey — Peas
Asparagus
Quail
Terrapin
Swiss Méringue
Plombière
Cakes — Mottoes — Candied Fruits
Oranges — Apples — Pears — Grapes — Nuts
Champagne — Sherry — Claret — Sauterne — Liqueurs
Coffee

New Year's calling was an established custom in the sixties and seventies, and a queer custom it was with gorgeous possibilities for Gilbert and Sullivan had they ever availed themselves; battalions of calling gentlemen and receiving ladies would have made a rarely effective chorus. Most of the large homes kept 'open house' on New Year's Day, the hostess assisted by several young lady friends, a first group to be relieved by others during the afternoon, for it was a long day, often beginning as early as 11 A.M. The first callers would be gentlemen with extended lists who were hopeful of reaching Mrs. Gwin's by dinner-time. Collations were served at all open houses, but Mrs. Gwin's spread surpassed them all, and after hot oysters, cold birds, jellied meats, salads, and desserts, with accompanying wines, there would be dancing for those still able to enjoy it.

If one were not receiving, it was in order to close the blinds of the house and shroud it in dim silence. Callers then merely left cards without asking for 'the ladies.' But cards were carefully counted, and any young man beholden for past hospitalities, who failed to pay his debt with a card left in person, was stricken from the list of the slighted hostess.

Speaking of menus and chefs, San Francisco restaurants have been noted for their cuisines since pioneer days. California had always richly supplied markets, for the Spaniards lived well long before the gringos came. As early as the fifties, Clayton's Restaurant in Commercial Street, and Martin's a few doors beyond, were better than most New York restaurants. Winn's Fountain-Head of Luxuries had a grand name, but in spite of it, excellent food. For terrapin and oyster suppers, we went to Captain Cropper's in Second Street. In the sixties this place was taken over by a man named Harkness, who did catering for social events. Terrapin and oysters were usually ordered, ready to serve, from Harkness.

But Peter Job was really the first caterer. He was an excitable little Frenchman and a most accomplished confectioner whose shop in Washington Street displayed intricate effects in frosting and spun sugar. Peter Job's was a popular place for ice-cream and cake on warm afternoons, and he frosted most of society's wedding cakes. Sugar doves and wedding bells adorned them.

Doubtless Peter Job frosted the wedding cake when Sue Sweringen married Judge Stephen J. Field. We went to the ceremony at little Grace Church in Powell Street. No decorations; no display of any sort — it was not yet fashionable. The bride wore white muslin, the flaring skirt all ruffled, and her sister, as bridesmaid, wore the same simple fabric. Distinctly I recall the squeak of Judge Field's shoes as he walked down the aisle. Brand-new, of course, and developing the squeak unexpectedly, no doubt. Not long afterward, Bell Sweringen married Andrew McCreery at Grace Church, but there were no guests. Bride and bridegroom drove up to the church alone one evening, and announcements after the marriage surprised society.

The Sweringen girls were all unusually bright and all had interesting careers — Mrs. Field as a hostess in Washington and Mrs. McCreery as owner of a stable of racing-horses in England where she was long one of the Prince of

Wales's set. It was said she inspired the character of 'The Sporting Duchess' in a play of that name once popular in London and New York. A third sister became Mrs. Condit-Smith, of Washington, and one of her pretty daughters married General Leonard Wood.

The Hall McAllisters moved down to South Park from the old family house in Stockton Street and gave a fancy-dress ball in the new house which made social history. I went as Summer in a flower-garlanded dress which trailed all around. Kate Robinson stepped on it. 'It's too long,' she said. I looked at her Pierrette costume all of two inches above her ankles.

'Yes, it is too long,' I answered. 'We might both profit if you added some of it to yours'; for such brevity as she displayed was daring, indeed, and likely to shock conservatives. Kate Robinson laughed and pirouetted to prove her assurance. She was a spirited girl, one of the really clever women in society later when as Mrs. Monroe Salisbury she became something of a social power.

Mrs. Frank Pixley was Marie Antoinette that night and very effective with her powdered hair and rose silk gown. She, too, was one of society's clever women, wife of an intrepid editor whose pen was feared by the weak brothers of politics. Frank Pixley owned a weekly paper, 'The Argonaut,' and himself wrote its trenchant editorials. Bret Harte was a contributor.

Of the McAllister house a true story has become legend in San Francisco. Hall McAllister lost it at poker to Captain Harry Lyon, a dashing gentleman from New Orleans who won it just in time to present it to his daughter for a wedding gift. Cora Lyon was married from the family home in Harrison Street and her post-honeymoon receptions were held in the house that was staked and lost in a game of poker.

Our new home in O'Farrell Street was uptown then, near the old place at O'Farrell and Jones Streets known as the 'Johnson Mansion,' where lived a happy colony of cats. Mrs. Johnson left them ten thousand dollars in her will — it may have been twenty thousand — and they all moved to a ranch in Sonoma County, where for all I know their descendants are still living.

Also near was the home of Joseph Duncan, a suave and cultured gentleman who was cashier of the Bank of California and whose fortunes crashed with Ralston's. He was known as a connoisseur of the arts and was often asked to select paintings and marbles for the palaces of his friends who knew little about them. His own house at Geary and Taylor Streets held many treasures. Isadora, his daughter, was born there about the time of the crash, and the family soon afterward moved to Oakland. She was still a small girl when she played the piano for her mother's juvenile dancing-classes and they all went abroad to live long before she dreamed of becoming a dancer.

We gave many musicales at the O'Farrell Street home when my sister Annie sang. She had a lovely voice. One evening Louis Gottschalk played her accompaniments. He was a dreamy-eyed youth, but already famous as a pianist. Felix Pioche, the French banker, brought him to one of our parties and we were delighted to welcome him.

Gottschalk lived for several years in San Francisco, where he gave piano lessons, and all his fair pupils fell in love with him or with his magnetic music. There was no end of gossip over one romance with a South Park belle which threatened to end in an elopement. But she was locked in her room; the musician departed for wider fame in the East, and in a year or two she married an Army officer stationed on Angel Island.

Adelaide Phillips, the contralto, was our guest of honor one evening. She had brought a letter to my mother from Mrs. Doremus, of New York, and dined with us several times, to delight us with her singing. Gottschalk was her accompanist.

I think it was the same season that the Vandewaters gave a reception for Mr. and Mrs. Bayard Taylor when the poet-traveler came to lecture on Sweden. Mrs. Taylor was a young German girl, daughter of a Herr Professor, whom he had married abroad and who obviously looked upon her husband as a very great man. He really was a leading figure in American letters, then, although I doubt if any one reads him avidly now. Mr. Taylor, one felt, shared his wife's estimate of her husband, and stood very tall and toplofty beside Mrs. Vandewater to meet her guests. Presentations were effected with reverence, and when the solemn privilege had been accorded, one passed on into a hushed assemblage. It was all rather pontifical. No one conversed with Mr. Taylor, but he delivered a few brief monologues — one on changes he noted in San Francisco since his first visit. He had followed the Gold Rush to write letters about it for the 'New York Tribune,' 'when the water came up to Montgomery Street,' a familiar phrase to recall the city's past era.

CHAPTER V

CIVIL WAR days in San Francisco were not greatly different, all considered, from the days of other years; the same swift rhythm and bright touch of excitement. Life always had a keen, stark quality which war may quicken in old, quiet places, and the stress and tension did not reach us. There were a few flares of excitement. A few passionate secessionists fell into the tragic mood, and a few friendships were strained. But there was no sharp bitterness of feeling and much of the drama was played lightly.

The only time we really felt the menace of war, I think, was in a brief crisis of uncertainty after news of the firing on Sumter reached us. The news of Sumter's fall came by Pony Express, and was chalked on blackboards in front of newspaper offices while papers were still on the presses. People stood and read it in silence and men discussed it quietly with grave faces. No one was sure of California; there had been much talk of seceding. And no one could know what had transpired in the nine days since our news had left St. Joe. War, of course, but what had happened? Northerners and Southerners alike felt uncertainty and apprehension.

Senator Latham, Thomas Selby, James Otis, and other Northern men held a conference, and a mass meeting of citizens was called. Where Post, Montgomery, and Mar-

MASS MEETING AT THE CORNER OF MARKET AND POST STREETS, MAY 11, 1861
At this meeting San Francisco declared in favor of adhesion to the Union

ket Streets conjoin, sand lots and converging streets made a broad, open field for the gathering.

'There may be trouble,' Father told us. 'You had better remain indoors.' Wise counsel, no doubt, but impossible to follow. We had no thought of attending the meeting. Women were not expected. But we drove across Kearney Street to watch the crowds assemble; men, with here and there a woman among them, going down Market and Post Streets, down Commercial and Clay, to turn south on Montgomery; thirty thousand in all, it was said.

From the improvised platform my father watched the crowd's response when orators declaimed on duty to the Union. Apathetic it was, until the young clergyman, Thomas Starr King, spoke. He was eager and impassioned, and his hearers caught the fire of his patriotism. When he ended in a wave of applause, San Francisco, which meant the State, stood for the Federal Government. Flags were unfurled on buildings, and election lithographs of Lincoln were dusted and set in windows. Southerners 'went softly,' Northerners refrained from overbearing patriotism, and a delicate balance of amity was maintained.

Many incidents that might have had tragic significance ended with a touch of comedy, the deportation of Dr. Scott, for example. This beloved pastor of Calvary Church was a secessionist without discretion. On the first Sunday after the news of Sumter, he preached a sermon for the South to a congregation including many Northerners. It was disturbing, possibly dangerous to public peace. Deacons remonstrated. But on the Sunday following, Dr. Scott once more invoked divine blessing on the rebel cause, and a few days later was discovered hung in effigy before his church.

This was naturally very shocking; and since it appeared that Dr. Scott could preach no neutral sermon, his friends decided on drastic measures. On the third Sunday, when the clergyman, still praying for the South, left his pulpit, he was met by several of those high in church affairs and led to a waiting carriage — Mrs. Thomas Selby's barouche. As they drove toward the steamship docks, Dr. Scott learned that he was actually *en route* to his old home in New Orleans. They placed him on board a Panama steamer, with tickets and provision for the trip, and he departed, protesting, no doubt, but with the good wishes of all concerned. At the close of the war he returned to resume his interrupted pastoral duties at Calvary Church quite as though nothing of any consequence had occurred.

I remember how Lucy Hall waved a rebel flag over the balcony of the Oriental Hotel when Confederate volunteers marched down Market Street on their way to fight for the South. There was no demonstration in the streets. To preserve that delicate balance of amity of which I have spoken, the Governor had forbidden it. But Lucy Hall's fiancé marched with the volunteers. She was a dashing, spirited girl, one of the belles of the Southern set, and when the men passed the Oriental, where she stood on the upper balcony, she leaned far out waving her rebel colors. Not an officer or soldier could salute them and hers was the only flag that waved in defiance of the edict. But she married a Northerner, after all, one of the young engineers who surveyed the Placerville Road.

Some of our friends went to the front. Judge Terry rushed to the scene of hostilities in Texas to fight for the South. General Halleck and Colonel Baker departed to join the Northern army and both gave distinguished service. Colonel Joe Hooker left his *fiestas* to fight for the Union; and several companies of volunteers. But California's greater contribution was in money, over a million dollars, nearly a million and a half, to the Sanitary Commission for which the entire country subscribed five million dollars.

Many who did not go to the war sent 'bounty men' in their stead. The price paid these hired fighters was anywhere from one to five thousand dollars, and it was an accepted custom to send them until it became deplorably certain that many of them 'jumped their bounty' and never saw service.

We were all going to 'the minstrels' in those days. They were the popular theatrical entertainment of the time with programs changed weekly. Always I thrilled like a child at the circus when the curtain rose to show the line of black faces across the stage and an urbane interlocutor said courteously, 'Gentlemen, be seated.' Songs and patter followed. I can still hear the sonorous tones of one basso-profundo going down to the bed of the ocean when he sang 'Rocked in the Cra-dull of the Deep.' Frillman, I think his name was. Billy Birch was a favorite end man who chanted a parody on a sentimental war song of which the chorus ran:

> 'Farewell, Mother, you will never
> See my name among the slain,
> For when I can jump the bounty,
> I'll come back to you again.'

Lists of the fallen sometimes held the names of friends or relatives and a few families were in mourning, but the note of gayety in San Francisco was never long silenced. We laughed for days over one fright which, it transpired, was caused by the most delightfully Gilbertian episode.

It was two hours after midnight, one night, when the sound of heavy guns wakened the city. At once every one thought of the Confederate raider Alabama, then being sought in Pacific waters. An attack on the Presidio, we decided, and remained sleepless the rest of the night, although firing ceased after fifteen or twenty minutes. Morning brought the explanation; a peaceful visit of H.M.S. Sutlej, with customary salutes exchanged, customary but untimely. The Sutlej had inadvertently entered port out of hours.

Because of uncertainty as to the Alabama's whereabouts, port orders were that no vessel should enter the Golden Gate between sunset and sunrise, and the Sutlej had sailed from Esquimault before this new regulation was known. That night a lookout stationed on Alcatraz — the island fortress at the inner portals of the Golden Gate — had discerned a large ship making her way through the fog into the bay, and immediately reported it. A shot was fired to bring the vessel to. This was ignored and a second shot was sent across her bow. At this the vessel hurriedly raised the United States flag and proceeded to fire a salute of twenty-one guns. She proved to be the friendly Sutlej, with Admiral Kingcome on board.

In return for her salute, the courteous reply of twenty-one guns was in order from Alcatraz. This was given while an alarmed city listened to the supposed bombardment — given all but one gun, as it happened. Only twenty shots were fired, and Captain Connelly of the British ship had kept careful count. He demanded the twenty-first. For some reason it was not forthcoming and the Captain informed the Commandant at Alcatraz that he would remain in port until the final gun of a proper salute was heard. Having so stated, he took his ship to the usual anchorage for British vessels at Sausalito. Next morning, when every one concerned was wide awake, the British ensign was raised with ceremony on Alcatraz and the twenty-first gun of a proper salute was fired. The Sutlej, perfectly satisfied, sailed away an hour later.

Northerners and Southerners in California were alike saddened when General Albert Sidney Johnston fell fighting for the South at Shiloh. He had been commandant of the Department of the Pacific before the war. When he resigned his commission to go to Richmond and enlist in the Confederate Army, he went with the good will of the city, where he had made himself sincerely liked. His loyalty under pressure from secessionists who had formed a plot to seize army posts and munitions in California, in the name of the Confederacy, had won especial admiration. The conspirators sent a committee to call upon the General in his office and request no more than his acquiescence in the plot. His resignation had gone to Washington, but it was a matter of weeks before General McDowell could arrive to relieve him, and meanwhile he was still a commanding officer of the United States Army. Knowing the purpose of the committee, he received it, and spoke first, affirming his allegiance to his uniform until he should be relieved, and a disappointed committee bowed itself out.

After General Johnston departed, Mrs. Johnston and their children went to live with her cousin, Mrs. Tod Robinson, in Powell Street. Mrs. Robinson was a staunch supporter of the rebel cause. She had been Mary Crittenden, of Louisville. Her husband, a lawyer who came West to practice in the new city, had died leaving her with too small an income for her needs, so Mrs. Robinson 'took boarders' in her Powell Street home. It was one of the few ways open to a gentlewoman to earn money. After the war, San Francisco, like the South, blossomed into many boarding-houses run by Southern ladies whose fortunes had gone with the Lost Cause.

Mrs. Robinson was a finely intelligent woman of courage and character who worked indefatigably for the losing cause during the war. She established something like a very limited Red Cross service, raising a fund for the relief of Confederate prisoners in the North. Her son was imprisoned at Rock Island.

One excitement of the war years was furnished by the Chapman Plot hatched by a band of Secessionists who planned to convert the sloop 'Chapman' into a sea raider to prey on Pacific Mail steamers in the name of the Confederacy. One of the conspirators was a nephew of John Bright. Another was a Mexican for whom many boxes of 'farm implements' were loaded on the 'Chapman' addressed to his ranch in Mexico. The 'farm implements' were in reality arms and ammunition. Learning of the plot before the 'Chapman' sailed, the city police boarded her, arrested the conspirators and confiscated the 'farm implements.'

We were all discussing it, and the John Bright nephew when one morning 'The Flag,' a violently patriotic newspaper which flourished briefly, came out with the astounding statement that Mrs. Tod Robinson had been one of the conspirators!

It was a bomb shell in South Park, and in all San Francisco where Mrs. Robinson and her family, dashing Kate Robinson and the Albert Sidney Johnstons, were so well known. Like the McAllisters, Gwins, Friedlanders and other Southern families, they had never forsworn their Northern friendships.

We talked of nothing else while Mrs. Robinson remained in seclusion and made her denials to the proper authorities. One of the conspirators, it developed, had in fact called on her to enlist her help, but to no avail whatever and this had been her only connection with the plot.

In time it all died down but for long afterward there

hung a faint halo of martyrdom over Mrs. Robinson's high-held head.

In the last years of the war, there was the excitement of new silver mines in Nevada. A Pony Express rider, idly prospecting in the Washoe country north of Virginia City, had come upon rich lodes, and the rush to the land of the Washoe Indians was on. In San Francisco, interest centered in the new Stock Exchange. Every one speculated in mining shares. A conviction prevailed that gold was gold and silver would remain silver, however the war might end.

Pony Express riders were out of jobs, so to speak, since the telegraph had crossed the Rocky Mountains. Over it flashed the news of Lincoln's assassination and death, and a sense of calamity fell like darkness over the city, as it did over the whole country north of the line. We still had with us the Knights of the Golden Circle, a secret society of secessionists, and there were many members of the Southern clans whose mourning was perfunctory, but the whole city mourned, nevertheless, and buildings were draped in the cerements of woe. How many yards of black bunting went into the expression of civic sorrow in those days!

CHAPTER VI

AFTER THE WAR

THE Presidio 'carried on' socially as well as militarily through the war years and afterward. So many gallant officers I knew are forgotten now. Vivid, dashing figures they were, many of them distinguished for service to their country. Their blue uniforms with brass buttons, and white stripes down the trousers for infantry, yellow stripes for cavalry, and red for artillery, are bright flashes of color in my memory of old San Francisco. General McDowell succeeded General Albert Sidney Johnston as commandant and brought with him from Washington, his aides, handsome Captain Jim Cutting, of New York, and Captain Franklin Haven, of Boston, both West Point men. Later, the General's aides were Colonel William Neal Dennison, son of Governor Dennison of Ohio, and General Whittier, who was a Bostonian and had the Beacon Hill reserve of manner, which was odd in the West. Also he was conspicuous by reason of being 'clean-shaved' when other men were wearing elaborate hirsute adornments. It was a day of something like facial landscape gardening for men. Hedges, parterres, and veritable jungles trimmed their features.

When General Halleck arrived, full of Civil War honors, to be Commander-in-Chief of the Pacific Department, his aides were Colonel Bob Scott and Captain Henry Huntington, and their wives, with Mrs. Halleck, made a charming trio. Mrs. Scott as Bessie Casey had been known as the prettiest girl in the Army. Mrs. Huntington was called the tea-rose for her lovely skin. Mrs. Halleck, imperious and handsome, was proud of her relationship to Alexander Hamilton, as any one might well be.

The Hallecks lived in a large house at Folsom and Second Street near Rincon Hill, where they gave a ball every winter, and where Captain Sumner and I once danced figures of the cotillion for the terpsichorean edification of other guests. It was the popular dance in New York, imported from Paris to supersede the Lancers.

The tall, ecclesiastic figure of Colonel Coppinger looms in recollections of the Halleck balls. Ecclesiastic except for the long Dundreary whiskers he wore — 'weepers' we sometimes called them, I suppose because they faintly suggested streams of tears flowing down either side of the face. He was tall and thin and dark, with an interesting austerity probably acquired during his service in the Papal Zouaves; an Irishman by birth, but a citizen of the world. He had come to America from Rome to fight in the Civil War, and from a private in the Federal Army had risen to the rank of Colonel.

A blithe spirit was Colonel Smedberg, who had served gallantly in the war and been severely wounded. Whenever a party dragged, Colonel Smedberg would suggest singing and proceed to open the program with 'Marching Through Georgia' in a fine baritone. The rest of the party joined in the chorus, and then Major Calif would contrib-

CAPTAIN JAMES CUTTING, U.S.A.
1864

PIERRE D'ORLÉANS
Duc de Penthièvre

ute 'When I was in the Army,' a favorite number at the minstrels. As soon as there was an opening, Cutler McAllister would lift his voice in 'One Fish-Ball' intoned with appropriate melancholy: 'The waiter roared it through the hall, "We don't give bread with one fish-ball,"' many times.

Pilot-boat parties were popular and the little tugboats chartered for a day would be scrubbed and polished with flag flying in honor of guests, cruising with them about the bay to stop at Sausalito, where a champagne lunch was always served. General Whittier gave one that I remember and unbent very pleasantly to join the chorus of 'One Fish-Ball' when it floated over the waters.

Grand opera arrived in '68. There had been opera in other years, but the Carl Rosa Company brought the first really grand season with all its social exhilaration. Audiences filled Maguire's Opera House dressed in their best, the women carrying nosegays in lace-paper holders to throw at the feet of the prima donna, statuesque Parepa Rosa. She was the wife of the manager, a towering Scottish Juno, while he was a slight, little Englishman whose name had been plain Charles Rose. The company sang in English and this was an interesting novelty. Italian opera had always before been sung in Italian. There was a handsome basso named Karl Formes, who remained in San Francisco when the company departed and for many years was a leader in musical affairs.

Mrs. Hall McAllister gave a party for Madame Parepa, who proved full of sparkle and high spirits. In spite of their incongruous figures, Madame and her husband danced well together, peasant steps in which she held her skirts high at the sides, and a charming tarantella. One of the guests who had heard Madame carol several numbers at the home of Felix Pioche a few evenings before, asked if she would sing.

Madame declined. 'Only when it is an engagement for money, I sing,' she explained with amiable frankness.

'But Madame,' the gentleman persisted, 'you sang at Mr. Pioche's the other night.'

'Ah, Mr. Pioche gave me a bracelet,' she answered, displaying on her rounded arm a circlet made of gold quartz medallions, the largest adorned with the letter 'R.' in diamonds.

For a while it was considered amusing to visit Professor Coombs and have one's head charted. Phrenology was the new way of fortune-telling, clearly more scientific than tea-leaves. Professor Coombs's parlors were crowded with patrons. He made a map of one's skull and read character, with prognostications, from its topography. But the Professor was eccentric and became more so. A person of benevolent aspect, he bore a certain resemblance to portraits of the first President, and people remarked on this until the poor man's head was turned and he took to wearing a Continental hat with knee-breeches, and calling himself 'Washington the Second.' For years he was a figure in the street scene, standing on corners or promenading Montgomery Street in buff colonial costume, holding aloft a banner inscribed with his title. Every one called him 'Uncle Freddie Coombs.'

So many quaint gentlemen, who in a modern city would face the indignity of being 'run in,' passed unmolested in Montgomery Street. 'Emperor' Norton was a favored ward of the town who could dine in any restaurant and imperially ignore the cost, buy theater tickets in any box office with no more than an imperial nod of thanks, and draw checks on San Francisco banks, although he owned not a dollar on earth. By common consent in the banking fraternity, his checks were honored, and he never drew one for more than twenty-five cents through some canny sense of restraint that preserved the imperial privilege.

During shopping hours one saw him in Kearney or Montgomery Street, walking toward some destination which I fancy was never reached, his old army uniform and military cap with its rakish feather worn with an air. A sword hung from his sword-belt and he sometimes carried a short, knotted stick which might have been a scepter. The whole town knew him.

Every now and then one of Emperor Norton's proclamations would appear in the press. They were relative to a number of things and newspapers always printed them. One dated August 12, 1869, dissolved and abolished the Republican and Democratic parties in the interest of peace, since it had been imperially remarked that their existence engendered dissensions. Another referred to the Emperor's wardrobe and requested replenishment. His uniform was always shabby, but some especial disintegration inspired the proclamation which read:

Know ye whom it may concern that W. Norton I, Emperor *Dei gratia* of the United States and Protector of Mexico, have heard serious complaints from our adherents and all that our imperial wardrobe is a national disgrace, and even His Majesty the King of Pain has had his sympathy excited so far as to offer us a suit of clothing, which we have a delicacy in accepting. Therefore we warn those whose duty it is to attend to these affairs that their scalps are in danger if our said need is unheeded.

Little was known of the Emperor's past. He had come to California from England in the fifties and for a time was a successful merchant. Business reverses had left him ruined financially, but with the pleasant delusion of grandeur which endured until his death in 1880.

Some time in the sixties the Great Unknown appeared in Montgomery Street to stir speculation and surmise. No one knew who he was or whence he came. He was faultlessly attired, but from beneath his polished silk hat fell a thick mane of black hair, and he walked with a curious flourish suggestive of the theater, his gold-headed cane held behind him. Some Hamlet drifted into harmless histrionic eccentricities, he might have been; or a person of note somewhere — here concealing his identity. He spoke to no one, preserving the aura of mystery, and went his way unconcerned by the staring public. Every afternoon he promenaded Montgomery Street absorbed in his own meditations. After a time curiosity waned and the queer figure was taken for granted. When finally newspapers announced that the Great Unknown would give a reception in Pacific Hall and there disclose his identity, admission twenty-five cents, no one was interested. A few newspaper reporters gathered to hear the secret, and to these the unknown revealed that he was a retired German tailor named William Frohm, which was scarcely worth twenty-five cents. Yet regarded as color in the pageant of the streets, William Frohm, with his mystery and picturesque presence, surely had his value.

Likewise the 'Razor-Strop Man,' who ambled through the rush of downtown neighborhoods in Quaker's garb, with an aspect of mild detachment. His baggy brown coat and trousers were topped by a broad-brimmed hat of yellow plush, and he was conspicuously clean-shaven in a day when priests and Quakers almost alone eschewed hirsute decoration. On his arm he carried a basket of razor strops, and with them, bottles of his own cough remedy which cured everything, including colds.

Striding by him one might see 'The American Eagle,' well nicknamed, for the tall, thin man, in tightly buttoned Prince Albert coat, stooped as he strode and a huge beak of a nose protruded from beneath his heavy black beaver hat. He peered from under the brim with cruel eyes — the most relentless of bill collectors, terror of delinquents in the eighteen sixties.

In the neighborhood of the Stock Exchange, one saw the 'Money King,' whose name was really King and who assumed 'Money' as a sort of trademark. He was a money-lender conducting business on any curb, and during the Bonanza years, the hope of derelicts and 'mud hens' to whom he lent small sums. A small gold badge in the lapel of his coat was his sign, engraved 'Money King ' In spite of the fact that his stovepipe hat was very dingy, his clothes shabby, and the shovel beard always in need of trimming, it was said the Money King was actually a prosperous gentleman who speculated wisely in stocks. It was his pleasure, as well as his business, to stand at the corner of Pauper Alley near the Stock Exchange and lend money.

'Mud hens' were depressing creatures — women who haunted the financial district speculating in stocks with all the feverish intensity of gamblers; or scuttled along Pine Street hugging some loss or gain to their souls. There was one whose husband had lost his fortune and died. She spent the rest of her days in the shadow of the Stock Exchange, buying when she could borrow from his friends and having no life beyond the street where fortunes vanished and appeared in figures chalked on blackboards.

We had, in these years, I am constrained to state, a few adventures with earthquakes. But slight tremors of the earth, occasionally classed as such by alarmists, were given, generally, very little attention. One in '65 was definitely an earthquake. It came on a Sunday morning of October while I sat in our pew at Grace Church listening to the Reverend Giles Easton preach the Word. Suddenly the church swayed and its timbers creaked. Every one started in alarm. Dr. Easton in the pulpit rose easily to the occasion.

'Be calm, my friends,' he said with lifted hands. 'It is all over.' Just then there was another shake and many of the congregation dived under pews. Dr. Easton repeated reassuringly, 'There is no danger, friends.'

SIR EDWARD SHELLEY

LADY SHELLEY

His assurance did not impress me. Transfixed, I wondered whether to dive or dash for the doors when a third shock set the walls to grinding on their foundations, and I fled down the aisle, out into Powell Street. There stood Dr. Easton in his white robes. He had made better time through the vestry doors.

The shake of '68 that did much damage to buildings on 'made ground,' the section where shallows of the bay had been filled in, seemed less severe to me, but we passed most of that day out-of-doors, since slight shocks followed the first one and swinging chandeliers or rocking-chairs that gently rocked by themselves strained the nerves.

After the war the city was filled with visitors. Travelers in America turned to California with its gold and romance which the late unpleasantness had left undimmed, and celebrities were thick among them. There was that curious personage, Sir Edward Shelley, who dined with us several times. He was a nephew of the poet. — 'Ah, did you once see Shelley plain?' — Browning's line comes to me as I write this, but Sir Edward would have answered no. His glorious young uncle left England before our friend's day. Yet he must have heard many intimate reminiscences in the family.

Sir Edward was an adventurous soul to whom civilization was just something to be endured while he was in it, and speedily escaped. As a young man he resigned a commission in the British Army to explore Africa, and for long, lived among the Kaffirs. He could tell of meeting Livingstone, who recorded the encounter in the heart of

Africa. Most of his conversation was of wild places of the earth. San Francisco was a way station on his journey to the South Seas. He sailed away for Honolulu and that was the last we saw of him; a tall, sun-browned man with English blue eyes set oddly in his dark face.

Somewhere in these years came Sir Richard Burton — then Captain Burton — who was the first European to penetrate the Holy of Holies at Mecca. He had learned the Koran by heart and could quote verses of it in strange-sounding words. With the British Consul, George Lane Booker, who was a pillar of society in San Francisco for thirty years or more, he dined at our home and told tales of his adventuring.

Like Sir Edward Shelley, he was burned brown by alien suns, but Burton's eyes were dark and piercing, and with his sunburn, gave him a deceivingly Oriental appearance which he fostered for disguises assumed in his travels. Once, starting on a railway journey, he had found it expedient to depart as a corpulent Arab. Beneath his robes he tied an air pillow, well inflated, and the effect was gained. Well out of the railway station, disguise was no longer necessary, so when the train entered a tunnel, Burton quietly removed the stopper from the cushion and allowed his corpulence to deflate. When the train emerged into daylight again, his collapsed appearance naturally astonished fellow travelers who stared at him in bewilderment and apprehension for the rest of the journey.

Then there was young Lord Richard Grosvenor so determined to see the Wild West that he made the tiresome trip across the plains by stage-coach. Delightedly he told of meeting Brigham Young in Salt Lake and 'three Mrs. Youngs!' There were twenty-one altogether, he added for climax.

A few years later, on a visit to Salt Lake I myself met several Mrs. Youngs, plain, disillusioned-looking women who lived together in 'The Beehive,' with 'Amelia's Palace,' the luxurious home of the favorite, just down the block. Brigham himself commanded any one's admiration for his qualities of leadership, his justice, and his honor in all business dealings. I heard it said many times by men who had business relations with him, 'His word is as good as another man's bond.'

Mr. and Mrs. Charles Kean played a season of tragedy at Maguire's in the sixty's, and at a reception given by General and Mrs. McDowell we met this quaint old couple of the theater, who had long left youth behind them, but were still effective players. Mrs. Kean as Ellen Tree had been the Ellen Terry of her day and had traces still of great beauty. But the whimsical face of her husband, set with odd little features, made him look more like the 'comic relief' in melodrama than a tragedian. Yet in younger days he had played 'Hamlet' with success and he was still finely impassioned in 'The Corsican Brothers' — almost great as Louis XI. I enjoyed talking with him at the McDowell party and told him of hearing Fanny Kemble in Dublin, and her display of temper.

'Just like her,' he said; adding that he remembered as

a boy the death of her aunt, the great Siddons, whom Reynolds painted as 'The Tragic Muse.' Charles was a son of Edmund Kean who played with Mrs. Siddons. I was sorry to read of his death a year or so later in England at the end of his tour of the world. The Keans had gone on to Australia from San Francisco.

General and Mrs. McDowell were indefatigable hosts in these post-war years. For the Duc de Penthièvre who came on a tour of the world, they gave a garden party at Fort Mason which was a splendid affair. This young Frenchman, cousin of Louis Philippe, had been a student at Annapolis for a time and was filled with friendliness for all Americans. Van Ness Avenue was not then cut through to Black Point on which the army post is built. To reach it, guests were conveyed in the army and navy tugboats which plied between Market Street docks and the bay posts, landing at a little wharf under the hanging gardens of Fort Mason. It was even then one of the most picturesque of army stations. A grove of black pines, which gave the Point its name, set off the gardens with their flower-trimmed lawns terraced down to waters of the Golden Gate. When it was *en fête* with striped marquees, groups of guests in uniforms and light gowns and many bright parasols against the background of hills and bay, the scene was altogether worthy of Penthièvre's enthusiasm which he freely expressed in perfect English. A review of troops in his honor before the party had greatly impressed him.

Mark Twain I never met, but we heard of him here and there after his return from the Sandwich Islands — were

CHARLES KEAN

MRS. CHARLES KEAN

in the audience at Maguire's when he made his début as a lecturer and amused us to hilarity with the story of his trip. Mrs. Low, wife of the Governor, was in a box with his friends that evening — every one of importance was there; and long afterward I read with delight Mark Twain's account of his agreement with the Governor's wife to look up at her when his quips went slowly, whereupon she would ripple forth her ready laughter to start the house. He tells that once in a slight pause, after some bit of pathos, his glance wandered idly over the house taking in Mrs. Low's box, where inadvertently it caught her eye —

I remember Mrs. Low in the box that evening, and her rippling laughter.

The young man's Hawaiian letters had been appearing in the 'Sacramento Union,' which was then read all over the State, and he was taken up by local literary lights, foregathering with Bret Harte and Charles Warren Stoddard in offices of the 'Golden Era,' which was then printing Harte's stories and verses. When, after he departed California, his 'Innocents Abroad' letters were published in the daily 'Alta-Californian, of San Francisco, every one read them little as any one guessed they were the first printing of an American masterpiece, destined for immortality as we reckon it.

Since Sir Francis Drake passed it by sailing northward, many British admirals have turned into the Golden Gate to anchor their ships in the bay. Admiral Farquhar came for long visits. He was an old friend of my mother's, a jolly little Scotchman she had known before her marriage, and they had always much to talk of, recalling days of their youth. One of his port calls was made during the Franco-Prussian War when his ship, the Zealous, remained in the harbor for many weeks, keeping in touch by telegraph and cable with London.

We had a house in San Rafael, across the bay from the city, that summer, and on his last Sunday in port, the Admiral came to tell us good-bye. It was in the heyday of the Sunday picnic when noisy picnickers crowded ferry-boats on the Sabbath, bound usually for Fairfax Park near San Rafael. Poor Admiral Farquhar, crossing the bay, found himself in the midst of an Irish picnic party — a Fenian picnic at that, and he in his British uniform! It was at the height of one of the Fenian agitations.

Very disapprovingly the Fenians eyed the British officer, with a disapproval that might at any moment become belligerent. As the ferry-boat ploughed past the Zealous, lying at anchor in the bay, one burly son of Erin addressed the Admiral:

'I've been tellin' these men,' he said, indicating a group, 'that they wasn't worth egg-broth or they'd have blown that ship out of the water where she stands. But have no fear, Sir, we'll not harm you.'

'Fear!' exclaimed the Admiral, safely at our house, 'my only fear was that some American newspaper reporter might discover me. I could see the headlines in the press — "British Admiral attends Fenian picnic! Indorses Movement!!"'

During this summer Mrs. Paran Stevens came out from New York with a party of friends who included young Lord Walter Campbell, son of the Duke of Argyle, and one Sunday when Lord Walter was our guest Admiral Farquhar invited us all, in his honor, to divine service on the deck of the Zealous. It was a blue-and-gold morning on the bay, and the uniforms of officers and men were bright in the sunlight. The trained voices of four hundred sailors chanting the Litany sounded across the waters like unearthly music; and never in a cathedral have I felt so deeply the beauty and inspiration of the service.

For contrast there was a frivolous occasion on another day when we were dancing on the same deck, and General Sherman, visiting San Francisco, came to call on the Admiral. The salute fired from one of the ship's big guns shook her from stem to stern and abruptly ended a dreamy waltz. I remarked that day that Lieutenant Leith danced often with Miss Lucy January, a pretty St. Louis girl who came on board with San Francisco friends. It was the beginning of a romance. They were engaged before the Zealous sailed, and as soon as he could thereafter, Lieutenant Leith resigned his commission and went to St. Louis to marry Miss Lucy. He made a fortune in the Southern city and then became Lord Leith of Fyvie with estates in Scotland. So they lived happily ever afterward.

Mrs. Stevens was a remarkable woman who might have had a success in politics had she been a man. She was not handsome, but irresistibly vivacious. No one could be dull in her presence. Countless stories of her homely wit were told, and her social success was as much due to personality as to wealth and determination. Her daughter Minnie, afterward Lady Paget, was a decidedly pretty girl. They came from New York in Mrs. Stevens's private car with a party of assorted guests who included Lord Walter, Mr. and Mrs. Joe Stone, of Cincinnati; a young Mr. Laird, son of the British ship-builder; Dr. de Lakst, Belgian banker; and Lord Walsingham, an entomologist who hoped to find in California a certain rare species of butterfly which he vainly sought in San Rafael gardens. At the Palace Hotel, where they stopped, Mrs. Stevens discovered Cyrus, late bellhop at the Fifth Avenue Hotel in New York which her husband had owned, now answering bells at the Palace.

Mr. and Mrs. Rulofson, of New York, who were living temporarily at the Grand Hotel adjoining the Palace, gave a party for the visitors. Invitations were for an informal evening, so guests were arrayed accordingly, all save Mrs. Stevens whose *toilette* would have served for a Royal Drawing-Room, and who wore necklaces and bracelets galore with her *décolleté* gown. It may be explained, however, that several necklaces were then the fashion. A diamond dog collar, favorite adornment of the Princess of Wales, would be combined with ropes of pearls; and if one fancied the idea and owned the jewels, a string of emeralds or rubies, or both, could be added to the display.

Supper was served that evening at one end of the long corridor on which the Rulofson suite opened. While we sat at table, some one asked Mr. Laird if his father's plant had not built an American battleship. 'Ah, yes,' answered

LAWRENCE BARRETT

BRET HARTE

the Britisher, a bit loftily. 'We built the Alabama, you know.'

'Ssh!' hushed another guest. 'Not so loud. These rooms [indicating doors in the corridor] are occupied by Captain Winslow, who *sank* the Alabama, you know.'

I doubt if Mrs. Stevens met Senator Fair's family on this visit, but Tessie Fair, who must have been a very small girl then, was, as Mrs. Hermann Oelrichs, to live for years in Mrs. Stevens's white marble château in New York, a picturesque house at Fifth Avenue and Fifty-Seventh Street, bought from the Stevens estate. Virginia Fair was married there to William K. Vanderbilt, Jr.

It was while we were living in San Rafael that Mr. and Mrs. Bret Harte were our neighbors and spent many evenings at our home. Mrs. Harte had a well-cultivated contralto voice, so there was always music when they came, with Bret Harte's irradiant wit to amuse us. His burlesques of people and everyday scenes, whether at the University of California where he lectured on modern literature, or in editorial offices of the 'Overland Monthly,' were wildly funny.

Harte was writing a play for Lawrence Barrett that summer, and the actor crossed the bay often to offer moral support and discuss its characters. They never did reach perfect agreement on it, and would argue until Mrs. Harte said they were unfit for human companionship. Then they would all come over to our house. Barrett was almost as amusing as Harte, and together they were better than the theater, although it was all so light and inconsequential that I remember none of their nonsense now. I do recall Barrett's saying he dreaded parts in modern drama; how he hated to wear a swallow-tail on the stage. 'Give me a toga every time,' he added. 'I'd rather play a noble Roman than any other character.'

The play, 'Two Men of Sandy Bar,' was not completed until long afterward in the East, where Stuart Robson and Charles Thorne finally produced it with indifferent success.

Harte was a good-looking man who would have been handsome except for the scars of smallpox which marred his face. His dark hair was thick and wavy, and with his mustache he wore a pair of slight 'side-burns' which extended halfway down the face from the temples in a masculine fashion that succeeded 'weepers.' There were two small sons in the Harte family then, the younger named for Thomas Starr King, who, of all Harte's California friends, was the one he genuinely admired. His poem, 'Relieving Guard,' written after Dr. King's death in '64, is, I think, his finest bit of verse. I have never been able to read it unmoved.

Mr. and Mrs. Harte were very happy together that summer, and we heard with much regret of their separation when Harte went abroad to live and his wife with the children remained in America. Neither ever came back to California.

Admiral Joseph Denman sailed through the Golden Gate on the old Sutlej when she paid her second call at our port. He was a brother of Lord Denman. With him was his wife, the Honorable Mrs. Denman, for wives of British navy officers were then permitted to accompany their husbands on voyages. Mrs. Denman was musical and had her piano on board. She liked to sing duets with Lieutenant Sir Lambton Lorraine, who had a powerful baritone and confided to me that he had to mute his tones almost to a whisper to avoid drowning out her little trill. Sir Lambton afterward distinguished himself in an accident in New York Harbor when he was in command of the Niobe, which rescued Americans from a burning ship, the Virginius. He was honored for this by the 'freedom of the city.' To this day I have no idea what that means. Free street-car rides that the police enjoy suggest themselves, but they hardly seem adequate.

Lord Charles Beresford was a junior officer on the Sutlej, a rollicking youth already noted as a wit and *raconteur*. He was delicious in an imitation of two sailors on the Sutlej reprehensibly burlesquing their commander's wife and her timidity. Lord Charles was walking his watch when he overheard them.

The Sutlej, it may be explained, carried sails for propelling power to add to steam, as many ships did then.

Said one sailor in Mrs. Denman's gentle tones, 'Oh, Joey, dear, isn't it very rough?'

'Yes, Grace, love, it is,' replied the other in the Admiral's accents.

'Joey, dear, won't you have the sails taken down?'

'Yes, Grace, love, it shall be done.'

At this point Lord Charles deemed it expedient to walk away, officially unaware of the dialogue.

The irrepressible young man went with me one morning when I selected a bonnet at a millinery shop in Clay Street and offered advice and criticism to the suppressed delight of the salesgirl and my own helpless mirth. The purchase finally accomplished, Lord Charles insisted on carrying the bandbox until we started home in a hired hack. Lord Charles and Cutler McAllister were, I think, the happiest spirits I have ever known with laughter always near them.

Poor little 'Sir' Robert Bridges! I remember him with profound sympathy, one titled visitor who appeared unhappy in the rôle of social lion. He was, in fact, terrified, and fled one day, bag, baggage, and samples. For he was no baronet; merely a timid little London salesman sent by his firm to the Wild West, where life was dangerous and lawless disorder prevailed according to his conviction. It occurred to him that a title might insure respect and civil treatment from the outlaws. So in the register of the Occidental Hotel he wrote 'Sir' before his name with no ulterior motive on earth. It did more than he hoped. With respect and civility it precipitated social attentions that were terribly disconcerting. He was bombarded with invitations. All that it was possible to refuse were refused, but one he had vainly tried to evade was to Mrs. Shillaber's 'Salon,' for so she called her weekly receptions where French was the language of the evening, although no one spoke it. There we met 'Sir' Robert, a harassed-looking

SIR ARTHUR FARQUHAR

LORD CHARLES BERESFORD

little man who dropped his *h*'s everywhere. A few days afterward he decamped leaving his confession behind him and no one mentioned him thereafter to Mrs. Shillaber. But for a long time Mrs. Shillaber's experience with 'Sir' Robert made hostesses wary of strange titles.

Some of our English visitors were all unprepared to find the degree of civilization which actually existed in this remote city, and came with sadly deficient wardrobes. The old Duke of Manchester and his son, Viscount Mandeville, hadn't a suit of evening clothes between them, but serenely accepted all invitations. With perfect aplomb and extraordinary effect, the Duke appeared at dinners and balls in a suit of brick-red tweeds with blue flannel shirt — his preconceived idea of a correct costume for the Wild West. 'I am a traveler,' he would blandly explain, 'traveling with as little luggage as possible. You will forgive my tweeds.'

No doubt he could have borrowed a dress suit for occasions, but he never did and was probably wiser in this than little Lord Milton, who likewise hadn't supposed 'swallow-tails' were found in California. Lord Milton raided the wardrobe of a stalwart friend and wore a suit six sizes too large for him, with trousers in thick rolls at the bottom and his hands pathetically lost in long, flapping sleeves.

Two young hunters, Lord Waterspark and Lord Berkeley Paget, came hunting bears in San Francisco and were surprised to find them only in a zoo. Crossing the plains they had brought down a buffalo and they longed for a bear to add to this triumph, but birds and rabbits were all they found in expeditions near the city. Mother was sympathetic and gave them a letter to Ned Beale at El Tejon, his ranch in the South. If there were no bears in the hills of El Tejon, she could rely on Ned Beale to 'plant' one. But it was not necessary. The hunters found two natives on this vast estate, which covered thousands of acres. It was one of the great ranches of California where old Spanish customs and traditions were preserved. General Beale, distinguished and witty, was a prince of hosts. A youth filled with adventures had furnished him an endless supply of stories, all colored with his rich humor. As a young officer just out of Annapolis, he had fought in the Mexican War, and a sword which hung on the wall at El Tejon was the gift of brother officers to commemorate some conspicuous bravery. After the Mexican War he resigned from the Navy to take charge of Indian affairs in the Southwest for the Federal Government. With General Stephen Kearny he marched into California from New Mexico in 1846. Kit Carson was their guide. He could tell with flashes of comedy of meeting his old commander, Commodore Stockton, in San Diego, and of holding the lazy little Spanish town, with General Kearny sick in bed, while Stockton went on to raise the American flag over Los Angeles. Commodore Sloat was then flying the Stars and Stripes over Monterey, and young Beale sailed north to meet him. From that year until his death, California was his home, although he served as American Minister to Austria under Grant and made many trips abroad. One of his daughters married a diplomat, Bakhmetieff, the

Czar's last Ambassador in Washington. Another became Mrs. John R. McLean and a son married James G. Blaine's daughter Harriet for his first wife.

The Beales had a home in San Francisco as well as at El Tejon. Mrs. Beale drove the first private carriage in the city, a large barouche drawn by two powerful horses imported with it from the East. The street stared when the Beale carriage passed, but soon there were broughams and landaus, Mrs. Donahue's glass coach, and the huge green clarence of the Baron Walkinshaws to keep it company.

Driving excursions were over the Howard Street planked road, which for part of its length was lapped by waters of the bay, to Mission Dolores; then down San Bruno Turnpike to the San José stage-road and on to Tony Oakes's, a wayside inn where horses of the San José stage were changed. Tony Oakes was the name of the proprietor. Some time in the sixties the Cliff House was built overlooking the Pacific Ocean, and then the fashionable drive was out Point Lobos Road to this historic resort.

On bright afternoons a procession of vehicles with many a spanking pair and fast trotter passed out O'Farrell Street to turn into Point Lobos Road, past the waste of undulated sand which became Golden Gate Park, to the ocean beach. For a short time the Ocean Side House was a favorite resort. The Hall McAllisters gave a dance there and we drove out another night for Mrs. John Felton's dance. But the place soon deteriorated into a shabby beer-hall.

Visitors were invariably driven out to the Cliff House, where the barking amphibians of Seal Rocks were considered a great attraction. For many years Old 'Ben Butler' sunned himself on the highest rock, occasionally lifting his head to bay like a dog at the moon, above the clamor of the other seals. When he died, old Ben's huge body was dragged ashore and stuffed to adorn the museum of Sutro Baths.

The Cliff House was a little flat-roofed building perched on the edge of the cliff at the entrance to the Golden Gate. From its balcony high above the breakers one gazed through binoculars at the seals or sighted ships beyond the Farallones. On clear days these distant islands were silhouetted against the horizon. There was an excellent cuisine at the Cliff House, specializing in fried Eastern oysters, and a bar famous for its mixed drinks. Mixed spirits, however, were never served to ladies. On cold afternoons we sipped port or sherry on the balcony while men drank high-balls, cocktails, or Tom-and-Jerry at the brass rail indoors.

A towering promontory back of the Cliff House was bought by Adolph Sutro, one of the Nevada millionaires, who built his home there with windows overlooking the sea, and gardens that are now a public park. Sutro was the most intellectual of the plutocrats, an English Jew who had gone to Nevada in the silver rush. The Sutro Tunnel, considered a brilliant piece of engineering, simple as it appears to be, had made his fortune. It was merely proving his idea that the Comstock Lode could be reached by boring into the base of the hill in which it was buried, instead of interminably down from the top. Sutro was

CLIFF HOUSE AND SEAL ROCK

allowed to try the horizontal approach and drew his line straight to the rich deposits of ore.

In San Francisco he lived very quietly. His ways were reclusive, although he served as Mayor of the city for a time and planned many public benefactions. But he had a taste for books and preferred his library to Nob Hill diversions. The library at Sutro Heights was that of a bibliophile. He was a lover of trees as well as of books, and eucalyptus groves of California are his memorial. It was he who first imported the Australian gum trees that have become so much a part of the landscape. The original arrivals were set in Sutro Gardens, where now they tower above all other trees with their long draperies of foliage. Sutro Forest, covering a waste of sand south of Golden Gate Park, was another of his contributions to the beauty of San Francisco.

'Stevedore,' the Vandewaters' old white horse, drawing a comfortable rockaway, was a familiar friend on the Cliff House Road; and likewise, 'San Mateo,' driven by D. O. Mills in a shining buggy, usually teamed with another fast-stepping bay. Often he drove them from the city to Milbrae, where he built a château and established a dairy. In the art gallery at Milbrae hung Reid's spirited painting of 'Sheridan's Ride' which had attracted much attention in the East. Countless chromo copies of it were made.

Lucky Baldwin was a sensation one day on the Point Lobos Road, tooling the first four-horse English coach to come to the West. James Ben Ali Haggin drove the second with a pair of bays and a pair of iron-grays. A pair of iron-gray carriage horses and a spotted coach dog were a fashionable combination for landau or barouche.

One equipage in the procession always attracted especial interest — Mrs. S. J. Hensley's blue seashell carriage drawn by four horses and filled with guests. The flowered bonnets of the ladies bobbed above white fur robes in the flaring blue shell with an effect attractively theatrical. Mrs. Milton Latham's brown barouche with yellow wheels, lined with light blue satin and drawn by two milk-white horses — the first to be seen in San Francisco — was another bright detail; with Mrs. Latham seated therein in all her piquant prettiness.

Art and the Old Masters became matters of popular interest in '66, when R. B. Woodward opened to the public the gallery of his home out on Mission Street. It was an unusual and interesting benefaction.

Woodward had commissioned Virgil Williams, a local artist who had studied abroad, to copy Old Masters in European galleries, until a collection of over one hundred was made. Williams took a studio in Rome and for several years worked on the curious commission. The results were excellent reproductions of Titians, Tintorettos, Leonardos, and Botticellis, among others; hung in the Mission Street gallery they doubtless were a cultural influence in the new city.

The private park surrounding the Woodward house was also opened to the public to become, as Woodward's Gardens, the most famous of San Francisco's old open-air resorts. It covered a sloping hillside, and the little valley, with gardens, artificial lakes and fountains, and an added zoo, was the delight of children. In a large tank, overlooked by a grand-stand, were barking seals and sea lions whose feeding was the crowning event of a day at Woodward's. Men carrying great baskets of raw meat, and long pitchforks to toss it, passed through the grounds on their way to the tank and were followed like the Pied Piper of Hamelin by an ever-growing company. The seals and the Old Masters were rival attractions.

CHAPTER VII

When I look back across the pageant of the years there is an especial brightness and touch of the bizarre about that sequence of the late sixties, the seventies and eighties. In it was the reign of the bonanza kings who built their palaces on Nob Hill, where Jim Flood's thirty-thousand-dollar brass fence glittered in the sun. The beautifully wrought metal flashed for the entire length of two blocks on the square where the brownstone mansion stood, and it was the sole task of one retainer to keep it bright. Passing any hour of the day one discovered him polishing away at some section of it. The huge cubic house is now the home of the Pacific Union Club, and the fence is still there, but with its pristine polish gone. When I saw it last, it was black as bronze. In brighter days it might have been a symbol of all the fantastic flamboyance of the time.

An incredible period it was, with its lavish expenditures and sudden luxury veneered over many crude ways of living. Strange homes, these Nob Hill palaces, the amazement of visitors from the Old World which had nothing like them. For that matter, they were unique in America. Very well I recall, on a visit to Chicago in later years, how insignificantly small mansions of the Gold Coast looked to one inured to Nob Hill.

Diagonally across California Street from the Flood house stood the Hopkins castle, whose gray towers could be seen from the bay and far south of the city. Terraced gardens fell away on the steep hillside at the back, and surrounding them was a mighty stone wall, forty feet high against the terrace of the lower level along Pine Street. There, massive oak doors swung on iron hinges to permit the entrance, not of armored knights on horseback, but of basket phaëtons, the family barouche, rockaways and broughams. A long looped 'S' of a driveway led upward to the house, and when lamps along its way shone at night, with the castle windows alight, the effect from the city below was enchanting.

Within, the house was a mess of anachronisms. One entered portals of a feudal castle to pass into the court of a doge's palace, all carved Italian walnut with a gallery around the second story where murals of Venetian scenes were set between the arches. These were the work of Jules Tavernier, French artist, who stopped in California after a trip to the South Seas, where he painted long before Gauguin.

A beautiful place in itself was this central court, as were many individual rooms in these anachronistic mansions filled with rare inlaid woods, marble mosaics, and rich furnishings. It was said that architects measured shelves in the libraries of some of them and ordered yards of books from dealers to fill the spaces, as they would order fixtures. Of the truth of this I am not certain, but astonishing effects in servants' liveries I well remember. The Negro coachman of one new millionaire wore a suit of white cloth with black velvet buttons as large as butter-dishes, and orange-topped boots — his own taste, I fancy.

In spite of its absurdities, the Hopkins house achieved a general effect of stately magnificence, a sort of Mrs. Malaprop dignity. And it looked enduring. But alas, this feudal castle was built of wood painted the color of stone, and it burned like any shanty in 1906 — as did all the Nob Hill palaces, with one exception, the brownstone house of James Flood with its brass fence.

Mark Hopkins was one of the 'Big Four' who built the Union Pacific Railroad; Huntington, Stanford, and Crocker were the others. They all lived on Nob Hill, where Huntington joined the colony after David Colton's death, when he acquired the Colton palace at California and Taylor Streets. Colton was the road's chief legal counsel and a man of discriminating taste, one must assume, for his house, copied from a famous white marble palace of Italy, was rarely beautiful. Many times I wished its chaste walls and classic columns were of enduring marble instead of white painted wood. It burned with the others in 1906, and its gardens are now Huntington Park.

Across Taylor Street the prodigious Crocker mansion billowed over its lawns; and across California Street was the homelike Tobin house, distinguished by reason of having what might be termed a hand-picked library. In its steep hillside garden played a family of happy children. One of them became a poet, Agnes Tobin, whose translations of Petrarch's sonnets gave her high place in literary London. Another became the American Minister at The Hague.

After Mark Hopkins's death, the Hopkins castle was closed for years. His widow went East to build a new home at Great Barrington, and married the young architect, Edward Searles, who planned it. The Nob Hill castle was part of his inheritance at her death, a white elephant of which he made generous disposal by presenting it to the San Francisco Art Association.

This truly magnificent gift brought the young Art Association out of rooms over the California Market, of all places, where art was pervaded with the aroma of fish and the sound of the butcher's cleaver was heard. Mingled with my memories of Private Views that opened Spring Exhibitions in the old rooms are scents of the market.

In its new home the Art Association gave annually a Mardi Gras ball which brought back for one night of the year the castle's lost splendor. In the setting of stately rooms, with their scintillating chandeliers, the bright costumes of Pompadours, Carmens, court gentlemen, and jesters made an unforgettable picture. One of the last of these balls before 'The Fire' was in honor of the young Duke of the Abruzzi, who came to San Francisco as officer on an Italian battleship. His very tall, straight figure, in long black domino, was conspicuous among the dancers, and with his brother officers he brought an added glamour to the Mardi Gras that year.

Just below the Hopkins castle stood the great, gloomy barn which was Senator Stanford's home. The death of young Leland Stanford, Jr., left a pervading sadness there, and afterward one inevitably thought of it looking at the frowning façade of the house, painted dark brown. But in earlier days the vast rooms had seen elaborate entertainments. Mrs. Stanford was a plain, gentle little body who liked beautiful things. Her collection of rubies was said to be the finest in the world and her laces were as exquisite as Marie Antoinette's.

Senator Fair planned a palace to outshine them all for the hillside block facing the Hopkins and Stanford houses, but only a granite wall enclosing the grounds ever materialized. Part of it now surrounds the terrace of the Hotel Fairmont built there by his daughters. The Fair family lived in a comparatively modest mansion on the Pine Street level of Nob Hill, and there Tessie Fair was married to Hermann Oelrichs of New York.

'Jim' Fair was one of the Con-Virginia 'Big Four' — Mackay, Fair, Flood, and O'Brien — who owned the consolidated silver mines of Nevada which in six years' time poured out three hundred millions — and went on pouring.

Flood and O'Brien had owned a restaurant in Montgomery Street, the 'Auction Lunch,' where an especially fine fish stew drew patrons from the Stock Exchange near by. Daily the proprietors heard talk of stocks and mining shares and together decided to invest. Results were overwhelming. Flood and O'Brien found themselves among the plutocrats and retired without delay from the restaurant business. About the same time a jolly little Irish barkeeper at the 'Auction Lunch' retired also into the plutocracy. He had been popular with patrons who sometimes passed friendly tips across the bar by which Tim profited until, suddenly, he too found himself rich. Tim had been courting an Irish girl, cook at the Toland home on Nob Hill. They were married now, and built a mansion with the surpassing splendor of a dais in the parlor where, enthroned like royalty, Hannah received visitors. Many called just to see the dais. It was really no more than an ingenuous expression of the will to rise in the world. But when the daughter of the household returned from an Eastern finishing school expensively finished, the dais disappeared from the parlor to become a family skeleton. Since this pretty daughter married into the aristocracy abroad, the story of Tim and Hannah proves to my mind something like efficiency in the 'Melting Pot.' Mrs. Toland, I fear, never appreciated this. In a theater lobby, at a charity ball, wherever her way crossed that of Mrs. Tim, she always greeted her regal ex-cook with a cordial 'Good-evening, Hannah.'

Dr. and Mrs. Toland belonged to the old South Park set, although their attractive Spanish home was near the Roberts house on the Washington Street slope of Nob Hill. Mrs. Toland's little windowless carriage displayed the first hammercloth seen in San Francisco, a square of maroon-colored felt finished with a fringe, which covered the coachman's box and imparted elegance, according to prevailing ideas on equipages, which were elaborate. There was even a prescribed difference in height between coachman and footman which conscientious carriage-owners found it difficult to keep. The supply of footmen was limited, and those who suddenly felt the need of one had to take any available.

The story of Tim and Hannah, true except for their names, has always seemed to me the perfect legend of our plutocracy, but there were others one could tell — of a spirited lady who gave delightful, epicurean dinners in the seventies and had acquired her social poise in dealing three-card monte in her youth.

General Beale related a story of a new millionaire which passed into the repertory of end men at the minstrels. The original hero was a gentleman whose career had begun as a door porter in Montgomery Street. Speculations in 'Gould and Curry' laid the foundation of a great fortune. In London one year, General Beale and Judge Boalt encountered this gentleman making the Grand Tour.

'Where are you going from here?' they asked him.

'To Rome,' he answered. 'I'm going straight through Spain to Italy.'

'But you can't do that,' they said. 'You can't go to Italy through Spain. Spain is a peninsula.'

'The deuce it is!' their friend replied. 'I always thought it was a monarchy.'

Legends and stories notwithstanding, the bonanza millionaires were interesting men, generally speaking. They had the adventurous spirit of pioneers who leave small security for a hazard of new fortunes and there is something attractive in this spirit always. Most of them were men of unusual character, John W. Mackay for one; and I have heard it told of Senator 'Jim' Fair that when he joined a company to come across the plains as a youth of eighteen, he took charge of the entire party when older men were demoralized and undone by hardship and fatigue, and brought it safely to the Coast.

Several were men of brilliant mentality. Collis P. Huntington was one of these. He was a large man with heavy shoulders, a personification of power. One saw him often riding in a California Street cable car which stopped before his door, and involuntarily one regarded him with respect that had nothing to do with his millions. Grip-men and conductors on the cars were all his friends. The Huntington family was never conspicuous in San Francisco's social scene. Clara Huntington, the adopted daughter, was educated abroad and there married Prince Hatzfeldt.

James Ben Ali Haggin was, I thought, most interesting of the plutocrats as a personality. A conservative gentleman in appearance, but with Oriental traces in lineaments and temperament, strikingly handsome with flashing black eyes and close-trimmed white beard, he was the son of a Turk — a wandering actor, it was said — who had married an American girl and settled in the South. James Ben Ali had been educated for the law before he followed the gold rush to California. The Haggins were all brilliant and handsome. A dark-eyed daughter, Rita, so we heard, wrote exquisite poems and herself burned them all before her death. She died of consumption in her youth.

There was a family of sons and daughters in the Haggin house on Taylor Street, a large gray mansard with stables behind it that were all the most fastidious horses could desire. Haggin owned some famous racers. The Tevis home was near by; Mrs. Haggin and Mrs. Tevis were sisters. This house, too, was filled with young people, and wonderful parties were given there. For one there were fireworks out on the bay so that guests at the Tevis ball could look from the broad windows of the house on Nob Hill down across the city and out to the bay's dark waters where starry rockets and flares were sent up for their divertisement.

The last entertainment in the famous old mansion was a dinner for Madame Sembrich and Madame Emma Eames on the night before the earthquake of 1906. It was burned down in the fire that followed.

Taylor Street on Nob Hill was charming in the seventies and eighties with a character of its own. Spacious homes set in flower gardens had none of the overwhelming attributes of Nob Hill palaces and were centers of attractive hospitality. Opposite the Haggin house William T. Coleman built a white Roman villa in a walled garden — a lovely old place. Near it in a long Spanish palace of white stucco, Senator George Hearst's family lived for a time. Mrs. Hearst was a gentle lady, extremely pretty in her youth. In later years she was noted for her philanthropy. We heard of many things she did for friends in misfortune which had nothing to do with her public benefactions. For one who had been left with a small income at her husband's death, she built a charming home on Jackson Street.

At the north end of Taylor Street was a house that had

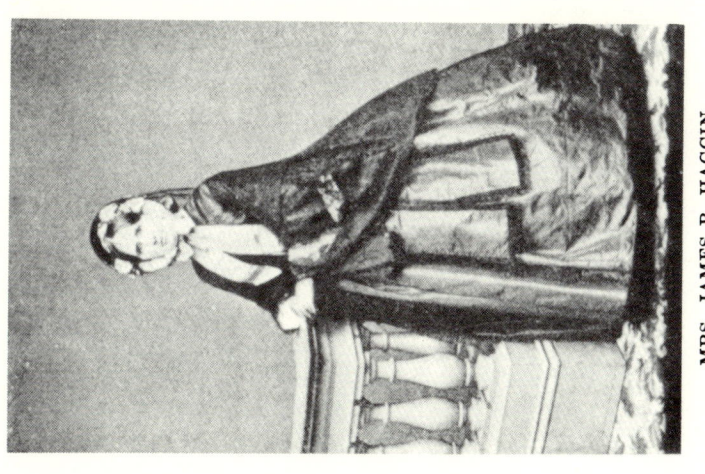

MRS. JAMES B. HAGGIN

JAMES B. HAGGIN

come around the Horn. It had made the voyage from New England in a sailing vessel, cut into sections to be put together in Taylor Street, and some confusion in this process had completely disorganized a proper New England domicile. It stood with a funny, rakish assumption of dignity, all out of drawing. There were curious set-backs and projections where the second story didn't fit over the first, and the front door found itself far down at one side with a blank wall where it should have been. Tenants became adjusted to its peculiarities, however, and lived there very comfortably, as they may still, since it survived 1906.

Other houses that had come around the Horn were more successfully assembled at the end of the voyage, and adorned neighborhoods of North Beach where a number of sea captains lived. One old sea-salt built a queer dwelling on top of Russian Hill — a low circular house with windows all around it, topped by a cupola, a replica of the roundhouse on ocean liners of the time. I liked to picture him sitting in it, perfectly at home, looking out across the Golden Gate to the sea.

A romance Barrie might have written belongs to old Taylor Street. Gently sad in the mid-Victorian manner, it couldn't have happened in a newer age. Its heroine was the daughter of a Nob Hill plutocrat who built a Spanish *palacio* in Taylor Street where the family lived. When the daughter was a small girl, they went abroad, to spend a season in Venice in a palace adjoining that of Robert W. Browning, son of the poet. Browning himself passed much time there that winter and made friends with the little girl next door. In a book of his poems he inscribed a verse written to her.

Some years afterward the family passed a season in London and through their friendship for the Brownings made other English friends, among them a young army officer of good family and no fortune. The little girl, now grown up, and the young officer fell in love and became engaged. But his income could not support a wife and her father had an adamantine prejudice against dowries. So they parted. The heroine came back to San Francisco, where, for all her youth and loveliness and her father's wealth, she lived a secluded life, doing much charitable work, rarely seen at a ball or party. Years passed, and she grew into middle age while her lover served in India and South Africa and fought through the Boer War. One day after long silence a cablegram came to Taylor Street. He was desperately ill in a London Hospital. Could she come to say good-bye? By this time the adamantine father had passed away and she was mistress of her own fortune. That day she took the train for New York on her way to London.

There is a happy ending. They were married in the hospital, where for weeks she nursed him and then, miraculously, he recovered. Once they càme back for a visit to Taylor Street and she had found the sparkle and happiness denied her youth. Sentimental and outmoded as I said, but Barrie's 'Quality Street' always made me think of it.

John W. Mackay brought his family from Virginia City in the early seventies, but they lived only a year or two in

San Francisco before Mrs. Mackay went abroad, with her children, to establish a home in Paris. I met her, one afternoon, calling on a mutual friend at the Occidental Hotel, and during the time she was in California, we were friends. She was a charming young woman then, vivid and witty, not at all overwhelmed by sudden wealth — not at all impressed by San Francisco society which had begun to take itself a bit heavily. Her social success abroad was never a surprise to me, for she had an easy, graceful independence that made her very engaging. I suppose her career as leader of the American set in Paris and as hostess at her London home was brilliantly unique; but to me her most interesting triumph is that she lives as one of the characters in Ludovic Halévy's noted novel, 'L'Abbé Constantin.'

Mrs. Mackay was Mary Hungerford, of Brooklyn, daughter of Colonel Hungerford, who fought in the Mexican War, and she had come to the gold country with her first husband, Dr. Bryant, whose death occurred soon afterward in Virginia City. It was their daughter who became Princess Colonna. When the young widow married John W. Mackay, he was no more than a very good-looking and successful miner with his vast fortune still in the offing, though already sighted by his keen eyes. Mackay was easily the brains of the Nevada Big Four. He was an outstanding figure anywhere, something of a Beau Brummel in his early prosperity. I have seen him step out of the Lick House into Montgomery Street in the light trousers and brown velvet sack coat of current masculine fashion, a broad felt hat above his keen eyes and sweeping mustache — to be followed by many admiring feminine glances. In later years he returned for visits to the West, and his old friends, Raphael Weill among them, wined and dined him. But Mrs. Mackay never came back.

The Lick House was California's first palatial hotel. Very palatial, indeed, we thought it, and took great pride in the long building extending from Post to Sutter Street in Montgomery, rising to the dizzy height of three and a half stories. The opening banquet in '62 was an event of many guests, speeches, toasts, flowers, and music. It soon became the fashion to dine at the Lick on Sunday evenings. The dining-room and lobby were beautiful rooms, with their flagged marble floors and fine woodwork. James Lick had been a cabinet-maker in his youth and for his hotel, built with California gold, he imported rare woods from South America and the Orient, doing much of the finishing and polishing with his own hands, reveling in the work. He was a sad-looking man, more or less of a recluse, who had literally dug his gold, or much of it, from the hills himself. He worked with his pick-axe until he was rich, when, instead of a palace on Nob Hill, he built baths and planned other public benefactions. The Mercantile Library, with its collection of books once one of the finest in the country (most of them were burned in 1906), owed much to him, and Lick Observatory is his memorial.

With all the new prosperity and wealth of the seventies, San Francisco changed greatly in appearance. Downtown was suddenly more metropolitan. Horse-car lines and a crowd of horse-drawn vehicles filled the streets. Two new hotels were neighbors of the Lick House in Montgomery Street, the Russ House, and the Occidental, all of five stories high, which on a new site replaced the old Oriental torn down to make way for a business block. Under them were smart shops. 'Colonel Andrews's Diamond Palace' was one of the sights of the town; a jewelry store of white marble with a sort of lobby where mirrored walls reflected the showcases and their display in flashing confusion — the final word in metropolitan splendor for a large clientèle.

Kearney Street, from Market north to Clay, was the popular shopping district, and one took a Kearney Street horse-car which turned at Broadway into Stockton, to ride over toward North Beach, where Newman and Levinson's little shop kept rare imported laces.

Residences were now built on the hills overlooking the Golden Gate, and South Park saw an exodus to new neighbors. A few imposing homes were built in the Mission District on the 'other side' of Market Street, among them the Phelan mansion, old-fashioned and attractive, with white marble statuary gleaming on its lawns, and the old Claus Spreckels house in Howard Street. But after the original residents deserted South Park, all 'South of Market Street' was considered unfashionable. The once hospitable homes became dingy lodging-houses. In Silver Street, between South Park and Rincon Hill, Kate Douglas Wiggin established her first free kindergarten for the poor children of the neighborhood, so lately the neighborhood of wealth.

There was never anything like civic beauty in those days. In residence districts one found a varied assortment of architectural freaks, and downtown still had a haphazard aspect, with low frame structures, surviving from the fifties, scattered among well-built business blocks. The Ferry Building at the city's entrance was a long brown shed facing a plank-paved plaza, not at all an entrance to impress arriving visitors. Moreover, as they stepped off the ferry-boat which brought them from the Overland Railroad terminus across the bay, they were assailed by a battalion of hotel 'runners' shouting the names of hostelries in a vociferous din. For years the Russ House runner was the star of the lot. His heavy bass boomed over and over, 'Russ-ouse, Russ-ouse,' with vigorous emphasis on Russ, beneath all the clamor of other indistinguishable names. It was a long step toward civic beauty when the new Ferry Building finally rose in place of the shed, its tall, slender tower, copied from the Giralda of the Cathedral in Seville, dominating this foyer of the city.

We had of course, the Mint, austerely classic and beautiful with its stone columns and the broad sweep of stone steps leading to the entrance; and there was the post-office on Washington Street, another classic effect in gray stone. But beyond these, public buildings were unimpressive. The new City Hall, far out on Larkin Street, was simply a mess. It was never completed, but still wandering vaguely over several blocks, with its unfinished wings and peeling stucco, making it look like an old ruin, it happily burned in 1906. The present Civic Center covers its site.

Through residence neighborhoods of the old city passed the colorful figure of the Chinese vegetable vendor in blue cotton blouse and trousers, padded slippers, and a broad hat like an inverted tray of woven bamboo. Over his shoulder he carried a flexible pole and, slung on either end of it, a huge basket overflowing with fresh greens and glowing fruits that bobbed rhythmically to his swinging gait. On Fridays the Chinese fishman followed him on his rounds and stopped at the curb to weigh silver fish in his scales. Chinese peddlers of silks and brocades, carved ivory and jade, carried their wares from house to house packed in cases that were tied in great squares of yellow cotton. It was an adventure to have one brought in with his pack. He would step softly into a room with many little bows and kneel on the floor to untie the knotted cloth; and presently the carpet would be covered with a fascinating confusion of bright silks, ivory fans, lacquer boxes, pale green tea-cups of 'Canton Medallion,' and carved sandalwood that scented everything.

I missed their visits when Chinatown grew progressive and a Chinese merchants' association did away with them. 'Eight dolla hop,' one would say holding a piece of brocade at arm's length while he knelt among his wares. 'You like him? All light. Fi dolla.'

Chinatown was endlessly fascinating. As early as the seventies it was said that thirty thousand Chinese were crowded into the quarter which extended northward on Dupont Street from California to Broadway, a district six blocks long and little more than a block wide. It was an enchanting little city where gentlemen in lavender brocade coats and puffed silk trousers were thick among coolies in their blue cotton. Their long queues were braided with strands of cherry silk. Little-foot women, with sleek heads and jade bracelets falling over their hands, leaned on their attendant maids in slow progress, the tiny feet shod in gold-embroidered silk; and adorable children, in green and cherry-red embroideries, laughed in the crowd of the lantern-hung street. It was, in short, a scene transported from Pekin. Windows of the bazaars were a blaze of color. Sweetmeat vendors were stationed along the curb, and over the gilded balconies of restaurants drifted the shrill music of singing slave girls. Everywhere the scent of sandalwood mingled with that of the fish markets.

Often we went shopping in Dupont Street, for silks, carved teakwood tables, and lacquer trays, and the Canton china that found its way into San Francisco dining-rooms. And often we brought home gifts of lichee nuts, jars of ginger, or white lilies growing in jade-green bowls — good-will offerings from the merchants.

These friendly aliens, with their love of bright hues, their strange theatrical customs, the tong wars and 'hatchet-men,' and all the mystery of life lived in subterranean levels, like geological strata, brought a flare of rich color to the pageant of the old city.

Violent agitation against the Chinese in the seventies left many people cold, so to speak, and especially cold were San Francisco housewives. For them the Chinaman solved a domestic problem. He was a marvelous cook through a genius for imitation, and his integrity was refreshing. Much of the responsibility of housekeeping could be safely left to a 'Number One Boy.' And Chinese servants were eminently good to look at in their long white blouses, padded slippers, and their heads shaved almost clean, just a patch of hair left to braid into a queue which was wound tightly about the crown.

One became adjusted to their ways. At ten o'clock every evening they set out for the quarter to visit the barber, the joss-house, and a gambling-game, and were unavailable after that hour. One of our friends had a 'boy' who serenely detached himself from his duties between two and four in the afternoon. The doorbell pealed vainly, and if she went to his room to knock and suggest a little service, the bland answer came gently through the door, 'Resting now.'

The house-boy of one of our friends was a marvel of silent efficiency named Sing. One morning in the third year of his service, our friend took her place at the breakfast table as usual and all the appointments were as usual. She rang for coffee. A totally strange boy appeared bearing the coffee-pot which he placed in its accustomed position.

'Who are you?' the mistress asked in amazement. 'Where is Sing?'

The new boy bowed several times. 'I am Sing's friend,' he explained. 'Sing go to China. I stay,' which he did to the family's entire satisfaction for six years.

Sometimes the presence of these reticent, soft-footed Orientals brought a stark flash of alien drama into quiet

Occidental homes. In the country house of other friends were a Chinese cook, Chuen, and a house-boy, Charlie — Chuen was a middle-aged man with a temper, but he was a perfect cook, so the temper was humored. Charlie was a youth not long from China. Some stupidity or carelessness on Charlie's part may have provoked the crisis. One morning the family was wakened by cries from the back piazza — Charlie's voice wailing over and over in pidgin English, 'I want my Mudder! I want my Mudder!' They rushed to the scene. Charlie was crouched on the floor with fending arms, blood pouring over his face from a cut in his head. Chuen stood over him with a hatchet. At sight of the master, he dropped it and padded away to his room. Charlie was cared for and a doctor summoned. But not the doctor nor any member of the family could extract from either Charlie or Chuen a word of explanation.

It developed, however, that Chuen had been a hatchet-man in Chinatown. The hatchet-man corresponded to the Occidental gun-man and functioned in tong wars. Chinese in America all belonged to tongs and the several associations were forever evening scores in long feuds. Each tong had its hatchet-men, and when war was declared, they were stationed with their hatchets in obscure doorways or alleys to chop down marked men of rival tongs. During tong wars, Dupont Street would be roped across and guarded by the police to prevent the entrance into Chinatown of disinterested 'foreigners,' who might be chopped by indiscriminate hatchets or struck by the bullets of the police.

THE SAND-LOT RIOTS

Chinatown was a really exciting place. It was thrilling even in smallpox epidemics when the police guarded all entrances and yellow plague flags were flying over the quarter. But for all the lack of sanitation and bland disregard for Western ideas of law and order, San Francisco never resented its presence. It was too fascinating in its life and color.

Anti-Chinese feeling was generated and stirred by a species of political party led by a fiery little Irishman named Dennis Kearney, who held meetings in sand lots. His followers, known as sand-lotters, soon included most of the city's hoodlum element which had no particular other interest at the moment and took up Kearney's cry, 'The Chinese must go!' This was persistently reiterated until a just resentment of white labor against low wage standards of coolies became the inspiration of senseless violence; and the Sand-Lot Riots resulted.

Lumberyards near the docks were threatened with burning, and the disorder grew so serious that a much-harassed chief of police longingly remembered the Vigilantes and appealed to William T. Coleman, once their leader. For twenty years the Vigilance Committee had been disbanded. Coleman had returned for several years' residence in New York, and was living a life of conservative affluence in his Taylor Street mansion, with no taste for violence. But the peace and safety of the city were imperiled, and he sent out a call for his old comrades. Many of them, like himself, conservative men of middle age, answered the summons. A committee was formed, but the days of Vigilantes were past, and the new body was known as the Citizens' Committee. Its members were unarmed except for pick-axe handles to be used in dispersing mobs. 'Coleman's Pick-Axe Brigade' it was called. But the pick-axe handle was effective, and Coleman's Brigade ended the rule of riot. I've always thought that San Francisco owed a greater debt to William T. Coleman than was ever publicly acknowledged.

The reign of Ralston was a brief and brilliant period. This most spectacular of the plutocrats dazzled the city with an extravagance rich and romantic. Everything was done in the grand manner. At Belmont, his estate south of the city, he lived like a prince of the Renaissance, with something of the same arbitrary generosity and richly careless hospitality. The horses at Belmont stood in stalls of polished inlaid wood and their harness was silver-mounted. The master lived in proportionate splendor. I sometimes wondered if any two men in Christendom could have been as different in tastes and ways as William C. Ralston and his partner, D. O. Mills, who was a pattern of conservatism almost austere. Together they founded the Bank of California, dislodging the old Tehema House from its setting at California and Montgomery Streets to erect a building for it in '64. The Tehema House, favorite hotel of miners and *rancheros*, meekly betook itself over to Broadway, where it stood in shabby, offended dignity until 1906.

We first knew Ralston when he married Lizzie Fry, the pretty niece of Colonel Fry, of the Army; were guests at the wedding in Calvary Church, on May 20, 1858, at two

WILLIAM C. RALSTON

MRS. WILLIAM C. RALSTON

o'clock in the afternoon, as an old engagement-book records. There had been no invitations. Simply, Dr. Scott announced from the pulpit on the preceding Sunday that the marriage would take place, and the church was filled with their friends, who gathered in the informal way that was then the fashion. There were no ushers, no bridesmaids: nothing to dazzle or amaze. But the wedding trip that followed startled society. It was a honeymoon camping party. Half a dozen ebullient young friends accompanied the bridal couple to Yosemite Valley, where they were guests of the bridegroom during a two weeks' honeymoon.

To reach Yosemite in those days it was necessary to make the last part of the trip on horseback over narrow mountain trails, and the Ralston honeymooners thus accomplished it — all of the ladies riding astride in bloomers! This was the crowning shock when news of it reached South Park.

The Ralstons lived in Tehema Street for a time, but not until they acquired Belmont down the peninsula were their lavish entertainments the amazement of the community. Belmont was a charming place in itself, once the property of an Italian gentleman, Count Cipriani, who had lived there, remote from his native land, for political reasons. He called it Cañada de Diablo, and in his day the house had been a modest villa. The new owner added wings and ells until a rambling white mansion wandered seemingly at random over the sloping hillside, all laid out in gardens. In a domed wing was the oval ballroom. Its walls were mirrored, and from the frescoed ceiling hung a great crystal chandelier whose reflected lights and sparkle filled the room. I have never seen a more effective setting for a ball.

Long wings of guest-rooms were filled for days at a time, and if it happened that there were no guests at Belmont, the prince gathered a company to drive down with him in his coach and whatever additional vehicles were required, for dinner and the night.

Mrs. Ralston once told me she was sitting at peace with the world one morning when the butler appeared to ask if there would be guests for dinner. 'Only the family this evening, Santino,' she told him. Just then the telegraph in her room clicked. It was before the days of telephones, and Ralston had installed a private wire from Belmont to his office in the city. She answered the call, and her husband's message was clicked out: 'Will be down with fifty guests for dinner.'

A ball at Belmont was always preceded by a banquet; that is, guests who came from the city were expected to dine at Belmont, and a dinner there was a banquet. One elaborate affair was given for our old friend Admiral Farragut on his return visit after the Civil War, with Vice-President Colfax sharing the honors of the evening. We found the Admiral aged that year. He danced but little in the old meticulous manner.

At a Belmont banquet for the Japanese Embassy headed by Baron Irakura, I marveled at the inscrutable poise of these Oriental gentlemen, encountering Occidental hospitality for the first time. Would they measure all of it by this example, I wondered.

Our Renaissance prince elected thus to play host to all distinguished visitors as much to make their stay a happy one as to impress them with California hospitality. He genuinely wanted them to like his city and spread its fame — a one-man Promotion Committee for sheer pride and delight in the place he had done much to build. The sweeping gesture of hospitality might have bewildered strangers. It used to be said that no sooner did a man of note sign his name on the register of the Palace or the Lick House than he was rushed, pen in hand, down to Belmont. This was an exaggeration. But even if it bewildered, the gesture was usually taken as it was given, in good will. Occasionally it gathered strange specimens. Once a British globe-trotter, discovered at the Palace Hotel, was driven down to Belmont for a stay of several days, but precipitately departed. The presence of the Ralston children at dinner the first evening, a family party, had distressed him, and he stated that children never dined with their elders in England. From this point he proceeded. Manners and customs of America were deplored and condemned, until the evening ended. At breakfast in the morning, he took up the theme once more, and was proceeding easily when his host rose in wrath.

Mr. Ralston banged a hard fist on the table. 'That will do, sir!' he thundered. 'I've stood as much of your impertinence as I intend to. The carriage will be at the door to take you to the train at eleven o'clock. See that you go!' And he strode out of the room.

Of Ralston's background I know very little. He came from Ohio in the early fifties with the business genius that made him conspicuous almost at once and the exhilarant personality that won popularity with all classes. His workmen all adored him, from the gardener at Belmont to a janitor at his bank. In many things he had a fine, discriminating taste. His homes were charming. A town house built in the Spanish manner on the Pine Street slope of Nob Hill had rare carved woodwork imported from abroad and floors of colored marble mosaics, the work of Spanish artisans. This, like Belmont, sheltered a 'Young Ladies' Seminary' in its decline.

Books and paintings were sometimes bought wholesale. When he was furnishing Belmont, he called one day at the studio of Thomas Hill where the walls were covered with the artist's paintings. Mr. Ralston glanced about. 'How much for the lot?' he asked. A generous price was paid and Hill's landscapes were hung all over Belmont.

The most theatrical of all Ralston's daring exploits was his raid on the Mint. It might very well have sent him to prison, but nothing whatever was done about it so far as I know, and it brought the Bank of California safely through a crisis. This was soon after the Civil War, when, for some reason of financial stringency, President Grant forbade banks to exchange gold bullion for coin at United States Mints. The order placed banks of the gold country in a peculiarly difficult position. In the vaults of the Bank of California, for example, there were tons of gold, but insufficient coin to meet an imminent run.

Directors were in despair when Ralston asked them to leave the situation to him. They fancied he might send some special urgent message to Washington where other appeals had been refused. Instead, he asked several trusted lieutenants to come to his office that night. What other arrangements he made were never revealed. But some time after midnight, Ralston and his men proceeded from the bank to the Mint in Commercial Street, a distance of several blocks, carrying bags of bullion; and they returned to the bank carrying its exact value in coins. The trips were repeated during the night until several tons of bullion had been exchanged for its equivalent in money, and the bank was ready in the morning to meet all demands. How Ralston gained access to the Mint remained forever unexplained.

His belief that San Francisco was destined to be a great metropolis and his pride in the city inspired Ralston to build the Palace Hotel, long the most luxurious hotel in America. It was, in truth, a little top-heavy in the first years with its vast proportions; but like Shepheard's of Cairo and the Grand Hotel of Yokohama, it was known around the world, and undoubtedly attracted travelers who might have globe-trotted straight through to the Orient to remain for more or less extended visits. The new trans-continental railroad and Pacific Mail steamers across the Pacific made a trip around the world easy and popular.

The hotel's great central court of white marble, with surrounding galleries of seven stories rising above it to the vaulted glass roof, was unique. Carriages drove into the court through wide doors and turned in a circular driveway cut in the flagged marble floor. It was warmed by huge braziers of polished brass filled with glowing charcoal, and when adjacent dining-rooms were filled and the galleries above were lighted, it was a lovely place. It was brilliant for the opening on October 2, 1875, when a banquet to General Phil Sheridan christened it. But before this triumph of his plans, the end had come for Ralston.

Newsboys called suddenly through startled streets, 'Ralston dead!' 'Ralston drowned!'

The city was stunned. For the public there had been no forewarning of a crash, but among Ralston's associates there had been uneasiness for some time over his extravagant expenditures. The Grand Opera House, which in Mission Street aspired to rival the Grand Opera of Paris, had been one long overshot. It was said that he owed the Bank of California four million dollars. Finally, at a meeting in the bank he was forced out of the directorate. From the meeting he went straight to North Beach, where a few hours later his body was washed ashore.

Accident or suicide? It was never definitely decided. An insurance company, convinced of the accident theory, paid the widow fifty thousand dollars. Ralston had been in the habit of bathing at North Beach, where there were several swimming clubs. In his overwrought state the sudden contact of cold water might have superinduced a stroke. He had swum far out when, without a cry, he sank. So a resplendent gentleman passed, unattended and unpanoplied at the end. His funeral procession was blocks long, so greatly was he revered by the public; by his associates as well, much as they might deplore his extravagance in business. At the opening of the Palace Hotel, Senator Sharon, who had been his creditor for two millions according to popular computation, paid him a generous tribute.

In the settlement of Ralston's estate, Senator Sharon acquired the Palace Hotel, with Belmont which he now made his home. The hotel was the pride of California, and the fashion of the city gathered there on Monday evenings for the band concert in the court. When, in 1879, General Grant came across the Pacific from Japan on his tour of the world, he was welcomed back to America in the court of the Palace, where galleries were hung with flags and garlands. Stationed in them were five hundred choristers who sang an ode of welcome with Madame Fabbri to lead them. Their voices filled the court to its high roof. Far below stood General Grant, surrounded by dignitaries, looking up toward the music.

General and Mrs. Grant were guests at Belmont for several days, and Senator Sharon gave in their honor a grand banquet and ball with many extravagant details and special trains from the city to recall the Ralston hospitality, but something was missing; some flourish or touch of romance which in Ralston's day had lent character to what might have been mere theatrical display. Belmont had become conventionally plutocratic.

Among diversions of this visit was a drive through Menlo Park, the new colony of country homes near Belmont where the Athertons, Eyers, Edgar Millses, and others owned large estates. James Flood had lately built there an enormous white castle surrounded by formal lawns, parterres, terraces and fountains, which he called 'The Towers.' Mrs. Flood implored Senator Sharon to stop at 'The Towers' with the illustrious visitors when they passed that way.

'If I do, Mrs. Flood,' the Senator demurred, 'you'll have a collation that will ruin everybody's appetite for the banquet at Belmont.'

Mrs. Flood protested that this she would not do. Just a snack, she would offer; the merest refreshment. And the stop was arranged.

Exactly as Senator Sharon had feared, a luncheon of many courses was served, and he was obliged to sit through it with an appearance of pleased enjoyment while his guests did it full justice. He watched, you might say, the edge of appetite for his surpassing dinner that night ruthlessly destroyed.

Flora Sharon's wedding to Sir Thomas Hesketh was the last elaborate social event at Belmont. The bridegroom came sailing through the Golden Gate on his yacht, Lancashire Witch, bound around the world from Liverpool, and they sailed away on her for the honeymoon, and back to England. The young Fred Sharons went to live in Paris, and the Senator did not long survive the Sarah Althea Hill affair. Belmont's glory had departed. After a period as a select seminary for young ladies, it became a sanitarium.

FLORA SHARON
Afterwards Lady Hesketh

The railroad down the peninsula from San Francisco to San José passed through colonies of country homes and for a ball at Menlo or San Mateo, as for one at Belmont, special trains were run from the city for guests. Burlingame, now the center of country life in California, was then a tract of land adjoining the W. D. M. Howard estate, 'El Cerrito,' and was laid out in vegetable gardens which supplied the Palace Hotel. Senator Sharon had acquired it with Belmont and the Palace from Ralston's estate and converted it to this use. After his death, his son conceived the idea of a Western Tuxedo, and the potato patches became parks and terraces.

The Howard family lived at El Cerrito in a queer maze of a house which had originally been a small cottage for brief country visits. The visits were prolonged and by degrees wings and extensions were added to increase the capacity and comfort of the house until it strayed over the landscape in an engaging way, with little colonnades connecting wings, oddly terraced rooms, and an air of consciously enjoyed caprice. The Howards gave many house-parties, and we drove from El Cerrito to picnic at Lake Merced, where I could always evoke a picture of the Broderick-Terry duel on the lonely shore.

Broad, level lawns of the William Barron place at Menlo Park were the marvel of the countryside. During the dry summers of California, lawns must be watered daily and sometimes twice each day, to preserve their verdure. Water in Menlo was scarce, principally supplied by artesian wells and correspondingly expensive, but the

Barron lawns were kept an inch under water for months. One could never walk on them in summer, but it was enough to come upon their green beauty on a hot, dry afternoon and be refreshed at the sight. Mr. Barron once said that a green velvet carpet over the land, frequently renewed, would be less costly, but he had a preference for grass.

Senator Latham bought the Barron place in the eighties and added to its beauty with fountains and an artificial lake where lotos blossoms rested on the waters. The lotos had been imported from Japan with the wistaria that draped verandas, and when they were in bloom strangers were welcome to drive through the grounds and enjoy their beauty.

The Latham stables, like those of Belmont, were finished with inlaid woods and costly fixtures. Surely horses never anywhere else had known the luxury they found in Old California. Lucky Baldwin's stable on Nob Hill overshadowed his house, and across the street another racing gentleman built one that surpassed it, with a modest home adjoining. A dozen others were scarcely less rich in appointments — all of which reminds me of Major Rathbone and his chandelier.

Major Rathbone had been American Vice-Consul in Paris before his marriage to Miss Atherton, when he came to California to live and built an Elizabethan country house near the Atherton estate at Menlo. In a San Francisco shop the Major selected fixtures for the new house — an especially handsome chandelier to illuminate and adorn the reception-hall. When the Menlo Park address was given, the pleased salesman remarked beamingly, 'Senator Latham selected one exactly like this for *his* Menlo Park place.'

'Indeed? Where did he put his?' idly asked the Major.

'In the stable, sir,' replied the salesman, still beaming over the happy coincidence.

CHAPTER VIII

WE were a pleasure-loving people in the old city, which was really so young that it seems absurd to call it old. But I mean, always, old in contradistinction to the new city built after 1906; and by pleasure-loving, I hasten to state, I mean nothing in the Babylonian manner, but a love for the lightness and sparkle of life. San Francisco has always adored a *fiesta*, a celebration of any sort. The original effervescence of pioneer days never altogether departed. Chinatown and the Italian Quarter seemed perpetually *en fête*, and even the streets of dives and dance-halls along the Barbary Coast were irrepressibly gay; never dark and devious like the slums of London or New York. A 'wide-open' town in miners' parlance meant just that, and anything wide open cannot at the same time be dark and devious. The Barbary Coast covered a few blocks along Pacific and Jackson Streets on the outskirts of Chinatown, where one-story frame buildings housed saloons and dance-halls with a few cheap variety houses. It was all mild enough as slums go in seaport cities.

In our love of gayety we filled the theaters. It was still the grand period of the stage and the grand players, many of them, came to California, where generous patronage repaid them for the long voyage. My memories of the theater in these years are a brilliant tapestry of many figures against backgrounds of old castles, sylvan scenes, and Roman orums. Booth's slim, black velvet Hamlet; the whimsical Rip Van Winkle of Joseph Jefferson; Clara Morris, lachrymose and appealing with a white camellia in her flowing hair; Matilda Heron, a more beautiful Camille who in her last days nearly starved to death; and lovely Adelaide Neilson. All these are in the pattern, and a hundred others: One figure of superlative, polished dandyism, deft and dapper, stepping with light, pointed steps; Billy Emerson singing 'Moriarity.'

'The ladies all sigh as I go by,
"Are you there, Moriar-i-tee?"'

A figure that the Chase portrait of Whistler in the Metropolitan Museum of New York always recalled to me.

Most vivid of all, the glowing presence of Ristori. It must have been in the early eighties that the Italian tragedienne came to the California Theater, an elderly woman then, but with the fire of her genius still flaming. One understood how in younger days she rivaled Rachel in Paris. With what power and depth of sympathy she played Marie Antoinette! I lived through scenes with the unhappy Queen herself, although Ristori spoke the lines in Italian, and I understood no more than a word here and there; the scene where she gathered her little son in her arms and swept across the stage to fling window-curtains aside and face the mob that was crying, 'Down with the Austrian!' the scene of her farewell to the King in prison on the eve of his execution; and her going forth to her own death. I wept quite helplessly through them all, and even now have not forgotten my grief. She was a magnificent old actress: Marchesa di Capronica in private life. One of her daughters was lady-in-waiting to the late Queen of Italy.

It may be that these grand old players would seem hopelessly archaic today; stilted and amusing to irreverent youth. But I cannot think so. Times have changed, it is true, and with them many things, including what might be called the mental or psychological technique of art. Moderns feel and express their art differently, but the fundamental spark must be the same — the essential flash of genius.

The opening of the California Theater, 'modern in every detail,' which Ralston built for Barrett and McCullough in '69, was a grand gala occasion; an evening of light and color, laces and flowers, as I look back at it. The city's wealth, beauty, and fashion were all there, the ladies in light silks with fluttering fans and their hair done in the new mode with long 'Follow-me-lad' curls over one shoulder — an audience of 'carriage folk.' Those who did not own clarence or barouche commandeered public hacks for the evening, and they rolled up Bush Street from Kearney, the horses' hoofs clattering on cobble-stones. The lobby with its mirrors fairly glittered with elated people assembling, long silk skirts sweeping the tessellated marble floor; and the elegant Barrett, in full evening regalia, stood smiling like a host welcoming his guests.

The play was 'Money,' from Bulwer-Lytton's novel, with John McCullough and Marie Gordon as Alfred Evelyn and Clara Douglas. But before the curtain rose on the first act, Barrett stepped from the wings and read a dedicatory

RISTORI AS MARIE ANTOINETTE

address written by Bret Harte. The friendship of these two men endured many years and Harte was among those who applauded 'Larry' from the boxes that night.

Marie Gordon was the wife of John T. Raymond, the Colonel Sellers of later seasons, who made a hit that night in 'Money' with the minor rôle of Graves, and was ever afterwards a favorite in San Francisco. She was pretty and gentle and had excellent taste in dress. One would never have taken her for an actress off the stage, since her gowns were quiet and she used neither paint nor powder. Ladies, of course, never used paint then, and even powder was disapproved. Very well I recall the excuses offered by a Southern friend when I found her powdering her nose one day. 'We all use it in the South,' she told me, elaborately casual. 'It's the warm climate; makes our faces shine, so we just use co'n-starch powder and never think a thing about it.'

McCullough was not good in a play like 'Money.' Classic tragedy was his forte. Modern rôles cramped him, and his voice was too heavy and booming in stage drawing-rooms. Yet I am forgetting an occasion when he read the part of one of Shakespeare's women in tones perfectly modulated to its demands. It was at the Ben Holladay home after a stag dinner for Barrett and McCullough; Mrs. Holladay had asked me to come in to help her entertain the men when they left the dining-room. It was a lovely party for me, the only woman guest of the evening. I sat on a sofa beside Judge Hoffman and went into gales of laughter at his nonsense. This happy soul had, strange to say, become the city's most popular pallbearer, a distinction unsought and desperately unprized, but there seemed nothing Judge Hoffman could do to escape it. It had reached a point where the first person a bereaved family thought of was Judge Hoffman, and at one funeral after another he served, totally unable to refuse a request from grief-stricken relatives to participate in final honors for the departed.

While we sat there on the sofa, some one asked Mr. Barrett to read, and the actor amiably consented. We heard his mellifluous tones addressing our hostess, 'May I have a Bible, Mrs. Holladay?'

'Oh, my hat!' groaned Judge Hoffman in a whispered groan. 'He's going to read the burial service!' This he did. Relentless Fate had pursued Judge Hoffman. Barrett turned to that part of Second Corinthians used at funerals and the too familiar lines came to the pallbearer on the sofa. But so perfectly were they read in the marvelous voice, with such quiet restraint of feeling, that for once he must have enjoyed them. Barrett's voice had a quality not to be resisted, the most moving voice I ever heard in speech.

There followed the *pièce de résistance* of the evening. In their conventional black broadcloth, with no other background than long lace curtains at the end of the rooms, Barrett and McCullough gave the 'Closet Scene' from 'Hamlet' with McCullough reciting the lines of the Queen. Incredibly fine it was, and it held the company gathered in the parlor spellbound as in a darkened theater.

The Holladay house on the crest of Holladay's Hill was a landmark for many years, one of the few old mansions to survive the fire of 1906. To reach it from Van Ness Avenue, one climbed a long, broken flight of wooden steps on the steep hillside, or, preferably, drove around to the easy western slope where a carriage-way led to the house. It was painted white, and the reception-rooms were charming in the manner of the sixties, with long French windows and draped lace curtains, long oval gilt mirrors, crystal chandeliers, and pale carpets with great medallions of roses. Small marbles — parlor statuary — were set here and there on gilded pedestals and paintings in gilt frames hung on the walls. Steel engravings might invade the parlor in this prevailing scheme of home decoration, but never bronzes, which stood about in halls and libraries where marbles rarely ventured.

From the cupola of the Holladay house one looked out over the Golden Gate and bay to glimpse the Pacific, and landward, to count six counties if so minded; Marin, to the north across the strait, Contra Costa, Alameda, Santa Clara, San Mateo, and the County of San Francisco, in a sweeping circle. It was a marvelous view which Adolph Spreckels coveted when he built his stone palace near by on Washington Street, on a site which was second choice, but which still offers six counties. The City of Glorious Vistas should be San Francisco's second name.

Ben Holladay, who found a place in the annals of the West as owner of the famous 'Overland Stage' line, was an original character. With his longish white hair he looked like a patriarch of the Old Testament, but he was a shrewd business man who had started life as a stage-driver in Oregon and eventually owned most of the stage lines in the Northwest. With all the plutocratic prominence that came to him, his manners never changed. They were always 'early Oregon' — forthright, a little rough, but commanding respect. Mrs. Holladay was charming, and, in spite of her husband's scorn for them, cultivated the social graces. Her two young daughters she took abroad to be educated, and both married Europeans, one, the Count de Pourtalès, and the other, Baron de Boussière. After the weddings they all came home for a visit in order that the two husbands might meet their father-in-law. But old Ben Holladay had no taste for titles. He betook himself to the wilds of Oregon and there remained for the duration of the visit. It was quite a visitation, nevertheless. Mrs. Holladay brought the young people across the continent in a private car, and with them two friends, Mrs. Eben Wright and Mrs. David Torrence, of Boston. They all stopped at the Palace Hotel and were indefatigably wined and dined by the local *beau monde.*

Both Barrett and McCullough were favorites in society, but McCullough's taste was more for the Bohemia then becoming part of San Francisco life, the circle of artists, actors, and writers who founded the Bohemian Club in rooms over the California Market. Harry Edwards, of the California Stock Company, was one of the founders. For Barrett and McCullough had formed a stock company at the new theater, which, remote as it was from dramatic centers, rated scarcely second to the old Boston Museum Company. It specialized in tragedy, and now that I think of it, we had, in our zest for life, a singular taste for tragedy in the theater. The unhappy ending was popular. Lear, Othello, Macbeth, Julius Cæsar, Virginius, Romeo and Juliet were old friends whose loves and deaths we witnessed many times. We were familiar with ancient kings and followed their misfortunes to final catastrophe with fine enjoyment. Charles Kean brought us a malevolent Louis XI. King Henry VI was played by a young Thespian from Australia, George Rignold, who had a flashing eye and a kingly stride. Barry Sullivan presented Richard III with histrionic fervor. In his company were two young men destined to shine in comedy, Louis James and William H. Crane. James was a rare Sir Lucius O'Trigger to Joseph Jefferson's Bob Acres in 'The Rivals.' This old comedy, with Jefferson and Florence, and the forever incomparable Mrs. John Drew as Mrs. Malaprop, so blandly complacent in her linguistic errors, is altogether my most delightful memory of the theater.

These two distinguished Thespians, Barrett and McCullough, were much identified with San Francisco life in the 'Old California' days. They took the keenest interest in a charity performance of 'Rosedale,' given at their theater by society amateurs, so called, and gave hours of their time coaching the players in their parts. 'Rosedale' was one of the favorites of the stock company's repertory, and General W. H. L. Barnes, who arranged the amateur performance, chose it for interesting comparisons that might be made with the professional production, principally, I fancy, for the comparison of his own acting of the hero with that of Barrett in the role. Barrett coached him indefatigably and the result was a triumph of reproduction. General Barnes was a conspicuous figure in those days, a brilliant lawyer and gallant officer of the National Guard, slightly ostentatious, but public-spirited and progressive. One of his chief concerns was the Mercantile Library, and it was to raise funds for this institution that he planned the production of 'Rosedale.' Tickets were sold at five dollars apiece, an unprecedented price then, and the theater was filled. It was a Red-Letter night, with all the delightful effervescence that belongs to a gala occasion; flowers over the footlights, bouquets tossed from boxes, speeches and applause. The amateurs really did cover themselves with glory.

General Barnes had another happy inspiration to relieve the Library's financial strees — the 'Mercantile Library Lottery,' which was a joyous success. Thousands of tickets were sold, every one talked of it and bought more tickets, and in the end, after prizes were paid, the Library found itself free of debt.

The 'Old California' had always an air, like a house where only happy people have lived. Something about it made any evening there a gala, if it was only one of tickets for two to see 'Dundreary' Sothern.

Half a dozen years after the fatal night at Ford's Theater in Washington, Sothern brought 'Our American Cousin' across the Continent. It was while watching a performance

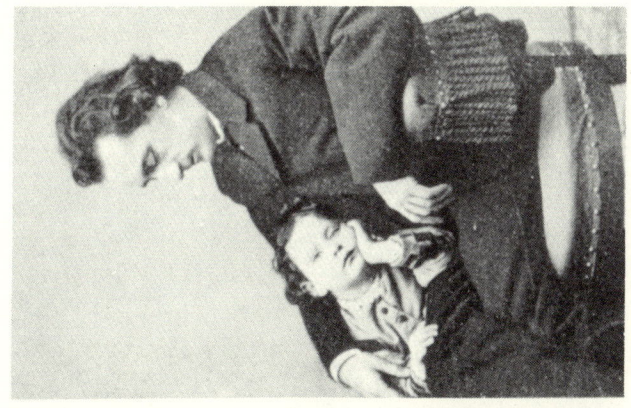

EDWIN BOOTH AND DAUGHTER

EDWIN ADAMS

of this comedy that Lincoln was assassinated by Wilkes Booth. I fancy it was many weeks before Sothern felt the comedy of Dundreary again, but when he played it at the California, he was irresistibly absurd, and from the first night won San Francisco's hilarious endorsement. The character was that of a witless English lord with monocle and 'weepers,' renamed for him 'Dundreary whiskers,' and a profound but imbecile seriousness in all things.

Sothern, himself, was droll as Dundreary in his own way. We rejoiced in his friendship but there is left only a general memory of his absurd, inconsequential wit. I do recall that Mr. McCullough said one evening at a dinner party that I had influenced him to engage Sothern for the California, and how pleasantly important I felt. Once when we met somewhere I had spoken of the English actor then delighting New York and asked why the California management had not called him west. There was the question of a very high salary, and Mr. McCullough's doubt that San Francisco would respond to the comedy of Dundreary, he told me.

'But of course it will,' I answered. 'Everyone has heard of Sothern's Dundreary and he would fill the theater for weeks.' And pondering this oracular utterance, McCullough had been moved to arrange the Dundreary season. Or so he assured me.

Sothern's original San Francisco engagement was prolonged and repeated, and during the last one I was present on the sad afternoon of Edwin Adams' farewell. Adams, a greatly loved member of the California company, had returned from a trip to Australia undertaken for his health, far gone in consumption. He longed to go to his old home in Philadelphia, and to enable him to make the trip, the farewell benefit performance was given. The play was Robertson's 'Home' in which he had acted many times the part of Col. White. That afternoon Sothern played the rôle. At the close of the performance the curtain rose again to reveal Adams seated in an arm-chair on the stage, looking very ill and wasted. Near him stood Sothern and McCullough. They both made speeches and then, from his chair, Adams said a few words expressing a gallant hope of returning to act again for his friends. I saw him watch the curtain descend amid flowers and applause. A few weeks later he died in Philadelphia.

Mary Anderson was a girl of seventeen when, in 1876, she made her San Francisco début as Parthenia. She was even then extraordinarily beautiful, with a rich contralto speaking voice. I never saw her act after her art matured, although once long afterward I saw her again in a theater. It was in New York when Maude Adams made her first appearance as Juliet at the Empire Theater, and the Juliet of other years applauded from a box. She was Madame de Navarro then, visiting New York from her English home, and a guest in the Vanderbilt box that night. Word of her presence soon passed through the audience, and one's eyes turned often from the stage to the beautiful, mobile face, tense with interest, in the box. She sat with her classic profile to the house, as lovely to look at as she had been in her girlhood. When Miss Adams and the Romeo, William Faversham, took their bows, she clapped with smiling delight.

Maude Adams was an excellent Juliet, I thought, with more of the wistful, elusive quality of youth than other Juliets commonly captured. But she never pleased the critics. Faversham, I liked better than most Romeos. One of Miss Adams's gowns made a deep impression on me as Ristori's laces had while I wept over Marie Antoinette — my feminine sense of the sartorial subconsciously alert. It was a long robe of creamy Irish lace thickly studded with turquoise to make it fall in heavy, graceful lines. No other daughter of the Capulets had such a dress.

But of all the Juliets I remember leaning over stage balconies, none was so bewitching as Adelaide Neilson, none so moving in the later scenes. She was at the height of her fame when she came to San Francisco in '77, a short while before her sudden death in Paris. It was a brilliant engagement of adulation and applause. We gave a very personal admiration to our stage favorites in that ingenuous age. To meet one was an adventure. Exciting, then, to receive a card in the mail one morning, to meet Miss Neilson at Mrs. John Faull's! I went in my best bonnet. She was entrancing at close range, vivid, sparkling, talking of her stage parts when she was questioned. Yes, she wept real tears, always. Her purple Isabella costume in 'Measure for Measure' was ruined by them and had to be often renewed. She was happy over the San Francisco conquest, and laughed much and lightly. A blue velvet hat on her very blonde head, when other women young and old wore bonnets tied under the chin, distinguished her costume. When news of her death so soon afterward shocked playgoers everywhere, I was glad to have this radiant memory of her.

Playing with Neilson that season was a romantic young actor named Henry Montague, first of the matinée idols. He wore his thick brown hair parted at one side and swept back from a noble brow, with two locks brought forward to form a hook on either temple, and before he knew it, the young man had set a feminine fashion. We wore 'Montague curls' for years. Poor handsome Henry Montague died in San Francisco the following summer when he had come again from New York to play Armand Duval to the robust Camille of Maud Granger. He was stricken with a sudden hemorrhage in his rooms at the Palace Hotel, where he passed away in a few hours.

While there were still kings in Hawaii, royalty sometimes came to call, sailing across the Pacific with a dusky retinue. Kalakaua's first visit in '74 was memorable. He arrived as guest on the United States warship Benicia with Minister Pierce, American Envoy to Hawaii, and there were floral arches, bands, and parades to welcome him, with balls and banquets to follow. I am not sure it was during this visit that a grand ball was given for the King at Mechanics' Pavilion, but I do recall of this ball much preliminary discussion, disagreement, and concern over the order of precedence for civic dignitaries and the ritual for royal presentations. In the end, however, it all went off very well.

ADELAIDE NEILSON

THE VISIT OF KING KALAKAUA

It was during the first visit that an enterprising manager arranged a concert in Pacific Hall and gained the King's consent to be present. This fact he widely advertised and, of course, it drew a crowd. By eight o'clock Pacific Hall was filled, but the royal armchair conspicuously placed remained empty. At half-past eight it was still very empty, and a distracted manager stepped to the platform. He begged the audience to be patient and announced that he had sent emissaries to fetch the King — dead or alive, no doubt, although this he left to inference. Presently the King arrived and made his way down the aisle to long overdue applause, and we all settled back to consider the concert.

His Majesty was good-looking in a dark brown way, and had dignity in spite of his short, rotund figure. He wore a uniform in the nineteenth-century European fashion for kings, and a pair of luxuriant black side-whiskers flaring away from his pleasant brown face.

One of the young officers of the Benicia, who was delegated to accompany Kalakaua to Washington that year, was Lieutenant Whiting. After he became a distinguished Admiral of the Pacific Fleet, he married Miss Etta Afong, of Honolulu, the pretty, piquant daughter of a Chinese merchant whose wife was Hawaiian. There were several Afong sisters. Two married American officers, and all received generous dowries from old Afong, who had made millions in the Islands. Mrs. Whiting lived in San Francisco for a time, an interesting and dainty little figure in the social scene.

King Kalakaua was destined to die at last in the Royal

Suite of the Palace named in his honor. He was stricken with pneumonia when returning from a trip to Washington, and died after a few days' illness. People gathered on the hills to watch the funeral ship sail out the Golden Gate, taking him home with flags at halfmast. A touch of symbolism in the scene — the wide gateway opening to the ocean, and the little ship sailing out, made it deeply impressive.

Queen Kapiolani and Princess Liliokalani, afterward the deposed Queen Lil, arrived in '87 on their way to attend Queen Victoria's Golden Jubilee, and there was great interest in their presence at the Palace Hotel. Nob Hill, entertaining them, was surprised to find their golden-brown beauty set off by very modish gowns. Mrs. Robert Louis Stevenson's daughter, Isobel Osbourne Strong, then living in Honolulu, had designed them, we were told, and the ladies wore them gracefully enough. Who could be entirely graceful in the heavy puffed polonaise skirts, tiebacks, and whale-boned basques of that day?

For the Queen's amusement, Senator John F. Miller, then Collector of the Port in San Francisco, commandeered the revenue cutter Shubrick for a 'water frolic.' Points of interest about the bay were few, but we cruised among the islands, stopped at a Chinese fishing village redolent of shrimps that were spread in great bamboo trays to dry, and called at Alcatraz, where Major Darling did the honors.

Governor and Mrs. Pacheco were old friends of the Hawaiian royalties, an inherited friendship of the Governor's whose Spanish forbears had trading relations with the Islands. Mrs. Pacheco I recall as one of the wittiest of San Francisco women. She once wrote a farce-comedy, 'Incog,' which had a great success in New York when Charles Dickson played it.

More interesting than Hawaiian royalty was a stout, florid gentleman, short of stature, but with a certain manner of unobtrusive importance, who came from his ranch near San José for visits to the Occidental Hotel. We often saw him dining there with members of his family. The first time, he had attracted my interest, and I asked Major Hooper about him — the Major was the urbane host of the hotel. He was General Ord, I learned, said to be a cousin of Queen Victoria, which, in truth, he was, and so like her he might have been her brother; of the House of Hanover by all his lineaments.

Large blue pop-eyes like the Queen's were an inheritance from his grandfather, George IV of England; for he was the son of James Ord, who was a son of the fourth George by his morganatic marriage with Mrs. Fitzherbert. James Ord had been sent to America in his childhood to be raised by the Ord family of Baltimore, whose name he took. General Ord, of San Francisco, was the son of this James Ord's American marriage. One heard very little about him. The family lived quietly at the ranch and preferred that their visits at the hotel should pass unremarked. But the old gentleman's unusual aspect inevitably excited curiosity, and the story of his ancestry was soon widely known. Yet he made few social contacts. I never saw him save in the devoted circle of his relatives, who treated him always with great deference.

Early in the present century the Ords came into public notice on two continents when Mrs. Fitzherbert's royal marriage was definitely established in England and the American family received a fortune from the Crown. Old General Ord had then gone on his way into eternity.

Through the eighties and nineties the Baldwin Theater had an important place in the city's life. It was part of the Baldwin Hotel Building at Market and Powell Streets, owned by Lucky Baldwin, who had won his name on the race-track. With a certain 1880 elegance of crimson plush and gilded trimmings, the Baldwin had an attractive, intimate warmth. The dress circle was raised above the orchestra circle, and in its long first row people 'dressed' as they did in the boxes, which gave brightness to the house. First nights were fashionable events. Visiting stars and stock companies would be welcomed with flowers and 'bravos' by an audience in evening clothes, laces and fine feathers — quite literally; for women often wore plumed hats perched high on their heads throughout a performance. One's view of the stage in those days was likely to be, and generally was, over an intervening hedge of millinery.

Daniel Frohman's Lyceum Company with Georgia Cayvan came every summer from New York; Daly's, with John Drew and Ada Rehan; the Empire Company, young Eddie Sothern as Lord Cholmondeley, Mansfield playing

Baron Chevrial dying at a banquet table while he raised his glass in a toast, with a realism fairly gruesome; Modjeska, who gave 'As You Like It,' with Maurice Barrymore as Orlando vanquishing the great Muldoon himself. These are a few who cross my memory of first nights at the Baldwin.

Modjeska's American début I recall at the 'Old California' long before, when she spoke English very brokenly, but acted with an authentic power that assured her success. She was the most appealing of all Camilles, and how many Camilles there were! Only Juliet rivaled *La Dame aux Camellias* as a favored rôle of all fair Thespians. San Francisco had then an interesting colony of Polish *émigrés* who welcomed Modjeska and her husband, Count Bozenta, when they came from their farming adventure in the South. Dr. Pawlicki, distinguished and brilliant, was their friend; and Sienkiewicz, who was to become the famous author of 'Quo Vadis,' had come with them from Poland. And there was my father's old friend, Captain Bielawski, ex-officer of engineers who was a draughtsman in the United States Land Office for years.

Edwin Booth played his last San Francisco engagement at the Baldwin, and I found his Hamlet as thrilling as in younger years. The poetry of his acting was a deathless quality. By that time San Francisco recalled that the great actor had once lived in a cottage out on the Mission Dolores Road, back in the eighteen-fifties when he came as a boy to California with his father; and he was welcomed with proprietary affection. His rooms at the Palace Hotel were kept filled with fresh flowers.

Fanny Davenport brought a gorgeous Cleopatra to the Baldwin with young Melbourne MacDowell to play Marc Antony. They were married soon afterward, and Fanny Davenport died before her happiness and beauty waned. She was handsome, rather than beautiful, with the well-rounded, slightly heavy pulchritude then admired.

Sparkling Rosina Vokes brought her English burlesque company, and sang, 'No matter what you do if your heart be true, and his heart was true to Poll.' She was dying of consumption on her last visit, but few of her audience could have guessed it, she played still with so much *verve*. Rosina Vokes was the most gifted of the famous Vokes family of the English stage, the wife of an English artist, Cecil Clay, who accompanied her on this tour. He would sit in an upper-tier box at the Baldwin through every performance, watching her with anxious, troubled eyes. It was all he could do. Her insistence on playing was not to be overcome, so he just trailed about with her until she was forced to give up. Actors do seem to have a courage peculiar to their calling. Georgie Drew Barrymore played with sparkle and lightness long after her health was broken. She died of consumption in Santa Barbara.

Lillian Russell sang at the Baldwin in her golden youth and wore a pink chiffon frock in 'La Cigale,' with a ruffled rose chiffon hat on her shining hair, to make a picture I remember. And there was the strangely lovely Mrs. James Brown Potter who came sailing through the Golden Gate from the Orient, one year, with her leading man, Kyrle Bellew. They were touring the world, playing anywhere from Capetown to Bombay and Honolulu, and so to San Francisco. This was several years after the Bishop's daughter-in-law had shocked Newport by reciting ''Ostler Joe' in a drawing-room, and then turned her back on the social tempest to go on the stage. Meanwhile, she had learned to act and proved an interesting Juliet to Kyrle Bellew's impassioned Romeo. She was singularly beautiful with her pale, delicately chiseled face, long dark eyes, and hair like burnished bronze with copper lights. In one act of 'Charlotte Corday' she wore a scarf of luminous emerald silk which had been especially dyed and woven for her in India. The effect against her pale beauty and gorgeous hair was a rare color study. Mrs. Potter's parents, Colonel and Mrs. Urquhart, had come from New Orleans and were living in Oakland, then — quiet, retiring people who must have looked upon this temperamental daughter as a lovely changeling.

Less beautiful than Mrs. Potter's, but more appealing, was Julia Marlowe's Juliet. Her husband, Robert Taber, was the Romeo. They were both very young and had just been married, and the romance delighted sentimental play-goers at the Baldwin.

There was a shining 'first night' when Georgia Cayvan wore her glass dress, and every one was eager to see this sartorial triumph in spun glass, which had been made in Bohemia for the World's Fair at Chicago and there exhibited before the actress acquired it. The fabric was delicately brittle, shimmering as crusted snow in sunlight, but flexible enough to be fashioned into an eight-gored skirt and modishly tight bodice with many glass ribbon bows. Gracefully and gingerly Miss Cayvan wore it in 'The Charity Ball.' I've wondered often what became of it — if eventually she broke it.

CHAPTER IX

WHEN Patti sang in San Francisco, the city went mad over her, a happy insanity that sent crowds following her carriage when she drove with Nicolini, or besieging the stage door to cheer when she appeared. Her piquant personality and winsome prettiness, with the heavenly voice, made her altogether irresistible, and she was generous with her singing. She would trill and carol far beyond the score, and often at the end of the opera, when she took her calls and caught flowers tossed to her from the boxes, would signal to the orchestra leader and the strains of 'Home, Sweet Home,' would silence the tumultuous audience. Or she might gaze pensively at a flower she held and sing 'The Last Rose of Summer,' which was a perfect *aria* for her voice, so crystal clear yet filled with color.

This was in '84 and the following year she came again for the first of her farewells. Colonel Mapleson, her *impresario*, conceived the idea of farewell tours which were repeated annually for years. He was something of a personage in those days, an impeccable Beau Brummel who decorated the foyer of the theater at every performance. Seats for the second season were sold out long before Patti and her troupe arrived, and anticipation was keen. Etelka Gerster, a lovely Hungarian who had been contralto in the first season, had been replaced by Madame Scalchi, an enormous Italian woman with the richest contralto I ever heard, like deep, wine-colored velvet. Photographs of Patti and Scalchi adorned shop-windows and there were displays of 'opera cloaks for the Patti season' — white brocade dolmans and pale velvet wraps trimmed with swansdown. Swathes of silk — peach-blow *moiré antique* or plum-colored *gros grain* — were labeled 'dress lengths for the opera'; and there were painted fans, lace handkerchiefs, pearl opera glasses, and opera bags to hold them, all for Patti's season. Its sartorial impetus was more than pleasantly profitable for merchants, and florists likewise profited, for the singer's rooms at the Palace were filled with flowers and set pieces galore passed over the footlights.

It was during this second visit that we met Patti when General and Mrs. Walter Turnbull gave a reception for her at their Van Ness Avenue home. She wore a little white bonnet on her birdlike head, and a polonaise gown of garnet silk, much too old for her, but in the prevailing fashion; and was bewitchingly pretty. Mrs. Turnbull had engaged three talented little girls, the Joran children, to give a musical program during the afternoon. The quaint little sisters, whose father was a music-master, played violin, 'cello, and piano. Two of them, Elise and Pauline Joran, afterward found fame abroad. Patti was delighted with their performance.

After one of their numbers, Mrs. Turnbull brought forward her small son, Walter, Jr., to meet the diva, so that he might recall the encounter in after years. Patti stooped to greet him. 'And what do you play on, my little man?' she asked, smiling. Walter, aged six, answered promptly. 'I play on the sidewalk,' he said, politely informative.

Etelka Gerster, who became so popular in Patti's first season, tragically lost her voice soon afterward, and, although we heard occasionally that physicians abroad promised her return to opera, I think she never sang again.

Jane Hading, beauty of the French stage, came to California with Coquelin the Elder, to play Molière in Mission Street. Except for brief seasons such as this, the old Grand Opera House had lost place, and was given over to blood-and-thunder melodrama. But for these seasons Fashion descended again upon Mission Street from Van Ness Avenue and Nob Hill, and the great crystal chandelier which hung darkly over the auditorium for 'ten-twent'-thirt'' sparkled once more. It was 'the largest chandelier in America' and a beautiful thing, notwithstanding, which hung there in Mission Street until the earthquake of 1906. Then it crashed into the pit below, just a few short hours after the old theater's last audience had departed. It was on the historic night when, as Ashton Stevens later said, Caruso changed the name of 'Carmen' to 'Don José.' The Metropolitan Company of New York had just opened a season to give the Opera House, as it proved, a glorious finale.

Coquelin as Tartuffe and Mascarille was the revelation of a great artist in a school of comedy new to the West, polished to fine, high brilliance. The company played in French, but in spite of this and the unfamiliar sophistication of their art, audiences flocked to see them and applaud.

Hading as Claire in 'The Ironmaster' made Mrs. Kendal's Claire seem very flat. She had beautiful henna hair worn parted and in the new 'Hading wave' which was soon the fashion, a loose, heavy wave that replaced crimps, which were never less than dreadful.

The Kendals — Mr. and Mrs. — English players, enjoyed a peculiarly Victorian vogue. It was generally understood that they were morally immaculate, socially correct and happily married. People who never entered a theater, except to see Shakespeare presented by some player they knew to be above reproach in private life, preferably Barrett, went to see the Kendals. It is astonishing to recall how many of these rigidly selective playgoers there were. But in spite of numbers, their influence on the drama seems to have been negligible. Even Mrs. Kendal betrayed them in a way when, to their deep dismay, she appeared as 'The Second Mrs. Tanqueray,' a lady with a Past.

Across the bay in Sausalito, where offshore all British ships in port were anchored, an English colony lived on the hillside, and there the Kendals were sedately entertained.

French restaurants of San Francisco delighted Coquelin as they invariably did visitors from the Old World. At Marchand's, or any one of several places, one could dine as well as in Paris for but slightly higher tariff. Seventy-five cents paid for the *table d'hôte* at the old Poodle Dog, an eminently epicurean feast served with wine.

In very Victorian days of the eighteen-eighties, 'perfect ladies' never dined in our French restaurants. At a few 'oyster grottoes' and a Vienna bakery in Kearney Street, they might regale themselves in a limited way if moved to eat in public. But these places palled, and a gradual, tentative invasion of the Poodle Dog and Marchand's became definite and established.

These gay old restaurants once inspired a member of the Bohemian Club to write a parody on the 'Marseillaise.' I never heard more than the last lines of it, given with all the vehemence and fervor of the original 'March on! March on! All loyal hearts, to victory or death!' The words of the parody were the names of four popular French restaurants, 'Marchand's! Marchand's! The Maison Riche, The Poodle Dog, The Pup!!'

Sarah Bernhardt dined often at Marchand's during her visits. She played many times in San Francisco and always to enthusiastic audiences. Half of them knew not a word of French, but she swept them all into the rush of her *tempo*. There was a nervous, swift-moving element in all her acting, and she had, of course, the essential flame which burned to the end, as it did in Ristori. Remembering her fragile grace in Camille and the barbaric splendor of her Empress Theodora, I wonder that she was ever called unbeautiful. Her voice like a wind harp's music, and the way she held her head, chin high to give a long, suave line to the slender throat, are still vivid memories of Sarah in her summer years.

She wore white a great deal, then, off the stage; long robes of creamy wool girdled below the waist, and long white veils wound about the turban on her frizzed red hair. The year she played Cleopatra at the Baldwin, young Mrs. Will Crocker gave a breakfast party for her on Nob Hill, to the rather shocked surprise of the neighborhood. Dinners and teas for bishops were more the Nob Hill idea.

Which brings me to Mother's clerical teas. She gave one annually for visiting clergy during the church convention in San Francisco, and for several years they were a great success, sprightly parties at which every one had a good time. A bishop properly mellowed may be delightful. Bishop Kip, who was one of the New York Kips, was always a perfect guest. Bishop Nichols had a happy sense of humor and told amusing stories of his visits to small parishes of the Wild West. Dr. Moreland, of St. Luke's, afterward Bishop Moreland, was from South Carolina, and could give Negro dialect recitations that were better than the minstrels. Dr. Lion, of St. Stephen's, sang well and willingly 'obliged.' Mother's clerical parties were really politely hilarious affairs. We missed Dr. Ewer, longtime rector of Grace Church, a temperamental cleric and perfervid preacher of the Word. He had entered the ministry in deep repentance for an early life of atheism and newspaper reporting. In that phase he had written a book, a burlesque of Spiritualism called 'Three Eventful Nights,' which was a sensation in the fifties. The brotherhood of Spiritualists, to his amazement, took it seriously and gave it profound attention.

Mrs. Ewer, it was said, had been a dancing-teacher in her youth, but this seemed incredible of her plump, placid presence. True or not, she was a shining success as a clergyman's wife with her immutable serenity. In later days we heard that Dr. Ewer had embraced Catholicism and become a light of the Roman Church, but what became of Mrs. Ewer I never heard.

A great religious revival swept over the city in the early eighties when Moody and Sankey converted sinners in the old Tabernacle in Turk Street, which overflowed at their meetings. These revivalists were not less renowned in their day than was P. T. Barnum himself. Theirs was a vast and beneficent influence, however short-lived it may have been, and their honors were well won. As did most of the town, we went one evening to hear them and saw a great audience exhorted into emotional transports.

Moody, the preacher, was a short, rotund gentleman, not impressive to look at, with his jungle beard, but possessed of unmistakable magnetic power. He stood easily with his Bible in his hand while he talked, and his first, casual manner would gradually become more intense, until his voice was deep with feeling, but he kept always his intimate, everyday speech and a sincerity not to be doubted. It was impossible for his hearers not to feel that he spoke to each one individually. At the close of the service he would grasp the hand of as many as could make their way to the pulpit, most of them sinners just brought to grace who would announce their reform with tear-wet eyes.

Ira D. Sankey led the singing and looked exactly like his name, tall, thin, and sanctimonious with long 'weepers.' He had a trained choir which sang the 'Moody and Sankey

Hymns' stirringly, and really popularized them. The 'Moody and Sankey Hymn-Book' became as familiar as 'College Songs,' and young people of the period, gathered about a piano, would render 'Washed in the Blood of the Lamb' with all the fervor they gave to 'Jingle Bells' or 'Champagne Charlie.'

The Moody and Sankey aggregation included also a 'lady elocutionist,' Laura E. Dainty, who recited 'Little Jim' and other parlor selections in a white nun's-veiling gown puffed at the back. Quite apart from the religious inspiration, Moody and Sankey meetings were worth all that was dropped in the contribution box.

Dr. Hugh Haweis was a zealot of another order who came in the early nineties on a preaching tour of the world with his violin. He was the famous rector of St. James's Church, Marylebone, in London, where his drawing power in the pulpit rivaled that of the great Spurgeon. Original as a clergyman may be in vestments of the Church of England, with many glints of humor, he had a pleasant way of breaking his discourse to play violin selections with fine musicianship. His theories on the uplifting effect of music had been written into a book, 'Music and Morals,' from which he quoted. Dr. Haweis was a small man with a decided limp, very noticeable when he stepped rapidly across a platform in the ardor of his address. It was said to be a souvenir of service under Garibaldi at the siege of Capua in his youth.

Church affairs played a more important part in the everyday life of past generations than they do today, and the visit of a famous clergyman was an event of note.

The son of Charles Dickens was a visitor when his father's books were still popular novels, and the son's readings from them, in the First Congregational Church, drew thrilled audiences eager to see one of the children of Gad's Hill Place. He was a fair, sad-looking gentleman with a melancholy droop to eyelids and mustache. Yet he read the trial scene from the 'Pickwick Papers' with keen relish of its humor. Not without apprehension we recalled stories of English ladies fainting in platoons when his father recited 'The Murder of Nancy Sikes.' But happily no one fainted in the First Congregational Church, although the younger Dickens's reading of this selection remains in my memory a vivid bit of histrionic horror; a dramatic *tour de force* doubtless reproduced inflection by inflection from his father's inspired rendition.

At an afternoon reception, Mr. Dickens's aspect of sadness was accentuated. He had little to say and that little was guarded. Wary of Americans he seemed. Lightly and inanely I asked him if he were tired of people perpetually lauding his father's books and deploring the criticisms of 'American Notes,' and his answer was, 'Ah! Personally I admire the United States very much and have enjoyed my visit.' Nothing could have been more discreet. Driven to the Cliff House, he listened patiently to the barking of seals, and in Golden Gate Park admired the Victoria Regia. It could never be said that the younger Dickens failed in appreciation of United States hospitality, and one felt that he would never write 'American Notes.' His mind was made up.

The Victoria Regia was a pond-lily; the largest in the world brought from the tropics to bloom in a pool in the Crocker Conservatory. So — now we had the largest chandelier, the largest flower, and some of the largest oil paintings in America. The Victoria Regia was an object of great popular interest. As I look back now, its blooming is one of the high lights of the eighteen-eighties. Every one talked of it. 'Have you seen the Victoria Regia?' served to open conversations at dinner-parties, or to change the subject. Every one went to the Park to look at it. In single file the citizenry passed around the pond to marvel at the great flare of petals. It really was a remarkable flower. The green leaf of its foliage measured several feet across and lay like the top of a pool table on the water.

Golden Gate Park, with the long panhandle entrance, had been laid out in lawns and driveways over several acres to become the city's favorite resort, filled with carriages on Saturday afternoons and Sundays. Crocker Conservatory was its great attraction. In it we saw orchids for the first time. There was a delicate pale blossom known as 'The Holy Ghost Flower' with a tiny curled petal like a white dove in its heart. I haven't heard of the Holy Ghost Flower or the Victoria Regia for years. Possibly they are extinct like Jacqueminot roses which have ceased to bloom.

The Japanese Tea Garden came to the Park with the

Midwinter Fair in '93, and remained, a charming souvenir, with its cherry bloom and waterfalls, tall stone lanterns, iris pools, and little tea-houses built out over waterways with stepping-stones. It is still the loveliest of places. This Midwinter Fair (still flashing forward) was a bright little exposition following the World's Fair in Chicago with some of the same exhibits and features. It was set in a valley of Golden Gate Park with charming little buildings and a Midway; and its season was a long *fiesta* for San Francisco. One wandered through eucalyptus avenues filled with Javanese, Arabs, Hindus, Samoans, and other picturesque aliens while Sousa's Band played, or Fritz Scheel's Vienna Orchestra. Once they both played at a concert of combined forces and this confluence of music attracted wide interest. It was a Niagara when they played together.

In the eighteen-eighties, high cart-wheel bicycles rolled through driveways of the Park, where horses shied at them, and no wonder. With riders perched high on the wheels, they had a curiously entomological aspect, like gigantic Daddy-Long-Legs.

One afternoon we saw Miss Minnie Warren and Commodore Nutt out for a drive, standing on the seat of their barouche to acknowledge greetings. Miss Minnie was about twenty inches high and the Commodore an inch or so higher. This must have been in the seventies, when they made a tour of the world with General and Mrs. Tom Thumb, at whose wedding in New York they had been bridesmaid and groomsman. Miss Minnie was a sister of the bride. They were all attractive little creatures, intelligent in miniature, and well-mannered. The Tom Thumbs were especially polished, accustomed as they were, according to Mr. Barnum, to 'All the Crowned Heads of Europe.'

Oscar Wilde's visit, not long after that of Charles Dickens, Jr., created no furor. It was long before his brilliant epigrams were widely quoted, before they were written, when he was deep in æstheticism, lecturing on 'Interior Decoration.' He was then wearing what afterward came to be known as a Fauntleroy costume, black velvet knee-breeches, short black velvet coat over a white silk blouse, black silk stockings and low shoes. It was not becoming, and he was not attractive, with his heavy face, one eye drooping, and an expression of utter ennui. For the life of me I can recall nothing of his lecture save the word 'dado,' to which he gave a peculiarly broad pronunciation. And I know nothing of how he passed his time in San Francisco. Doubtless he was frightfully bored, and looked upon California as a sort of No Man's Land where he spoke to penguins. The response naturally would be apathetic.

But something of the old, ingenuous enthusiasm of early days, contagious and exhilarating, flared again for Irving and Terry when they came with the London Lyceum Company to play at the old Grand Opera House. The whole city turned out for them. Press agents had very little to do with the overwhelming interest. We were lovers of the theater and for years had heard of the English actor and entrancing Ellen Terry. Those who saw them in London brought back accounts of lavish productions and distinguished acting; of a King Richard and Shylock, of a Portia and Beatrice, original and brilliant. When these all finally came to America and advanced across the continent in the royal progress of a special train, we were naturally keyed up to concert pitch.

People stood about the Palace Hotel for hours to catch a glimpse of the stars, and the sight of Irving's long, thin form crossing the court, followed by his little fox terrier, Fussy, or of Miss Terry muffled in veils attended by her efficient-looking daughter, Miss Craig, apparently repaid them.

The day before seats were placed on sale at the theater, a line formed from the box office, extending out Mission Street for blocks. All night it waited. Camp-stools, pillows, and substitutes paid by the hour to hold places, were resorted to, while small restaurants of the shabby neighborhood served trays of coffee and sandwiches. Ticket speculators were few. Those who waited were for the most part agents of groups of playgoers who paid them for the service; and some were enthusiasts there on their own account.

Never a more exciting 'first night' filled Mission Street with a crowd of spectators gathered to see the audience arriving. 'Nance Oldfield' was given first, with Terry blithe and charming; a short comedy in which Irving had no part. Then we were swept into the cumulative horror of 'The Bells.' It was the sort of thing light-hearted San Francisco adored. We watched the guilty innkeeper haunted by ghostly sleigh-bells that rang on the sleigh of the traveler he had killed until he was driven to a nightmare death by the everlasting sound. As Mathias, the innkeeper in 'The Bells,' Irving doubtless gave one of the most extraordinary exhibitions of histrionic power the theater has known. The reaction that night was a wild ovation. People stood on their seats to see the actor bowing before a storm of applause. It was a great night; but in calmer moments I preferred 'Becket' to 'The Bells.'

Tennyson's poetic drama written for Irving was new then, and it was produced with all the splendor of setting that made Lyceum productions the pride of theatrical London. Ellen Terry looked like the Blessed Damozel as Fair Rosamond; and Irving played the majestic character of the Archbishop with intellectual fire and a spiritual quality poignantly beautiful. His hurried, nervous mannerism of speech, so often condemned, I recalled in Charles Kean. In both actors it seemed to me the natural expression of intense feeling.

During his stay, Irving was elected honorary member of the Bohemian Club and so enjoyed its hospitality that he made a parting gift to each fellow member of a permanent pass to his Lyceum Theater in London. Bound in soft leather and adorned with his nervous signature, they are souvenirs in a number of San Francisco families.

Like most of California, I was unaware of the presence of Robert Louis Stevenson when he lived for a year or two in San Francisco before fame had found him. He was married there in 1880 to Mrs. Osbourne, of Oakland, at the home of Dr. Scott, but almost no one knew of the wedding. Mrs. Scott and Mrs. Virgil Williams were the only witnesses. Virgil Williams, the painter, was one of Stevenson's few friends in California. Together they would go to the Bohemian Club in its rooms over the California Market, where R. L. S. found several congenial souls; Dr. George Chismore, who wrote poems while he practiced medicine; and Charles Warren Stoddard. But I doubt if any he met thought the fragile young man would live long enough to set the world on fire.

His second visit I remember when he came with his wife, after a residence in Europe, where literary honors were heaped on him. They stopped at the Occidental Hotel, but Stevenson was too ill to be lionized. It was in the mid-eighties when he sailed out of the Golden Gate on Dr. Merritt's yacht, the Casco, bound for the South Seas, never to return.

After his death in Samoa, Mrs. Stevenson came back to live in San Francisco, and it was then California first knew her as a personage. She built a house on the Hyde Street crest of Russian Hill overlooking the Golden Gate, an Italian villa that was tremendously refreshing in its straight, clean-cut proportions. We were living through the East Lake period in home architecture when sudden ells and angles cut rooms into queer shapes and made wild exteriors, with roofs that slanted low or aspired to peaks, without reason.

The roof of the Stevenson house was perfectly flat; a terrace from which one looked out over the inspiriting expanse of bay and hills; still is, no doubt, since the house withstood the 1906 disaster, and the last I knew was a Carmelite retreat. There was a walled garden where tea was served, and the house was filled with souvenirs of Samoa; Stevenson's books and the Saint Gaudens medallion of R. L. S. over a fireplace, dominating the place.

Mrs. Stevenson was a fascinating woman: not beautiful nor finely brilliant, but with originality and a vivid personality that one felt the moment she entered a room — a stocky little person indifferently gowned, with a crown of short gray curls above piercing black eyes. This was long before the advent of the bob and Mrs. Stevenson's coiffure was considered eccentric, as were her cigarettes in that unenlightened day; which troubled her not at all. She had an independence delightfully complete.

Once in the Montecito home where her last days were spent, she showed me new wallpaper in the dining-room, a pattern of violent red apples in a confusion of green leaves. 'You don't like it,' she amiably surmised. 'No one does. They tell me it's dreadful. But I like it'; which was that.

While she lived on Russian Hill, the Stevenson monument designed by Bruce Porter was set in the Plaza — or Portsmouth Square, as it is now called. The little bronze ship with sails spread survived the fire of 1906 and is still a shrine for R. L. S. enthusiasts.

Brief and brilliant seasons in the old Grand Opera House drew fashion there again in its declining days. Emma Nevada came home from Paris to sing there, a Nevada girl

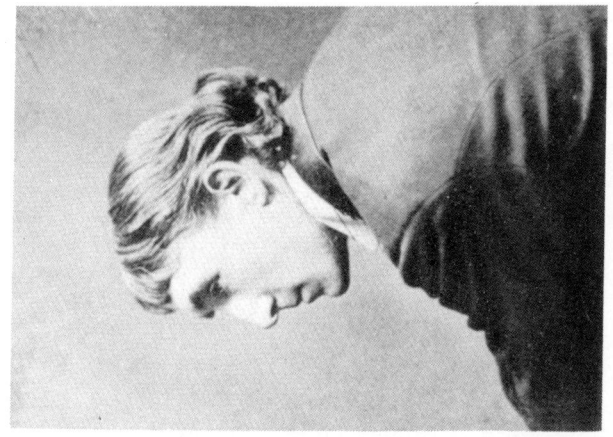

HENRY IRVING

ALBANI AS ELSA IN 'LOHENGRIN'

who was called the perfect 'Mignon.' She named her little daughter for this favorite rôle.

Albani sang there, but I remember her best filling the Mechanics' Pavilion with her voice. It was at some celebration in the Fair season, and she stood on the bandstand in the center of the huge building, sending her fine, strong tones up among the rafters in 'The Star-Spangled Banner.' Albani was an American woman who took her name from her native city, Albany; one of the great singers of her day and an especial favorite with Queen Victoria.

Stars of the Metropolitan Company in its greatest days sang in the old Mission Street Opera House, and San Francisco's reaction was very like that of a country village when the circus is in town. It was all glamorous and thrilling for a biennial period of six weeks. When Damrosch conducted 'Die Walküre' with Schumann-Heink's deep golden-bell voice, or 'Tannhäuser' with Nordica, and Bispham to sing 'The Evening Star,' the old opera house seemed bursting with music and enthusiasm. Mancinelli conducting 'Carmen' for Calvé, with her careless beauty and fire, strained the old walls again, and Caruso singing Canio's Lament, drew 'Bravos' to shake the chandelier.

But no more thrilling music could have been heard beneath the largest chandelier in America than Julia Ward Howe's 'Battle Hymn of the Republic,' sung by a huge audience in her honor. It was at the Decoration Day Memorial Services of the Grand Army of the Republic in 1888. She sat on the stage surrounded by old soldiers, and they said she looked like a white-haired priestess of peace sitting there while the strains of her war song rang through the place.

Mrs. Howe had come to California to lecture on the Woman's cause of which we were beginning to hear much, and to visit her sister, Mrs. Adolphe Mailliard, who had been Annie Ward before her marriage to one of the Bordentown Mailliards, whose forebears came to America with Joseph Bonaparte. The Adolphe Mailliards had been living for a number of years on their ranch near San Rafael, a place of picturesque gardens where Mrs. Howe's pretty young daughter, Maude, afterward Mrs. Elliott, of Newport, visited them one winter. Mrs. Mailliard died there in 1895, just a few months before she and her husband were to celebrate their golden wedding.

One afternoon at a tea, Mrs. Howe spoke informally of women's clubs in Boston. We had scarcely emerged from the sewing circle, although a Browning Circle flourished under the leadership of Mrs. Norris, the mother of Frank and Charles G. Norris. She had been an actress in her youth, and read 'In a Balcony' with fine expression. But nothing like a modern women's club was known, and those Mrs. Howe described, in which art and letters were discussed in an atmosphere of social friendliness, were a new idea. An inspiration, in fact; for not long afterward the Century Club was founded by Sarah D. Hamlin, with Mrs. George Hearst for its first president, to become honorary president when her term expired. It was the first women's club of distinction in the West, and the first women's clubhouse was the Century's in Sutter Street below Van

Ness Avenue, whence spread a definite cultural influence.

For years, membership in the Century carried a certain *cachet* of intellectualism, and it was, in a way, responsible for much of the new impetus toward erudition which went rather wild for a time. The transition from sewing-bees to afternoons with the Pre-Raphaelites, for example, was not accomplished without its amusing phases. But the wonder is, it was accomplished at all in so short a time.

This new vogue for erudition was, of course, a detail or manifestation of the Feminine Renaissance then beginning to be felt by the most indifferent mid-Victorians, if only because their daughters wanted to go to college. It is strange to have known the time of my youth when, it seems to me now, the female brain was deliberately stunted in its development; and to know also the present when girls go to college as a matter of course, practice professions, and find careers in politics. It is my belief that the feminine intuition we heard so much of in my young years was no more than subconscious cerebration; conscious cerebration being discouraged in women, the process was forced into the subconscious.

In San Francisco a charming woman, who was also a distinguished physician, did much to encourage conscious cerebration. Dr. Charlotte Blake Brown came from the Woman's Medical College in Philadelphia to practice medicine in the early seventies, when, according to popular prejudice, any lady who went in for learning must be a spinster without charm, while one who entered a profession, except that of acting, would be hard-visaged and militant. Dr. Charlotte was none of these, but young, attractive, married, and the mother of three children, an anomaly that required difficult readjustment among the prejudiced. Long before the close of her career, however, it was generally accepted as a fact that intellectual and professional women might be charming.

In her later years Dr. Brown was strikingly handsome, with silver-white hair and brilliant dark eyes — the least 'advanced'-looking woman imaginable, yet her quiet influence for the advancement of women was very great. She founded the Children's Hospital, with its training school for nurses, which opened economic possibilities to girls who theretofore had the choice of teaching school or music, with little else if they dreamed of independence. There were few shop girls then and no stenographers.

I know few details of Dr. Brown's life save that she came to California across Panama as a child in 1850, lived for a time with her people in Chile, and was then sent back East to school to be graduated from Elmira College. Her marriage followed and she came West again, to the Arizona frontier. After her three children were born, she decided to study medicine and entered the Philadelphia institution from which she was graduated in 1874. She practiced for thirty years in San Francisco and was especially distinguished as a surgeon. The bare record of her life may balance much pale, superficial living among women of her time — on whom in a way it was imposed.

CHAPTER X

SOMEWHERE in the eighteen-nineties was lost much of the ingenuous charm of the old city — never all of it; but with a new generation came a new metropolitanism, patterned, however remotely, on that of New York. We acquired a social leader of the Ward McAllister order — a young man from Baltimore who organized subscription dances known as the 'Greenways' and led innumerable cotillions. The sons and daughters of Apollo belles and beaus danced at the Greenways.

In those days young San Francisco was taught to polka and to waltz, to trip the schottische and Varsovienne, at Lunt's dancing-school, which was almost a social institution in the eighties and nineties. Professor Lunt was built like Von Hindenburg, but he was light as thistledown on his feet. I can see him now leading a cotillion, waltzing lightly down the long room in his Prince Albert coat, with his fierce mustache, followed by a troop of waltzing youths and maidens. Among them might have been discovered the young Frank Norris. Lunt's dancing-school was in Polk Street; the future novelist may have dreamed of 'McTeague,' the Polk Street dentist, while he danced the German.

An assistant dancing-master, Mr. Reynolds, was as strange a type for the part as Professor Lunt. He looked like a financier of scholarly tastes, with his sparse, iron-gray hair and finely cut features. Patiently he balanced before the infant class, counting in a sing-song voice, 'One-two-three, One-two-three. Turn out them little toes-two-three'; for his English was a bit faulty in spite of the scholarly appearance.

Little girls were wearing long 'shavings' curls then. Wet strands of hair were plastered around curling-sticks and brushed dry to form the hollow tubes; a process that severely tried juvenile patience. The little girls' mothers wore bustles, tie-backs, and Langtry bangs, for the fame of the Jersey Lily and the fashions she set reached us long before she came to California to fall in love with it and buy a ranch. General Barnes selected the place in Lake County and Langtry bought it 'sight unseen.' In spite of the wild country — it was miles beyond St. Helena, the nearest town — and a ranch-house of little comfort and no luxury, it pleased her and she planned to establish a stock farm there to raise famous racers. The house was elaborately refitted and furnished. I remember hearing of a carload of furniture that went up from Chadburne's store in Market Street. The Lily's brother came out from England to be manager and there were great expectations. But, after all, Langtry spent only that first summer at the place, which was sold a few years later.

The Jersey Lily, so admired for her face and form, was never, to my mind, half so lovely as Mrs. James Brown Potter, who was for a time her rival in London, one of the few women for whom Lord Kitchener ever expressed any admiration.

The nineties were a quaint period I've since learned. Young moderns refer to it as the 'Mauve Decade,' but we called it *Fin de Siècle*, and thought it very sophisticated and advanced. It was the fashion to be 'end of the century' in everything — which meant to be modernistic with an added flash of the bizarre. Aubrey Beardsley's drawings, for example, were very *Fin de Siècle* and so was the 'Yellow Book' of London, in which they appeared and which one found at Doxey's fascinating bookshop in the Palace Hotel. Its yellow cover with splashes of black expressed the quality, which was an elusive one, difficult to convey. The latest fashion from Paris was not necessarily *Fin de Siècle*, while a home-built gown of foulard in dashing zigzag pattern might be. 'Lady Windermere's Fan,' as drama, was distinctly so; and Mrs. Patrick Campbell, exotic and mysterious. But Daudet's 'Sapho' distinctly was not, nor was Olga Nethersole, the English actress who played it through a storm of horrified protest.

'The Lark,' published in San Francisco, was eminently *Fin de Siècle*. We were inordinately proud of it and of the fact that its fame reached London. Gelett Burgess, Bruce Porter, and Ernest Peixotto were its editors, and the small five-by-seven periodical, printed on butcher's paper, first gave the world that immortal quatrain on 'The Purple Cow':

> 'I never saw a Purple Cow,
> I never hope to see one.
> But I can tell you anyhow,
> I'd rather see than be one.'

Somewhat later its author, Gelett Burgess, produced a sequel:

> 'Ah, yes, I wrote "the Purple Cow" —
> I'm sorry now I wrote it,
> But I can tell you anyhow,
> I'll kill you if you quote it.'

Novels by a new writer, Mrs. Atherton, were daringly *Fin de Siècle*, or so we thought, and learned with amazement that she was the beautiful young Mrs. Atherton, of Menlo Park. More daring than hers was a novel by Amélie Rives, 'The Quick or the Dead,' which was surreptitiously read by conservatives and generally considered very shocking. But when 'Trilby' appeared serially in 'Harper's Magazine,' tastes had broadened, and almost no one was seriously distressed by Du Maurier's picture of life in the Paris Latin Quarter in all its delightful informality. The Trilby craze was terrific. We wore Trilby hats, Trilby coats, Trilby slippers, and what not; ate Trilby chocolates, played Trilby waltzes, and developed a 'Trilby type' in beauty. When the play was given at the Baldwin, with Wilton Lackaye as Svengali, the house overflowed at every performance. It was said the lovely voice that sang 'Ben Bolt' in the wings for the heroine belonged to a Mills College girl, Mabel Gilman. She afterward went on the stage in New York and became Mrs. Corey, of Paris.

I cannot recall in these years the first time I used a telephone. One adjusts so easily to many things in passing which seem, looking back, great and radical changes, as indeed they were. I recall the first telephone in our home when so few of our friends had installed them that there were only tradesmen to call up; but not the first time I lifted a receiver from the hook and heard a distant voice. It was a thrill, without doubt, but so soon accepted as part of everyday living that the first strangeness was forgotten. Just as I've forgotten the first horseless carriage I ever saw, although I do recall the first few driven in Golden Gate Park, where they looked so bobby and absurd with no horses in front.

I remember, too, the experience of a friend when she first talked over 'long distance.' She was the wife of Judge Wallace, one of the wittiest of San Francisco jurists. Mrs. Wallace called up her brother, Judge Ryland, in San José, and she told me that when at her home in Van Ness Avenue she heard his voice across fifty miles, it frightened her. Adventuring into the supernatural, it seemed.

The year the first horseless carriages appeared in the Park would have been when slowly circling the bandstand we listened to selections from 'The Mikado.' The 'Pinafore' craze had been succeeded by one for Gilbert and Sullivan's new Japanese opera. Its lilting airs were whistled, sung, played, and chorused all over the land. Traveling troupes presented it in San Francisco and there was a season of 'The Mikado' at the Tivoli — that picturesque old villa of opera in Eddy Street which gave the greatest pleasure to San Francisco music-lovers for many years. It had started as a beer-garden in Sutter Street, where the Jewish synagogue afterward stood. Men went there for good beer and the excellent music served with it — so excellent that the Tivoli Garden began to be patronized for its music, with beer a mere incidental. Finally the proprietors branched out to build the Eddy Street Opera House, a white villa with lattices and trailing vines and a balcony opening to an outside gallery where refreshment was served between acts. A stock company was organized to give opera at popular prices and then the proprietors branched still further out, and engaged famous prima donnas and tenors to sing short seasons with the stock company. So that, for example, one heard Zélie de Lussan, a great Carmen of her day, and even Tetrazzini in 'Lucia,' for fifty or seventy cents. There was a little soubrette named Gracie Plaisted who went on like the brook with undiminished *verve* while prima donnas came and passed.

After the matinée on Saturday afternoons, Market Street from Powell to Kearney was a popular promenade, where many of the city's interesting figures passed in review — actors, writers, politicians, and celebrities of the sporting fraternity, with pretty women to send them flaunting glances. A bright procession, never fashionable like the old march on Montgomery Street, but well worth reviewing. One might see, for example, Joaquin Miller, Poet of the Sierras, wearing his blue flannel miner's shirt, a broad felt hat, and trousers stuffed into high boots, although he hadn't been near a mine in years. Or 'Pompadour Jim,' the young bank clerk who was making a name for himself as an athlete at the Olympic Club. 'Gentleman Jim' was a later title which James J. Corbett won with the championship in the ring.

There would be 'White Hat' McCarthy, a funny little

Irishman who wore always an enormous white beaver hat which, over his odd little figure, looked very top-heavy, like pictures of the Mad Hatter in 'Wonderland.' White Hat was a familiar character on the race-tracks and about the hotels. He had friends in all classes and foregathered with millionaires at the Palace bar in the same easy goodfellowship with which he met his race-track friends in other places.

White Hat McCarthy was the originator of a joke heard, I suppose, around the world in its day. There came to live in San Francisco for a year or two a tall, rangy Englishman, Lord Talbot Clifton, who was much impressed by the personality of White Hat. The two became great friends and one often saw them crossing the Palace Court, little White Hat who reached Clifton's elbow, taking two steps to his long companion's one. They went together to Del Monte for a visit and the Englishman signed his name in the register. 'Lord Talbot Clifton and valet.' White Hat regarded the signature, then scrawled beneath it, 'White Hat McCarthy and valise.'

Ambrose Bierce was another figure of the Market Street parade, conspicuous for his really striking good looks. He had a shock of blond-gray hair that curled over his head and beneath the brim of his hat, with brilliant sea-blue eyes. Bierce wrote a daily newspaper column, seemingly inspired by a perpetual exasperation with human stupidity to which he was never reconciled. It was widely read and much quoted. He was never a prophet without honor in his own country.

Chris Buckley, the blind political boss whom Bierce excoriated, might stand briefly with friends on a Market Street corner, but one saw him more often driving with one of his disciples behind a pair of fast trotters. He was a man of singular power who in spite of blindness had gained control of city elections and the loyalty of many henchmen. Unscrupulous in politics, but faithful to friends, stories were told of his many charities.

Local politics had fallen almost altogether into the hands of professional politicians when James D. Phelan ran for Mayor and was elected — 'The Millionaire Mayor,' until it was discovered that, in spite of being the victim of great wealth, he was the most tireless and progressive mayor the city had known. Mr. Phelan was the popular president of the Bohemian Club for years, when 'Uncle George' Bromley spread there the genial glow of his wit.

'Uncle George' was a brother of Isaac T. Bromley, of the 'New York Tribune,' noted as an after-dinner speaker. But his own wit was far more spontaneous than Isaac's, so those who heard them both declared. It seemed to fall as the gentle dew from heaven. 'That reminds me —' he would say whenever there was a pause, and I suppose he had no idea on earth of what it reminded him until he was well under way. But the story, whatever it was, was always a good one. He was a famous night owl, lingering in the club lounge as long as there was any one willing and able to sit up a little later for companionship.

Once when he was aged and venerable the club entertained a visiting celebrity, who was delighted with the old gentleman's humor and marveled at midnight that it was still fresh. Others of the company fell away and still the wit of Uncle George charmed the visitor until there was none left but these two. Once or twice in the small hours the guest, feeling the need of sleep, ventured to suggest an adjournment and was overruled. 'It's early yet,' Uncle George would say, and go on with his story.

At 5 A.M. the desperately sleepy guest firmly announced his intention to depart. 'But it's early yet,' Uncle George protested. 'Don't go! What shall I do the rest of the evening?'

Among clearly remembered figures of these later years is Judge B——, the only person I ever knew who had survived a really thorough attempt at suicide. When it strangely failed, he accepted his destiny of life with a resignation courteous and detached. The adventure left him with the scar of a long slash across his throat and a genuinely ironic attitude toward living which made him different, especially from the sort of weary-of-life people who cling so tenaciously to it. After his retirement from the bench in San Francisco, Judge B—— had found it difficult to reëstablish his practice. In time he was reduced to desperate need, although his friends, including ourselves, never guessed this. The first knowledge of it came in newspaper headlines one morning. Judge B—— had been found lying unconscious on the beach below the Cliff House, his throat cut from ear to ear. He had gone from the room, where he lived alone, to the ocean beach in the early evening, taking a razor in his pocket. There were still people strolling on the sands, so he waited until the beach was deserted. Then he waded out into the ocean and, when the waters reached his shoulders, slashed his throat and fell unconscious into the waves — which perversely washed him ashore. After that, he waited until death came of its own accord a few years later, and in the interim often dined with us, an interesting and cheerful guest, only slightly sardonic. Something of his serene immunity to the temper of fate, so difficultly gained, I've never forgotten.

Then there is little Mr. Chang; no reason to recall him except that he was so engagingly unique, a quaint little Korean gentleman who looked briefly at the Occident from a hotel window and then hurried home. Also he reminds me of the strange career of a San Francisco gentleman, who became Prime Minister of Korea. It sounds like stage extravaganza, but this quiet, conservative gentleman, Clarence Greathouse, one of the perennial bachelors of the South Park set, actually did find himself Prime Minister of the Hermit Kingdom, living in a palace in Seoul where he ended his days. It had come about simply enough. Mr. Greathouse, who read law and wrote editorials for San Francisco newspapers, was appointed American Consul-General in Yokohama, where his knowledge of international law impressed statesmen of the East. At the end of his consular service, the King of Korea sent for him to be the royal advisor on certain matters. His counsel, it appears, was invaluable, for the King made him Prime

CLARENCE GREATHOUSE
Adviser to the King of Korea

MR. CHANG FROM KOREA

Minister for life, and Mr. Greathouse never came back to South Park. When, after his death, his mother, who had lived in his palace in Seoul, desired to return to her old home in Kentucky, Mr. Chang was appointed by the King to serve as honorary escort across the Pacific. He cut off his queue for this ordeal of travel, and discarded robes of silk for English tweeds fashioned by a Japanese tailor.

We asked him to dine with Mrs. Greathouse, and it happened that for a few moments before dinner Mr. Chang was left alone in the living-room. When we descended again from regions above, he had vanished. Not a trace of him. It was disconcerting and alarming. It might even be international if we had permanently lost Mr. Chang.

A messenger was sent to the Occidental Hotel in the wild hope that he might find his way back there. They arrived almost together, Mr. Chang and the messenger. Some homing instinct had led him safely through perilous streets in the right direction. It was made clear to him that we desired his return and awaited his presence at dinner, although he spoke no English and the messenger knew no Korean. Mr. Chang in turn made it clear that he would remain at the hotel. The incident was closed. He had escorted Mrs. Greathouse to our home, but dining with foreigners was not part of his duty as honorary escort. A few days later, Mrs. Greathouse saw him safely off on the steamer for Korea and herself departed for the sequestered quiet of Versailles, Kentucky, which must have seemed drab after all the exotic color and strange ceremony she had known.

She told us many details of the life in Seoul. The little Queen of Korea, assassinated by rioters who broke into the royal palace, had been her friend. Mrs. Greathouse had dined at the palace a few evenings before the tragedy. The Queen was a gentle, pretty creature, she said, highly intelligent; and her dreadful death plunged the King into deep grief. He had found refuge from the mob in the Russian Legation, believing her safe. It had been an uprising of a party favoring Japanese influence in Korea above that of Russia, favored by the rulers. Mrs. Greathouse told how assassins pursued the little Queen who ran before them from room to room of the long, low palace until in the last refuge they overtook her and killed her with swords.

In the last of these *Fin de Siècle* days came the Spanish-American War. The city was suddenly filled with soldiers, transports lying out in the bay, and much concomitant gayety. For the presence of the troops, camped on Presidio hills, the sailing of transports for the Philippines with bands, flowers, and pretty girls waving farewells, and endless parties for officers and men, made another long *fiesta* for San Francisco. No one thought of the grim side of war. It hadn't any very grim side in the Philippines, for that matter; the total losses of the campaign were twenty men, no officers. In Cuba it was more like war, but General Shafter, so long in command at Fort Mason, who fought at Santiago, came safely home again with his men, and it was all over in less than a year. As wars go, a very decent war.

The new century belonged to younger generations.

Grandchildren of my friends married and built homes out on the hills above the Presidio and looked politely vague if one remarked that just a few years ago this was all a waste of sand.

On a silver gray day of November, 1905, I looked back from the deck of a ferry-boat crossing the bay and saw San Francisco for the last time. My home thereafter was to be in a distant place, and this, that had been my home for nearly fifty years, seemed instinct with living individuality at the end, regretful for the parting; possibly because I had seen it grow, street by street, from the ramshackle town of the eighteen-fifties.

The Ferry Tower rose slim and graceful against the background of hills, all covered over with homes. They reached the slopes of Twin Peaks beyond the Mission. Palaces of Nob Hill loomed against the sky and Russian Hill's high gardens were green above skyscrapers of Montgomery Street. On the crest of Telegraph Hill a group of eucalyptus trees stood in silhouette and the long docks below were busy with the commerce of many ships.

It was a beautiful city. No amount of architecture unrestrained could destroy the setting; the hills sweeping upward from the bay where islands were green after early winter rains, and beyond, through the Golden Gate, the far horizon of the Pacific. Sea-gulls slanted their long wings over the widening stretch of water as I watched the city recede in the silver light.

Had I known how soon it would lie in ruins, I might have

turned back, disarranged plans and the course of events, to stay until the end. Yet, had I also known how soon it would be rebuilt in new beauty, I might still have gone my way, as I did, with a feeling of sadness and pride.

THE END

INDEX

INDEX

Abruzzi, Duke of the, 181
Adams, Edwin, his farewell to the stage, 219–20
Adams, Maude, as Juliet, 220–21
Advent, Church of the, and Rev. Marion McAllister, 76
Afong, Chinese merchant, 223
Afong, Etta, marries Admiral Whiting, 223
Alabama, the, Confederate raider, 146; and Mr. Kaird, 167
Alaska, Russians from, settle in California, 43
Albani, Madame, sings in Mechanics' Pavilion, 247
Albert, Prince-Consort, 5, 7
Alcatraz Island, 37; the sunset gun, 120; saluting the *Sutlej*, 146–47; a royal visitor and Major Darling, 224
Alden, Admiral, and Mrs., entertain on the *Active*, 88; Bishop Kip and a vote of thanks, 89–90
Allen, Major Robert, and the Diablo expedition, 71
Alnwick Castle; croquet and archery, 11
Alta-Californian, and the first printing of *Innocents Abroad*, 163
America, return to, 21; united by cable to Europe, 118
American Theater and the Mount Vernon ball, 123
Ames, Fisher, and a decanter of wine for Washington, 133
Ames, Pelham, of Boston, 83; marries Miss Hooper of South Park, 132; the wine for Washington, 133–34
Anderson, Mary, born in Sacramento, 98; her stage début, 220; applauds another Juliet, 220–21
Angel Island, 140
Angel's Camp, 101
Anza, Spanish explorer, 43–44, 109
Apollo balls, 80–81
Apollo belles and beaux, 83–84; their children, 251
Arguello, Don Luis, Spanish governor, his grave at Mission Dolores, 52
Arizona, the Spanish padres march from, 43; the Prince of, 78; Indians, 109

Art in early days, at the Mechanics' Fair, 95–96; Virgil Williams and the Woodward Gallery, 176–77
Ashe, Dr., U.S. Navy Agent, and Judge Terry's clash with the Vigilantes, 45–46; host for a torchlight parade, 92
Ashe-Bolado marriage, a Spanish-American alliance, 84
Aspinwall, Panama, 28
Aspinwall, William, and William T. Sherman, 39
Atherton, Alejandra (Mrs. J. L. Rathbone), 208
Atherton home at Menlo Park, 206, 208
Atherton, Gertrude, and a daughter of the De La Guerras, 112; becomes a novelist, 254
Atlantic, the, brings Jenny Lind to America, 2
Atlantic cable laid; San Francisco celebrates, 118–19
Auction Lunch, the, restaurant owned by Flood and O'Brien, 182
Australia, Lola Montez sails for, 54; Menken's horse shipped to, 56

Baker, Colonel E. D., at Broderick's funeral, 125; in the Civil War, 145
Bakhmetieff, Madame (Nellie Beale), 173
Baldwin, Lucky, drives a four-in-hand, 175; his Nob Hill stable, 208; and the Baldwin Theater, 226
Baldwin Theater, first nights, 226–30; *Trilby* season, 254
Barbary Coast, 80, 210
Barnes, General W. H. L., plays Barrett's rôle in *Rosedale*, 217–18
Barnum, P. T., and Jenny Lind, 23, 237; and General Tom Thumb, 248
Barrett, Laurence, and Bret Harte, 167–68, 213; at the California Theater, 212–13, 216, 217, 218; and the popular pallbearer, 214
Barron, William, and his brother, Pepe, 83; the cost of lawns at Menlo Park, 207–08
Barrymore, Georgie Drew, her death in Santa Barbara, 228

Barrymore, Maurice, with Modjeska 227
Beale, General Edward S., at El Tejon, 172; with General Kearny and Kit Carson on the march to California, 172; Minister to Austria, 172; his daughter marries a diplomat, 172–73; Mrs. Beale imports a barouche, 173
Beardsley, Aubrey, and the *Yellow Book*, 253
Beckwourth, James, explorer, 22
Bell, Judge Thomas, and Mammy Pleasants, 126
Belletti, Signor, and Jenny Lind, 23
Bellew, Kyrle, with Mrs. James Brown Potter, 229
Belmont, home of Ralston, 199; famous guests, 200–01; an unwelcome critic, 201; in its decline, 202, 206; acquired by Sharon, 205; Grant's visit, 205–06; Flora Sharon's wedding, 207
Benicia Barracks, 71
Beresford, Lord Charles, and Lady Denman, 169; helps select a bonnet, 170
Bernhardt, Sarah, in her youth, 58; her grace and splendor, 235; a Nob Hill breakfast, 236
Berreda, Señor, Spanish Minister to Chile, 28
Berreda, Señora, and daughters, Mrs. Harry Sherman and Mrs. Willis Polk, 28
Berton, Swiss Consul, 120
Bielawski, Captain Maurice, 227
Bierce, Ambrose, 257
Bierstadt, Albert, 121
Big Four, the, of Con-Virginia, 182, 184; of the Union Pacific Railroad, 180
Birch, Billy, of the minstrels, 145–46
Bispham, David, 247
Black Bart, bandit, 105–06
Black Point, 162
Blaine, James G., 173
Blair, David B., 114; Mrs. Blair (Lady Yarde-Buller)
Blanding, Mrs. William, 123
Blue-stockings, 13
Bluxome, Isaac, secretary of the Vigilance Committee, 73
Boalt, Judge, 184
Bohemian Club, celebrities of Red Room dinners, 57, 58, 59; founded, 79; Midsummer Jinks, 79; two famous epicures, 134, 216; the *Marseillaise*, 235; Uncle George Bromley, 258–59
Bolado-Ashe marriage, 84
Bonaparte, Joseph, and the Maillard family, 248
Bonanza kings, 178; palaces of, 179, 180, 181; plutocrats of the Auction Lunch, 182, 183, 184; leaders among, 185–86, 188, 189, 190
Booker, Sir George Lane, British Consul, 160
Booth, Edwin, 211; his San Francisco home, 227, 228
Booth, John Wilkes, 219
Boston Museum Stock Company, California Company compared to, 217
Botts, William, son of Governor Botts of Virginia, 76; his ballroom speed, 80–81; introducing the lancers, 117
Bounty Men of the Civil War, 145–46
Boussière, Baron de, and Baroness, née Holladay, 216
Bowie, Dr. A. J., and Mrs., and six hours for dinner, 134
Bozenta, Count, 227
Brannagan, Mike, a San Francisco character, 38, 49, 51
Breckinridge, John C., elected Vice-President, 91, 92, 93
Bridges, Sir Robert assumes a title, 170–71
Briggs, Bill, gambler, 41
British Columbia, 67
Broadway, New York, in the 1850's, 25; Oakland, 113
Broderick, Senator David, the duel with Terry, 124; death of, 125, 128
Broderick-Terry duel, 85, 124–25, 130, 207
Bromley, Uncle George, of the Bohemian Club, 258–59
Bromley, Isaac, 258
Brontë, Charlotte, in London, 12
Brown, Dr. Charlotte Blake, 249–50
Browning, Robert, and the little girl next door, 187–88
Browning, Robert W., 187
Brownings, the, visit London, 12
Buchanan, James, elected President, 91–93; a toast to, 119
Buckley, Chris, blind political boss, 258
Bull, Ole, 22
Burgess, Gelett, and *The Purple Cow*, 253–54

INDEX

Burial at sea, 32[1]
Burlingame, center of country life, 207
Burton, Sir Richard, and a story of deflation, 160

Calhoun, son of John C., 81
Calif, Major, 152
California, covered wagons, 1, 108; government land surveys, 12, 70–71; currency of early days, 51, 102; gold strikes, 97; the gold country and mining camps, 97–98, 101–02; Indians, 108–09, 110; discovery of gold, 110; talk of Secession, 142; contribution to Sanitary Fund, 145
California, Bank of, founded by Mills and Ralston, 198; gold from the Mint in a crisis, 202–03; Ralston forced out of directorate, 204
California Society of Engineers, honors Colonel Ransome, 70
California Theater, 211; opening, 212; under Barrett and McCullough, 216–20
California, University of, Colonel Ransome's account of Diablo expedition preserved in Bancroft Library, 70; Bret Harte lectures, 167
Californians, characteristics, 2, 56, 114, 210; as trans-continental commuters, 91
Calistoga Hot Springs, 87–88
Calvary Church, Secessionist sermons, 143; Dr. Scott deported, 144; William C. Ralston's marriage, 198–99
Calvé, Emma, 247
Cameron, Sir Roderick, and Lady, of New York, 22
Campbell, Mrs. Pat, is *fin de siècle*, 253
Campbell, Lord Walter, son of the Duke of Argyle; attends church service on a battleship, 165–66
Campbell, Uncle Dick, of Siskiyou, 105
Cardigan, Earl of, leads the Light Brigade, 20; General Hooker's resemblance to, 117
Carl Rosa Opera Company, 153
Carlisle, Earl of (Lord Morpeth), 17
Carlyle, Thomas, in Cheyne Row, 12
Carnegie, Mrs. (Mrs. J. D. Stevenson, of Nob Hill), 123–24
Carolan, Mr., and a neighbor, 96
Carroll, Tucker, of Virginia, 23
Carson City, Nevada, 100
Carson, Kit, 172
Caruso, Enrico, and the last night of the old city, 233; in an earlier season, 247
Casey, Miss Bessie (Mrs. Bob Scott), prettiest girl in the army, 152
Casey, James, hanged by Vigilantes, 34, 36, 43, 52
Castle Crags, 106
Cayvan, Georgia, 226; her glass dress, 229–30
Cazadero, Bohemian Club jinks at, 79
Century Club, 248–49
Chang, Mr., of Korea, 260–61
Chaperons in London, 5
Chapman Plot of Civil War, 149
Chase, Judge Salmon P., gives advice on a crate of chickens, 26–27
Chase, William, his portrait of Whistler, 211
Chile, 28; Henry Meiggs in, 81; 87; 250
Chileño Quarter of San Francisco, 34, 43
China, granite from, 49
Chinatown, 47, 193–94; tong wars and hatchet men, 196–97; 210
Chinese fishing village, 224
Chinese labor, 49, 110; peddlers, 193; servants, 194, 195, 196; a cook who was a hatchet man, 196; 'The Chinese Must Go' riots, 197–98
Chinese Theater, Pierre Loti's visit, 47
Chismore, Dr. George, friend of R. L. S., 245
Cipriani, Count, of Belmont, 199
Civil War, 69, 117
Civil War days, news of Sumter and a mass meeting, 142–43; Dr. Scott deported, 143–44; a rebel flag waves, 144–45; departures for the front, 145; the Sanitary Fund, 145; bounty men, 145–56; the *Sutlej* salute, 146–47; General Albert Sidney Johnston, 147–48; fund for Southern prisoners, 148–49; Chapman Plot, 149; Mrs. Tod Robinson and *The Flag*, 149–50
Clarendon, Earl of, and Fanny Kemble, 19
Clark, Senator William, and Ward McAllister, 77
Clarke, General, at the Presidio, 122
Clay, Cecil, husband of Rosina Vokes, 228
Clemens, Samuel L. (Mark Twain), his début as a lecturer, 162–63
Clerical teas, 236
Cliff House, 173; described, 174; 239
Cliff House Road, 128, 175

INDEX

Clifton, Lord Talbot, and White Hat McCarthy, 257
Coast Range Mountains, 70
Coit, Mrs. Howard (Lily Hitchcock), member of Fire Department, 65; witnesses a tragedy, 73
Cole, Dr. R. Beverley, physician of Vigilance Committee, 73
Coleman, Mrs. Evan J. (Lucy Gwin), 80
Coleman, Robert, killed in the Balkans, 74
Coleman, William T., head of Vigilance Committee, and the execution of Casey and Cora, 35–36, 43; 73; his personal appearance, 74; his home, 186; ends the Sand Lot Riots with a Pickaxe Brigade, 197–98; San Francisco's debt to, 198
Colfax, Schuyler, Vice-President, 200
Collins Line of steamships, 2, 27
Colonna, Princess, Mrs. Mackay's daughter, 189
Colton, David, his Italian palace on Nob Hill, 178
Comstock Lode of Nevada and Sutro Tunnel, 174–75
Condit-Smith, Mrs., née Sweringen, 138
Contra Costa Hills, 63, 66
Coombs, Professor, phrenologist, 154–55
Coppinger, Colonel, U.S.A., served with Papal Zouaves, 152
Coquelin, B. Constant, at the Bohemian Club, 58; plays Molière in Mission Street, 233
Cora, Charles, hung by Vigilantes, 35; married before execution, 36, 43, 56
Cora, Belle, widow of Charles Cora, 36
Corbett, James J., 'Pompadour Jim,' 256
Covered wagons, 1, 108
Crabtree, Lotta, 69
Craig, Miss, daughter of Ellen Terry, 243
Crane, William H., 217
Cranston, Hiram, of the New York Hotel, 21
Crittenden, A. P., killed by Laura D. Fair, 84–85
Crittenden, Mary (Mrs. Tod Robinson), 148, 149, 150
Crocker, Charles, of the Union Pacific 'Big Four,' 180
Crocker Conservatory, Golden Gate Park, 240

Crocker, Mrs. William H., entertains Bernhardt, 236; home burns and *The Sower* is saved, 96
Crystal Palace, London, 5; royal visitors at Great Exhibition, 8
Cunningham, Captain, U.S.N., and the *Toucey* launching, 119
Currency of early days, lack of small change, 51; gold dust, 102
Curtis, Johnny, stage-driver, 107
Cutting, Captain James, U.S.A., 151
Cutts, Miss Addie (Mrs. Stephen A. Douglas), 84
Cuyler, Captain Richard, U.S.N., 119

Daingerfield, Judge, and daughter (Mrs. James R. Keene), 102
Dainty, Laura E., with Moody and Sankey, 238
Daly Company, first nights at the Baldwin, 226
Damrosch, Walter with Metropolitan Company, 247
Dana, Richard Henry, at Yerba Buena, 43; a later visit, 66; *Two Years Before the Mast* quoted, 66–67
Darling, Major, receives royalty at Alcatraz, 224
Davenport, Fanny, marries leading man, 228
De la Guerra, Don Pablo, 112
De la Guerra descendants, 112
De Lakst, Dr., Belgian banker in Mrs. Paran Stevens's party, 166
Delessert, Eugène, member of the Vigilance Committee, 33, 34, 40, 42; his uncle, Benjamin Delessert, French philanthropist, 33; his brother, Edouard Delessert, French explorer, 33
De Long, George, killed by bandits in the Balkans, 74
De Lussan, Zelie, as Carmen, at the Tivoli, 256
Del Monte, 257
Denman, Admiral Sir Joseph, 168–69; Hon. Mrs. Denman, and Lord Charles Beresford, 169
Dennison, Col. William Neal, U.S.A., 151
Derby, Earl of, his shabby castle, 9
Diablo, Mount, surveying expedition, 70–71
Dickens, Charles, in Devonshire Terrace, 12; quoted, 50; his reading of *The Murder of Nancy Sikes*, 239

INDEX

Dickens, Charles, Jr., reads *Nancy Sikes* in San Francisco, 239; discreetly approves America, 239–40
Dickson, Charles, actor, in *Incog*, 225
D'Israeli, 12
Dolores, Mission, 44; cemetery, 52; wedding of Lola Montez and Pat Hull, 52; 175
Donahoe, Joseph, starts on world tour, 120
Donahue, Peter, his boiler factory, 72; Mrs. Donahue's glass coach, 173
Donner Lake, 100
Donner party, the lost, 100–01
Doremus, Mrs., of New York, and Adelaide Phillips, 140
Douglas, Stephen A., marries Miss Cutts, 84
Douro, Marchioness of, daughter-in-law of Duke of Wellington, 17; arranges presentation to Queen Victoria, 17; 18
Doxey's bookshop, 253
Drake, Sir Francis, 163
Drew, John, of Daly's Company, 226
Drew, Mrs. John, as Mrs. Malaprop, 217
Driving days, 175–76
Drury Lane Theater, Herbert Spencer and George Eliot attend, 12
Dublin, the season, 13, 14, 15; Theater Royal, 19; review of troops and a tragedy, 20; marriage in, 21
Dueling, the Broderick-Terry duel, 124–25; ends with Johnson-Ferguson duel, 130
Dumas, Alexander, and Lola Montez, 54; his circle and Menken, 55
Du Maurier, George, and *Trilby*, 254
Duncan, Isadora, her childhood in San Francisco, 139
Duncan, Joseph, father of Isadora Duncan, 139
Duncombe, Sir Philip, leads family prayers, 10

Eames, Emma, 186
Earthquakes, of 1865, 158–59; of 1868, 159; of 1906, 77, 78, 233; see also Fire of 1906
Easton, Rev. Giles, and the earthquake, 158–59
Edwards, Harry, founder of Bohemian Club, 216
El Dorado, gambling hall, 41
Eliot, George, sees *Merry Wives of Windsor*, 12
Elliott, Maud Howe, 248
El Tejon, the Beale ranch, 172, 173
Emerson, Billy, of the minstrels, 211
Empire Theater Company, 226
England, sailing for, 2, 3, 4; country house visits, 9, 10, 11; first cable message to, 118; see also London
Epicures and gourmets, 134, 135
Eucalyptus trees imported by Sutro, 44; 175
Ewer, Rev., and Mrs., 236–37
Eyre family of Menlo Park, 206

Fabbri, Madame, sings for General Grant, 205
Fair, James G., bonanza king, 167, 182; courage in a crisis, 184–85
Fair, Laura D., kills A. P. Crittenden, 84–85
Fair, Tessie (Mrs. Hermann Oelrichs), 167, 182
Fair, Virginia, marries W. K. Vanderbilt, 167
Fairfax, Lord Charles, of Virginia, 81–82
Fairmont Hotel, 182
Farallones, the (islands), 174
Farquhar, Admiral Sir Arthur, and a Fenian picnic, 163–64
Farragut, Admiral David H., establishes Mare Island Navy Yard, 86; early adventures, 87; at White Sulphur Springs, 87–88; 90; leaves Mare Island, 119; visits Belmont, 200
Fashions of the 1850's, 3, 6, 25–26; the well-dressed man, 47, 189–90; hirsute adornments, 151; weepers, 152
Faull, Mrs. John, and Adelaide Neilson, 221
Faversham, William, as Romeo, 221
Felton, Mrs. John, gives a dance, 173
Feminine Renaissance, 249–50
Ferry Tower, 192, 263
Field, Judge Stephen J., in Hill vs. Sharon case, 125–26; attacked by Terry, 127; his wedding shoes, 137
Fin de Siècle, 253–55, 262
Fire of 1906, Ward McAllister's adventure, 77–78; a Millet painting saved, 96; Nob Hill palaces burn, 180; City Hall destroyed, 192; Holladay home survives, 215
First Congregational Church, 63; 239
First Unitarian Church and Thomas Starr King, 63

INDEX

Fisk, Colonel Jim, and Josie Mansfield, 127–28
Fitzgerald, Lord Otho, reverses in the waltz, 15
Fitzherbert, Mrs., and George IV; a California descendant, 225–26
Flag, The, accuses Mrs. Robinson, 149
Flood, James, his Nob Hill palace, 79; the brass fence, 178; the Auction Lunch, 182–83; Mrs. Flood entertains General Grant, 206
Florence, William, in *The Rivals,* 217
Foard, Julia (Mrs. Joe Tilden), 132
Foard, Mrs., and her hoopskirts, 132
Formes, Karl, 153
Fort Gunnybags; *see* Vigilance Committee headquarters
Fort Mason, in the Fire of 1906, 77; Broderick's death, 124; a garden party, 162
Fort Point, 44, 120
Fort Ross, Russian settlement, 43
Francis, Sam, marries Harriet McAllister, 76
Franklin, Lady, widow of Sir John, 67–68
Frémont, General, for President, 91, 93–94; his ranch at Mariposa, 117–18
Friedlander, Mr. and Mrs. Isaac, of South Park, 134–35, 149
Frohman, Daniel, his Lyceum Stock Company, 226
Fry, Colonel, and Miss Lizzie (Mrs. William C. Ralston), 198

Garden, Mary, and Sibyl Sanderson, 103
Gautier, Madame, wife of the French Consul, 119
Geary, Colonel John W., postmaster, 59
Genteel tradition, the, 104
George IV of England and American descendants, 25–26
George Law, the, bound for Panama, 27–28
Gerster, Etelka, sings with Patti, 231, 233
Gibb, Don Daniel, 84
Gibson, Lieutenant H. G., of the Presidio and Washington, 122
Gilbert and Sullivan, 136; *Pinafore* and *The Mikado,* 255; a Gilbertian episode, 146
Gilman, Mabel (Mrs. Corey), and *Trilby,* 254

Glyn, Miss, as Cleopatra, 12
Goddefroy, Alfred, at the McAllister party, 76, 81
Gold, new lodes, 97; Marshall's discovery, 110
Golden Era, The, and Bret Harte, 163
Golden Gate, sailing through, 37; from Russian Hill, 44; the *Storm King* sails out, 120; from Lone Mountain, 128; Drake sails by, 163; Kalakaua outward bound, 224; 263
Golden Gate, the, voyage from Panama, 28, 30, 31; burial at sea, 32
Golden Gate Park, a waste of sand, 173; the Victoria Regia, 239–40; Japanese Tea Garden, 241; horseless carriages, 255
Goldschmidt, Otto, marries Jenny Lind, 23
Gonzales Ranch, 71
Gordon, George, of South Park, 131–32
Gordon, Mrs. George, sells Mayfield to Senator Stanford, 132
Gordon, Marie, of the California Theater Stock Company, 212–13
Gordon, Miss Nellie, of South Park, 131–32
Gottschalk, Louis, pianist, plays at the Ransome home, 139; a San Francisco romance, 140
Gough, Lord, hero of the Sikh Rebellion, at Lord Hawarden's, 16; Lady Gough and their unique castle, 16
Gould, Jay, 128
Grace Church, 62, 63; in *Two Years Before the Mast,* 66; Judge Field marries Miss Sweringen, 137
Grand Hotel, party for Mrs. Paran Stevens, 66
Grand Opera House; Sibyl Sanderson's home-coming, 103; rivals the Paris Opera House, 204; the 'largest chandelier,' 233, 240, 247; the Irving-Terry season, 243–44; brilliant seasons, 246, 247, 248; Mrs. Howe and the *Battle Hymn,* 247–48
Granger, Maud, as Camille, 222
Grant, General U. S., 72, 117; at the Palace Hotel, 205; with Mrs. Grant at Belmont, 205–06; guest of Mrs. Flood, 206
Grass Valley, gold strikes near, 97, 101
Great Exhibition at Crystal Palace, 5; royal visitors, 8
Greathouse, Clarence, Prime Minister of Korea, 260–61

INDEX 273

Greathouse, Mrs. M. E., returns from Korea, 260–61; tells of Queen's death, 262
Greenough, Mrs., of Washington, 74; testifies in Limanteur Case, 74–75
Greenway dances, 251
Grosvenor, Lord Richard, meets Brigham Young, 161
Guinness, Arthur, of Dublin, dining at his home, 13
Guinness, Arthur Lee, house-parties at Stillorgan Park, 14, 15, 16
Guinness, Benjamin, Lord Mayor of Dublin, 14; his sons, Lord Ardilaun and Lord Iveagh, 14–15
Gwin, Miss Lucy (Mrs. Evan J. Coleman), her début at the Apollo ball, 80; at White Sulphur Springs, 87
Gwin, William M., 80, 87; opposes Broderick for election to Senate, 124; his South Park home, 132
Gwin, Mrs. William M., 87; as a South Park hostess, 132, 136

Hading, Jane, with Coquelin, 58; the Hading wave, 234
Hager, Judge John S., and Mrs. John Wood, 68; at the McAllister New Year party, 76
Haggin, James B., his four-in-hand on the Point Lobos Road, 175–76; most interesting of the plutocrats, 185; his family, 185–86; Mrs. Haggin a sister of Mrs. Tevis, 186
Haight, Miss Sarah, and the Mount Vernon ball, 123
Halevy, Ludovic, Mrs. John W. Mackay and his *L'Abbé Constantin*, 189
Hall, Lucy, waves a rebel flag, 144–45
Halladie, A. S., invests the cable car, 52
Halleck, General Henry, takes command of Department of the Pacific, 151; Mrs. Halleck and the annual balls, at their Folsam Street home, 152
Hallock, John Y., sails on a world tour, 120
Hamlin, Sarah D., founds the Century Club, 248
Hammond, John Hays, his birth and christening, 113
Hammond, Lafayette, of South Park, 122
Hammond, Colonel and Mrs. R. P., parents of John Hays Hammond, 113

Hart, Mr. and Mrs., parents of Mrs. J. D. Stevenson, arrive from Australia, 123
Harte, Bret, and Thomas Starr King, 62, 168; his mother, 113–14; and Mark Twain, 163; with Mrs. Harte in San Rafael, 167–68; and Lawrence Barrett, 167–68, 213
Harvard, an alumnus sells his wardrobe, 48
Hatteras, Cape, wreck of the *Central America*, 33
Hatzfeldt, Prince, marries Miss Huntington, 185
Haven, Captain Franklin, aide to General McDowell, 151
Haven, Joseph, at White Sulphur Springs, 87; comedy on board the *Active*, 89–90
Hawaii, the royal family on canvas at Mechanics' Fair, 95; colonists from, 110; Mark Twain's visit, 162, and his lecture on, 163; Honolulu, 120, 133; *see also* Kalakaua, and Kapiolani
Hawarden, Lord, a house-party for the Duke of Wellington, 16–17
Haweis, Rev. Hugh, of London, on a musical preaching tour of the world, 238
Hayne, Dr., and Julia Dean Hayne on the *George Law* bound for California, 28; a crisis on shipboard, 31
Hayne, Julia Dean, her New York success, 68; repeated in San Francisco, 69; her daughter marries a Langhorne of Virginia, 69
Hays, Colonel Jack, Texas Ranger and Sheriff of San Francisco, 112–13; and a block on Oakland's Broadway, 113
Hearst, Senator George, 186
Hearst, Mrs. George, her generous charities, 186
Heenan, Johnny, marries Adah Isaacs Menken, 55
Hesketh, Sir Thomas, his wedding to Miss Sharon, 206
Highwaymen, Wells-Fargo treasure raids, 99; a generous bandit, 100; Black Bart, 105–06
Hill, Sarah Althea, in Hill *vs.* Sharon case, 125–26; marries Judge Terry, 126; spectacular tragedy, 127
Hill, Thomas, painter of Yosemite, and Princess Louise, 96; a sale to Ralston, 202

INDEX

Hitchcock, Lily (Mrs. Coit), honorary member of the Fire Department, 65; witnesses a tragedy, 73
Hitching posts, 56
Hoffman, Josiah Ogden, of New York, 24; his daughter, Matilda, and Washington Irving, 24
Hoffman, Judge Ogden, of San Francisco, 24; a popular pallbearer, 213–14
Hoffman, Southard, 24; his daughter, May, 24
Holladay, Ben, a dinner for Barrett and McCullough, 213–14; and the Overland Stage, 215; an original character, 215–16
Holladay, Mrs. Ben, 213–14; her social graces, 216; daughters marry titles, 216; home from Europe for a visit to Ben Holladay, 216
Holladay mansion on Holladay's Hill, 215; the view of six counties, 215
Holt, Mrs. Thomas (Addie Smith), friend of Mrs. Stephen A. Douglas, 84
Hollywood, Theodore Roberts, of, 57; a ranch on its site, 70
Honolulu, *see* Hawaii
Hooker, Colonel Joe, gives fiestas on his ranch, 117; in the Civil War, 117, 145
Hooper, Augusta, wedding to Pelham Ames, 132; and the loss of an heirloom, 133–34
Hooper family, of South Park, 132–33
Hooper, Major, of the Occidental Hotel, 225
Hopkins, D. A., Sheriff of the Vigilantes, stabbed by Terry, 45–46
Hopkins, Mark, of the Union Pacific 'Big Four,' 180; his castle on Nob Hill, 178–79; presented to the Art Association, 181; Mardi Gras balls, 181
Horn, Cape, route to San Francisco, 1, 104, 124; houses brought in sections, 102, 186–87
Horseless carriages, 255
Howard, W. D. M., his home becomes the post-office, 59; at El Cerrito, 207
Howe, Julia Ward, hears the *Battle Hymn* sung in her honor, 247; and the Century Club, 248
Hull, Pat, husband of Lola Montez, 53, 54
Huntington, C. P., of the Union Pacific 'Big Four,' 180; his striking appearance, 185
Huntington, Clara, marries Prince Hatzfeldt, 185
Huntington, Captain Henry, U.S.A., 151–52; Mrs. Huntington, 'the tearose,' 152
Hyde Park, Queen Victoria drives with Prince Albert, 8–9

Indians; Modoc tribe, 108; Washoes of Nevada, 109; Spanish of Southern California, 109; a Washoe tragedy, 109
Inge, Mrs., her colored cook, 89–90
International Hotel, the *table d'hôte*, 38–39; 'Wild West' under the windows, 44–45; 70
Irakura, Baron, of the Japanese Embassy, at Belmont, 200
Ireland, a season in Dublin, 13; country house visits, 14–18; presented at the Irish Court, 18, 19; marriage to Captain Neville, 21; a County Wicklow honeymoon, 21; *see also* Dublin
Iron Church (Trinity), 40
Irving, Henry, stirs San Francisco's enthusiasm, 242–43; brilliant opening in *The Bells*, 243–44; at the Bohemian Club, 244
Irving, Washington, a glimpse of, 23
Izards and Pinckneys of South Carolina, 123

James, Louis, actor, 217
January, Lucy (Lady Leith), and romance on the *Zealous*, 165
Japanese Tea Garden in Golden Gate Park, 240–41
Jefferson, Joseph, as Rip Van Winkle, 211; in *The Rivals*, 217
Jenny Lind Theater becomes Hall of Justice, 41
Jewett, H. S., portrait painter, 95
Job, Peter, confectioner, 137
Johnson, George Penn, fights a duel, 130
Johnson, Governor J. Neely, and the Vigilance Committee, 35
Johnson Mansion and the Johnson cats, 139
Johnson, Robert, of the Apollo balls, 81
Johnston, General Albert Sidney, sorrow for his death, 147; the honor of an officer, 147–48; 151

INDEX 275

Johnston, Mrs. Albert Sidney, 148
Joran, Elise and Pauline, play for Patti, 232
Justh, Emil, one of the Apollo bachelors, 81

Kaird, British shipbuilder and the *Alabama*, 166–67
Kalakaua, King of Hawaii, a ball in honor of, 222; late at a concert, 223; death in San Francisco, 224
Kapiolani, Queen of Hawaii, on Nob Hill, 224
Kean, Charles, recalls Fanny Kemble, 161–62; as Louis XI, 217
Kean, Mrs. Charles Kean, the Ellen Terry of her day, 161
Kean, Edmund, and Mrs. Siddons, 162
Kearney, Dennis, and the Sand Lot Riots, 197
Kearny, General Stephen, the march to California, 172
Keene, James R., Bear of Wall Street, 102
Keeney, Mrs. C. C., 122
Keith, William, painter, 96
Kemble, Fanny, reads *Hamlet* in Dublin, 19; 161
Kendal, Mr. and Mrs., English players, 234
Keyes, Major E. D., at the Presidio, 122
King, James, of William, editor of the *Bulletin*, shot by James Casey, 26, 34
King, Thomas Starr, 62; his speech for the Union, 143; Bret Harte's tribute, 168
Kingcome, Admiral, and the *Sutlej* bombardment, 146–47
Kingston, Jamaica, 27
Kip, Bishop William, and 'Kip's Melodeon,' 63; 66; presides at a farce, 89–90; 236
Kirkham, Major, 114
Kirkham, Leila (Lady Yarde-Buller), artificial light at her wedding, 114–15
Kitchener, Lord, 252
Knights of the Golden Circle, secret Secessionist society, 150
Korea, the Prime Minister of, from South Park, 260–61; King of, 260–62; assassination of the Queen of, 261–62

Lackaye, Wilton, as Svengali, 254
Lancers, the, at the Governor's ball, 116–17
Langtry, Lily, buys a ranch, 252
Lark, The, 253
Latham, Senator Milton S., the Latham tomb, 128; his Rincon Hill home, 130–31; gardens at Menlo Park, 208–09
Lathrop Station, the killing of Terry at, 127
Law and Order Association, opposed to Vigilantes, 35, 45
Lee, Lieutenant Custis, at the Presidio, 122
Lee, Robert E., 122
Leinster, Duke of, 15
Leith, Lieutenant (Lord Leith of Fyvie), a California romance, 165
Lick House, the first palatial hotel, 94, 189; James Lick's pride in, 190; 201
Lick, James, miner and philanthropist, 190
Lick Observatory, 190
Liliuokalani, Princess (Queen Lil of Hawaii), 224
Limanteur Land Case, Mrs. Greenough testifies, 74
Lime Point lighthouse, 121
Lincoln, Abraham, 72, 143; news of assassination, 150; 219
Lintivie, Comte de, French Consul in London, 10; the Comtesse and Tum-Tum, 10
Lion, Rev. William, of St. Stephens, 236
Liszt, Franz, friendship for Lola Montez, 54
Liverpool, 2, 66
Lockwood, Rufus, on the *Golden Gate*, 32; drowns at sea, 33
London, a gay season, 5; balls and chaperons, 5–6; Drawing-Room at St. James's Palace, 7; the Great Exhibition in Crystal Palace, 5, 8; Hyde Park, the Queen passes, 8–9; literary circles, 12; and Lola Montez, 52–53; Menken's visit, 55; from London to Italy, 184
Long Wharf, 48
Lorne, Marquis of, in California, 96
Lorraine, Lieutenant Sir Lambton, sings with Lady Denman, 169
Los Angeles, surveying expeditions, 70; Admiral Stockton raises U.S. flag, 172
Loti, Pierre, at the Chinese Theater, 47–48
Lotta, 69

Lotta's Fountain, 69-70
Louise, Princess, paints the Santa Barbara Mission, 96
Low, Governor F. F., 163
Low, Mrs. F. F., and Mark Twain, 163
Lunt, Professor O. A., and Lunt's Dancing School, 251-52
Lyceum Theater, London, 242; passes from Irving, 244
Lyon, Captain Harry, wins a house, 138-39; his daughter, Cora, 139

MacDowell, Melbourne, marries Fanny Davenport, 228
Mackall, Major and Mrs., on the *George Law*, 28
Mackay, John W., and the 'Big Four,' 182; his character, 184-89; brings his family to San Francisco, 188; a Beau Brummell, 189-90
Mackay, Mrs. John W., in San Francisco, and social success abroad, 189
Maguire's Opera House, Menken in *Mazeppa*, 54; Mrs. John Wood and japonica flowers, 68; the Wallacks in Shakespeare, an interrupted performance, 93; Mr. and Mrs. Charles Kean, 161; Mark Twain and Mrs. Low, 163
Mailliard, Mrs. Adolphe, sister of Julia Ward Howe, 248
Manchester, Duke of, sees Lime Point Lighthouse, 121; wears tweeds at a ball, 171
Mancinelli, conductor of Metropolitan Company, 247
Mandeville, Viscount, his deficient wardrobe, 171
Manhattan memories, 21-27
Mansfield, Josie, an early romance, 127; and Jim Fisk, 128
Mansfield, Richard, as Baron Chevrial, 226-27
Mapleson, Colonel, and Patti, 231
Mardi Gras balls, 181
Mare Island, and Ward McAllister, Jr., 78; change for White Sulphur Springs, 86; and Admiral Farragut, 86, 88, 90; a navy wedding, 89; Great Britain lands her envoys, 90, 91; the *Toucey* launched, 119
Mariposa, General Frémont's ranch, 93
Marlowe, Julia, as Juliet, 229
Marshall, James, discovers gold, 110
Marye, George T., 82-83

Marye, George T., Jr., Ambassador to Russia, 83
Marysville and Notre Dame Convent, 102, 104
Massenet and Sibyl Sanderson, 103
McAllister, Cutler, of the McAllister clan, 75, 76, 78; his favorite song, 152; and Lord Charles Beresford, 170
McAllister, Hall, 75, 76; a famous poker bet, 138-39
McAllister, Mrs. Hall, her social graces, 76; the fancy-dress ball in South Park, 138; reception for Parepa Rosa, 153; at Ocean Side, 173
McAllister, Harriet, marries Sam Francis, of New York, 76; approves the Prince of Wales, 76-77
McAllister, Judge, and Mrs. M. H., bring their family from Georgia, 75; their San Francisco home, 76
McAllister, Rev. Marion, of Church of the Advent, 75-76
McAllister, Ward, of San Francisco and the New York 400, 75
McAllister, Ward, Jr., the 'Crown Prince,' 75; and Senator Clark, 77; in the 1906 earthquake, 77-78
McCarthy, White Hat, and Lord Talbot Clifton, 256-57
McCloud River, 108
McClung, Major, killed at the Palace Hotel, 73
McCreery, Andrew, wedding at Grace Church, 137
McCreery, Mrs. Andrew (Bell Sweringen), of the Prince of Wales's set, 137-38
McCullough, John, and the California Theater, 212-13, 217, 218; at Ben Holladay's home, 213-14; in San Francisco's Bohemia, 216; and Edwin Adams's farewell, 220
McDowell, General Irvin, commands Department of the Pacific, 151; with Mrs. McDowell at Fort Mason, 162; a garden party for the Duc de Penthièvre, 162
McLean, Mrs. Louis, 123
McNulty, Dr. and Mrs., on the *George Law*, 28
McPherson, Lieutenant, popular at the Presidio, 76, 122; killed in the Civil War, 122
Mechanics' Fair; the first and later fairs, 94-95
Mechanics' Pavilion, 94-95; ball for

INDEX

King Kalakaua, 222; Albani sings, 247
Meiggs, Henry, moves to Chile, 81
Meiggs's Wharf, 33, 81
Melba at the Bohemian Club, 58
Menken, Adah Isaacs, and *Mazeppa*, 54–55; and Swinburne, 55
Menlo Park, the Selby home, 131; other estates, 205–09
Mercantile Library, 190; lottery, 218
Merced Lake, the Broderick-Terry duel, 124; picnics, 207
Merrion Square, Dublin, 13
Merritt, Dr., of Oakland, the *Casco*, 245
Merritt, Lake, 114
Metropolitan Grand Opera Company and Sibyl Sanderson, 103; Caruso as Don José, 233; biennial seasons, 247
Metropolitan Theater, New York, and Rachel, 24
Metropolitan Theater, San Francisco, and Mrs. John Wood, 68
Mexican land grants in California, the Limanteur case, 74; and Edwin M. Stanton, 111
Mexico and the Chapman Plot, 149
Midwinter Fair, 241
Mikado, The, 255
Milbrae, home of D. O. Mills, 175
Miller, Joaquin, Poet of the Sierras, 102, 256
Miller, Senator John F., and Hawaiian royalty, 122
Millet, J. F., *The Sower*, 96
Mills, D. O., establishes a bank in Sacramento, 98; drives on the Cliff House Road, 175; founds Bank of California with Ralston, 198; contrasting temperaments, 175
Mills, Edgar, cousin of D. O. Mills, in Sacramento, 98; sails on a world tour, 120; Menlo Park home, 206
Milton, Lord, borrows a dress suit, 171
Minstrels, the, 145–46
Mint, U.S., 101; a building of classic beauty, 192; Ralston's raid, 203–04
Mission District, 176–77; 191
Mission Dolores, 44; the wedding of Lola Montez, 52; 173
Mission Road, 60, 61
Modjeska, Helena, 58; her American début, 227
Modoc Indians, 108
Molière in Mission Street, 58, 233
Monson, Judge A. C., and the letter 'R,' 83

Montague, Henry, and Montague curls, 222
Monterey, Sherman's rose tree, 40; 110
Montez, Lola, a bride in San Francisco, 52–53; her book on beauty, 54
Moody and Sankey revivals, 237–38
Moody, Dwight L., 237–38
Moreland, Bishop William, in dialect recitations, 236
Morpeth, Lord (Earl of Carlisle) familiar with America, 17
Morris, Clara, a lachrymose Camille, 211
Mowery, Sylvester, 'Prince of Arizona,' 78
Muldoon, William, and Shakespeare, 227

Napa City, 86
Napa Valley, 85
Naylor, Peter, and the lancers, 117
Neilson, Adelaide, 211; as Juliet, 221; at a reception, 221–22
Nethersole, Olga, as Sapho, 253
Nevada, first land surveys, 70; 95, 100; Indians of, 109; new silver lodes, 150; Sutro Tunnel, 174; Con-Virginia, 182
Nevada City, mining town, 101
Nevada, Emma, at Grand Opera House, 246–47
Neville, Amelia Ransome, and San Francisco of the 1850's, 1, 2; voyage to England, 2–4; a London season and country house parties, 5–12; presented to Victoria, 6–8; in Ireland, visits to the Guinness home and Lord Hawarden's castle, 13–21; the Duke of Wellington, 16–17; presented at Irish Court, 19; Lord Cardigan of the Light Brigade, 20; marriage to Captain Neville, 21; returns to America, 21; in New York, 21–27; the voyage to California, 27–33; first impressions of San Francisco 34–44; the Wild West, and Judge Terry, 44–46; afternoon calls, 49–50; the Paris bonnet in *Two Years Before the Mast*, 67; at the McAllister home, 76; balls and parties, 80–81, 116, 119, 123; Admiral Farragut, 86, 88, 200; judging needlework at Mechanics' Fair, 94; stage-coach trips, 99, 101–07; dining with E. M. Stanton, 111–12; introducing the lancers, 116; the Presidio ball of 1859, 121–22; six

hours for dinner, 134–35; Judge Field's wedding shoes, 137; and Kate Robinson at the McAllister ball, 138; dancing the first cotillion, 152; the earthquake of 1865, 158–59; and Bret Harte, 167–68; and Lawrence Barrett, 167–68; buying a bonnet with Lord Charles Beresford, 170; and Mrs. Mackay, 189; at Belmont, 200; the Holladay dinner for Barrett and McCullough, 213–14; and John McCullough, 219; and Adelaide Neilson, 221–22; and Charles Dickens, Jr., 239–40; leaving San Francisco, 263–64

Neville, Captain Thomas J., marriage to Amelia Ransome, 21; 27; in California, 101

New Helvetia, Sutter's lost empire, 109–11

New Orleans, 31, 53, 126, 138; Dr. Scott banished to, 144

New Year calls, 135–36

New York, sailing from, 2; mansions compared to old castles, 9; in the 1850's, 21–27; sailing for Panama, 27; Lola Montez in, 53

New York Hotel, 21–24; the first Peacock Alley, 23

Niantic, the, clipper ship becomes a hotel, 48

Nichols, Bishop William Ford, 236

Nicolini and Patti, 231

Nob Hill, 63, 79, 95, 124; palaces of, 178–83, 190; and Queen Kapiolani, 224; and Bernhardt, 236; 263

Nordica, Lillian, and Wagner seasons, 247

Norris, Charles G., 248

Norris, Frank, 248, 251

Norris, Kathleen Thompson, 58, 102

North Beach, bus line to, 51; a lace shop, 191; death of Ralston, 204

Northumberland, Duke of, and Alnwick Castle, 11

Norton, 'Emperor,' 155–56

Notre Dame Convent, 102, 104

Nutt, Commodore, and General Tom Thumb, 241

Nye, Captain, of the *Pacific*, and Mrs. Flutterby, 4; 24

Oakes, Tony, of San Bruno Turnpike, 173

Oakland in 1851, 71; and Colonel Jack Hays, 113; in the sixties, 114; Isadora Duncan, 139; Mrs. Robert Louis Stevenson, 244

O'Brien, William S., of Flood and O'Brien, 182

Occidental Hotel and Sir Robert Bridges, 170; and Mrs. John W. Mackay, 189; and Mr. Chang, 261

Oelrichs, Mrs. Hermann (Tessie Fair), buys the Paran Stevens's château, 167; her wedding, 182

O'Gready, Mrs., of the Guinness family, 14, 16

Ord, General, of the House of Hanover, 225–26

Oregon, boundary line, 95, 102; stage-line to, 104; covered wagons bound for, 108; and Ben Holladay, 216

Oriental Hotel, a new home, 70; center of social life, 72; Vigilantes at *table d'hôte*, 73; Mrs. Greenough's age, 74, 75; waiting for news of 'Buck and Breck,' 93, 95, 120, 132; a rebel flag, 144

Ormsby, Jenny, mother of Sibyl Sanderson, 103

Oroville, 101

Orr, John, his epitaph, 129

Osbourne, Mrs., marries Robert Louis Stevenson, 244

Otis, James, for mayor, 116; and the Civil War mass meeting, 142

Overland Monthly and Bret Harte, 167

Overland Stage, starting east, 98; and Ben Holladay, 215

Pacheco, Governor Romualdo, 224–25

Pacheco, Mrs. Romualdo, writes a comedy for Charles Dickson, 225

Pacific, the, voyage to England, 2–4; lost at sea, 4; brings Rachel to New York, 24

Pacific Club in Steve Whipple's place, 78; the Parrott Block explosion, 78–79; and Baron Fairfax, 81–82; *see also* Pacific-Union Club

Pacific Mail Steamship Line and Hugh Whittell, 129; 132; and the Chapman Plot, 149; 203

Pacific-Union Club and Ward McAllister, Jr., 77; in the Flood mansion, 79

Paget, Lady (Miss Minnie Stevens), 166

Paget, Lord Berkeley, hunts big game at El Tejon, 171–72

Palace Hotel, on site of St. Patrick's Orphan Asylum, 72; shooting of Major McClung, 73; Mrs. Paran

Stevens and Cyrus, of the Fifth Avenue Hotel, 166; built by Ralston, 203; described, 203–04; acquired by Senator Sharon, 205; the welcome to Grant, 205; vegetables from Burlingame, 207; Mrs. Holladay's visit, 216; Henry Montague's death, 222; death of Kalakaua, 224; Booth's rooms filled with flowers, 228; Henry Irving crosses the court, 243; Doxey's bookshop, 253; White Hat McCarthy, 257

Palo Alto, 132

Palou, Francisco, Spanish padre, 43

Panama, sailing for, 27; crossing the Isthmus, 28–29; kidnaping by natives, 29–30; steamers from, 37; mail by way of, 59

Paris, and Lola Montez, 52; Menken's death, 55; Sibyl Sanderson and Massenet, 103; Mrs. Mackay's social success, 189; Emma Nevada's Mignon acclaimed, 246–47

Parrott Block, a landmark, 49; houses Pacific Club and Wells Fargo offices, 78

Parrott, John, builds the Parrott Block, of Chinese granite, 49; 131

Patti, creates a furor, 231; at reception, 232; unconscious repartée, 233

Pawlicki, Dr., of Madame Modjeska's circle, 227

Peixotto, Ernest, and *The Lark*, 253

Pelham, Dr. James, 29; Mrs. Pelham, 29–30; Sally Pelham kidnaped on Panama, 29–30

Penthièvre, Duc de, at Fort Mason, 162

Père la Chaise Cemetery, Menken's grave, 55

Perley, D. W., and Josie Mansfield, 127–28

Phelan, James D., mayor, and president of the Bohemian Club, 258; the Phelan mansion, 191

Phillips, Adelaide, sings at the Ransome home, 140

Pickaxe Brigade and the Sand Lot Riots, 198

Pico, Don Pio, last Spanish governor, 112

Pierce, Mr., Minister to Hawaii, 222

Pinafore, 255

Pinckneys and Izards of South Carolina, 123

Pioche, Felix, and Gottschalk, 139; and Parepa Rosa, 154

Pitt River, 104

Pixley, Frank, editor of the *Argonaut*, 138

Pixley, Mrs. Frank, at the McAllister ball, 138

Placerville Road, highway over the Sierra Nevada Mountains, 100; a feat of engineering, 100–01; an engineer marries, 145

Plaisted, Gracie, of the Tivoli, 256

Platt, Horace, and Ysaye at the Bohemian Club, 58

Plaza, the (Portsmouth Square), 40; U.S. flag raised, 42; 57; starting for the Presidio ball, 121; Broderick's funeral, 124–25, 128; the Stevenson Monument, 246

Plumper, the, a 'middie' and Lady Franklin, 67–68

Point Lobos Road, the fashionable drive, 173

Polk, Willis, marries a daughter of Señor Berreda, 28

Pony Express, inaugurated, 59–60; unbroken speed for two thousand miles, 60; William M. Gwin, a promoter, 80; brings news of Sumter's fall, 142; a rider discovers silver lodes, 150

Porter, Bruce, and the Stevenson Monument, 246; and *The Lark*, 253

Port Said and the 'wickedest city,' 44

Portsmouth Square, see Plaza

Portuguese Flat and a bear story, 106

Potter, Mrs. James Brown, arrives from India, 228–29; and 'Ostler Joe' at Newport, 229; as Charlotte Corday, 229

Pourtalès, Count de, and the Countess, née Holladay, 216

Presidio of San Francisco, 28; the Officers' Club, 44, 74; the tenth anniversary ball, 121–22; after the Civil War, 151

Prevost, Captain, of H.M.S. *Satellite*, calls on Captain Farragut, 90

Pringle, Edward, and the Apollo balls, 83

Pruet, of the Vigilance Committee, 35

Pullman, Mrs. George (Harriet Sanger), 98

Purple Cow, The, and *The Lark*, 253–54

Rachel, as Camille, 24; her illness in America, 24; return to Europe and death, 25

INDEX

Ralston, William C., and Joseph Duncan, 139; a Renaissance Prince, 198; marriage and honeymoon party, 198–99; buys Belmont, 199; balls and banquets, 200–01; an English critic, 201; raiding the Mint, 202–03; financial ruin and death, 204; Sharon's tribute, 205; the California Theater, 212
Ralston, Mrs. William (Lizzie Fry), marriage, 198–99; fifty guests for dinner, 200
Randolph, Mrs. Harrison, and the Mount Vernon ball, 123
Ransome, Miss Annie, 27; sings to Gottschalk's accompaniment, 139
Ransome, Colonel Leander, goes to California, 2; decides to remain, 26; welcomes his family, 38; honored by Society of Engineers, 70; government land surveys and a ranch on the site of Hollywood, 70; the Diablo expedition, 70–71; his personal character and a tribute from Judge Swayne, 71–72; and Baron Fairfax, 82; adventures with road agents, 99; and Edwin M. Stanton, 111–12; and the Civil War mass meeting, 143
Ransome, Mrs. Leander, 2, 3; in London, 5, 6, 7; shopping in New York, 25; a crate of chickens, 26; Judge Chase explains a joke, 26–27; in San Francisco, 49; opinion of Edwin M. Stanton, 111; big-game hunters and a letter to General Beale, 172; clerical teas, 236
Ransome's Point, Mount Diablo, 70, 71
Rathbone, Major J. L., and his chandelier, 208–09
Rathbone, Mrs. J. L. (Alejandra Atherton), 208
Rattlesnake at dinner, 88
Raymond, John T., at the California Theater, 213
Red Bluff, 101
Redding, 101; and Joaquin Miller, 102
Rehan, Ada, and Daly's Company, 226
Reynolds, Mr., of Lunt's dancing school, 251–52
Reynolds, Sir Joshua, his painting of Mrs. Siddons, 162
Richardson, Colonel William, first American resident of Yerba Buena, killed by Charles Cora, 35; 43, 56
Rignold, George, tragedian, 217
Rincon Hill, 39–40, 122, 131

Ristori, her conquest of Paris, 24; at the California Theater, 211–12; laces of Marie Antoinette, 221; and Bernhardt, 235
Rives, Amélie, publishes a sensational novel, 254
Roberts, Theodore, becomes an actor, 57
Robinson, Kate (Mrs. Munroe Salisbury), 138, 149
Robinson, Mrs. Tod, and the Rebel Cause, 148; accused by *The Flag*, 149–50
Rock Island, Federal prison, and Mrs. Robinson's son, 148
Rocky Mountains, crossed by telegraph, 150
Roff, Henry, of the Pony Express, 60
Rosa, Carl, and his opera company, 153; dances at the McAllister home, 154
Rosa, Parepa, prima donna, 153; a bracelet for singing, 154
Rosenthal, Toby, painter, 95
Rulofson, Mr. and Mrs., entertain Mrs. Paran Stevens, 166
Russ, Henry, 61
Russ Gardens, 60–61
Russ House, miners' and ranchers' hotel, 61; the star 'runner,' 192
Russell, Lord Cosmo, at a house-party, 16
Russell, Lillian, in her golden youth, 228
Russian Hill, 43; the Stevenson house, 145–46; 263
Russian River, 43
Ryland, Judge of San José, 255

Sacramento City, 48; metropolis of the mining country, 97–98; and the Overland Stage, 98–99; and the Placerville Road, 100–01; Sutter's Fort, 110; the Governor's ball, 116
Sacramento flood, 98
Sacramento River, 48, 98, 104
Sacramento Union, the, and Mark Twain's Hawaiian letters, 163
Sacramento Valley, a prophecy, 71
Salisbury, Mrs. Munroe, 128
San Bruno Road, 173
Sanchez, R. Bernardo, of the Apollo balls, 81
Sanderson, Sibyl, her girlhood, 102; at the Grand Opera House, 103; death at Cannes, 104

INDEX

Sanderson, Judge and Mrs., parents of Sibyl Sanderson, 103
San Diego, held by General Kearny, 172
Sand Lot Riots, 197
Sandwich Islands, *see* Hawaii
San Francisco, colorful past, 1–2; spirit of the people, 2, 64, 210; first view of, 37–38; points of historic interest, 40–44; shops, 42, 57, 191, 253; 'wickedest city,' 44, 210; street scene, 46, 191; rapid growth, 49, 130; parlors of the period, 50; bus lines and street cars, 51–52; hitching posts, 56; fashionable promenade, 57, 59; informalities of mail service, 59; discomforts of living, 63–65; fires, 64–65; Fire Department and Lily Hitchcock, 65; described in *Two Years Before the Mast*, 66–67; Custom House known as 'Virginia Poor House,' 91; the 'Buck-and-Breck' campaign, 91–93; Stock Exchange, 97, 157–58, 182; restaurants, 136–37, 234–35; Civil War mass meeting, 142–43; changes of the 1870's, 190–94; City Hall, 192; Civic Center, 192; 'glorious vistas,' 215; religious revival, 237–38; Market Street parade, 256–58; destroyed and rebuilt, 263–64
San Francisco Art Association, 181
San Francisco churches, general, 61, 62; Trinity, 40, 62, 63; St. Francis d'Assisi, Mission Dolores, 44; First Unitarian, 62; Grace, 62, 63, 66, 137, 236; St. Mary's, 63; St. Luke's, 63, 236; First Congregational, 63, 239; St. Patrick's, 72; Advent, 76; Calvary, 143–44, 198–99; St. Stephen's, 236; Tabernacle, 237
San Francisco fire of 1906, 2, 96; Nob Hill palaces burn, 180; City Hall destroyed, 192; Holladay home survives, 215; *see also* Earthquakes
Sanger, Harriet (Mrs. George Pullman), 98
Sanitary Committee of Civil War, 62; California's contribution, 145
San Joaquin Valley, 71
San José, city, and Notre Dame Convent, 104; stage road, 173; Ord ranch near, 225; a long distance call, 255
Sankey, Ira D., of Moody and Sankey, 207–08

San Mateo, 207
San Rafael, Bret Harte in, 114; a summer home, 164; Mr. and Mrs. Harte are neighbors, 167; the Maillard ranch, 248
Santa Barbara, Princess Louise paints the Mission, 96; the De la Guerras, 112; Georgie Drew Barrymore's death, 228
Santa Clara College, 104
Sausalito, anchorage for British ships, 147; English colony, 224
Scalchi, Madame, with Patti, 231–32
Scheel, Fritz, his orchestra at Midwinter Fair, 241
Schumann-Heink, and Wagner at the Grand Opera House, 247
Scott, Captain Bob, and Mrs., at the Presidio, 152
Scott, Rev. Dr., of Calvary Church, 50; deported during Civil War, 143–44; at Ralston's wedding, 199; at Stevenson's wedding to Mrs. Osbourne, 245; Mrs. Scott, 245
Seal Rocks, 173–74
Searles, Edward, and the Hopkins Castle, 181
Selby, Thomas, for mayor, 116; Rincon Hill hospitality, 131
Selby, Mrs. Thomas, 131; and Rev. Dr. Scott, 144
Sembrich, Marcella, at the Tevis home, 186
Serra, Junipero, comes to Yerba Buena, 43; at Mission Dolores, 52; 109
Shafter, Mary, 129
Shafter, Judge McMillen, 72
Shafter, Judge O. L., and fashion of the fifties, 47; and the Atlantic cable, 262
Shafter, General William, 262
Sharon, Flora (Lady Hesketh), 206
Sharon, Mr. and Mrs. Fred, 206
Sharon, Senator William, and the Hill *vs.* Sharon case, 125–26; as Ralston's creditor, 205; host at Belmont, 205–06
Shasta, a metropolis of the gold country, 97; described, 102, 104
Shasta, Mount, 104
Shasta Springs, 41
Shelley, Sir Edward, nephew of the poet, 159–60
Sheridan, General Phil, 204
'Sheridan's Ride,' famous painting at Milbrae, 175

Sherman, General William T., as a banker in San Francisco, 39–40; in Monterey, 40; 117
Shillaber, Mrs., and her salon, 170–71
Shurtleff home brought around the Horn, 102
Siddons, Sarah, and Charles Kean, 162
Sienkiewicz in California, 227
Sierra Nevada Mountains, the Placerville Road, 100; stage-coach days, 104–07
Sillem, Willy, collects a bill in Chile, 81
Siskiyou County, 107
Sisson's Inn, 104, 106
Sisson, William, mountaineer, 107–08
Sloat, Commodore J. D., buys Sherman's house, 40; raises flag over Yerba Buena, 42; in Monterey, 172
Smedberg, Colonel William R., 152
Sonoma County, General Vallejo in, 110, 112; 139
Sonora, the, brings news of Atlantic cable, 118
Sothern, E. A., and 'Dundrearys,' 83; at the California, 218–19; and Edwin Adams, 220
Sothern, Edward H., as Lord Chumley, 226
Sousa, John Philip, at the Midwinter Fair, 241
South Park, 57, 122; described, 132; hospitable homes, 132–35; a famous ball, 138; Hall McAllister house lost at poker, 138–39; 183; the exodus, 191; and the Ralston honeymoon, 199
Spanish-American marriages, 84
Spanish-American War, 262
Spanish grandees, 112
Spencer, Herbert, takes George Eliot to the play, 12
Spreckels, Adolph, 215
Spreckels, Claus, 191
Stage-coach travel, and adventures, 98; 100–08
Stanton, Edwin M., and the Sutter case, 111; a taciturn guest, 111–12
Stanford, Leland, buys Palo Alto, 132; and the 'Big Four,' 180; his Nob Hill palace, 181–82; and Leland, Jr., 181; and Mrs. Stanford, 182
Stanford University, 132
Stearns, Don Abel, 84
Stevens, Ashton, critic, and Caruso's Don José, 233

Stevens, Miss Minnie (Lady Paget), 166
Stevens, Mrs. Paran, 166–67
Stevenson, Captain J. D., 123–24, and Mrs., 124
Stevenson, Robert Louis, and Virgil Williams, 95; marriage, 244–45; at the Bohemian Club, 245; Stevenson Monument in Portsmouth Square, 246
Stevenson, Mrs. Robert Louis, 224; 244–45; her vivid personality, 246
Stewart's, A. T., in New York, 25
St. Francis d'Assisi Church, 44
St. Gaudens medallion of R. L. S., 246
St. Germains, Earl of, viceroy of Ireland, 18; presented to, 19; and ex-President Van Buren, 20
St. Germains, Lady, 18
St. Helena, the Langtry ranch near, 252
Stillorgan Park, home of Arthur Lee Guinness, 14–16
St. James's Palace, the Royal Drawing-Room, 7–8
St. Joseph, Missouri, and the Pony Express, 59, 142; and the Overland Stage, 98
St. Luke's Church, 63, 236
St. Mary's Church, 63
Stockton, city, 117
Stockton, Commodore, raises flag over Los Angeles, 172
Stoddard, Charles Warren, and Bret Harte, 163; and R. L. S., 245
Stokes, Edward, 128
Stone, Rev. A. L., 63
Stone, Mrs. A. L., her interesting ancestry, 63
Stone, Mr. and Mrs. Joseph, of Cincinnati, 166
Storm King, the, clipper ship, 120
St. Patrick's Church, 72
Street characters: Professor Coombs, Emperor Norton, the Great Unknown, the Razor-Strop Man, the American Eagle, Mud-Hens, Money King, 154–58
Strong, Ysobel Osbourne, 224
Sullivan, Barry, as Richard III, 217
Sumner, Captain, leads a cotillion, 152
Sumter, Fort, news of its fall, 142–43
Sutlej, H.M.S., and the salute from Alcatraz, 146–47
Sutro, Adolph, 174–75
Sutro Forest, 175

INDEX 283

Sutro Heights, 174
Sutter County, once New Helvetia, 111
Sutter, General John, and his empire, 109–11
Sutter's Fort, 98, 110
Sutter's Mill and discovery of gold, 110
Swayne, Judge Noah, his tribute to Colonel Ransome, 72
Sweringen, Bell (Mrs. Andrew McCreery), 137–38
Sweringen, Sue, marries Judge Stephen J. Field, 137; and Mrs. Condit-Smith, 138
Swift, John F., potential diplomat, 39
Swinburne, Algernon Charles, and Adah Isaacs Menken, 55
Switzerland, Sutter family from, 110
Swords, Colonel Thomas, 120–21; and Mrs. Swords, 120

Taber, Robert, and Julia Marlowe, 229
Tahiti, Pierre Loti arrives from, 47
Tahoe, Lake, and Tallac House, a tragedy of Indian life, 109
Tavernier, Jules, and murals of the Hopkins Castle, 179
Taylor, Mr. and Mrs. Bayard, at a South Park reception, 140–41
Taylor Street and a romance, 187–88
Tehema House, miners' hotel, 198
Telegraph Hill, and the Chileño Quarter, 34, 43; first sight of, 37; the signal of ships sighted, 37, 92, 93; last view of, 263
Telegraph, trans-continental, 150
Telephones, first used, 254–55
Tennyson, Alfred, brings his bride to London, 12; *Charge of the Light Brigade* and Lord Cardigan, 20
Terry, Judge David S., the stabbing of Hopkins, 45–46; the duel with Broderick, 124–25; in the Hill *vs.* Sharon case, 126; marriage to Sarah Althea Hill, 126; his death, 127
Terry, Mrs. David S., first wife of Judge Terry, 45–46
Terry, Ellen, and Ellen Tree, 162; the conquest of San Francisco, 242–43; her beauty as Fair Rosamond, 244
Tetrazzini, Luisa, sings at Lotta's Fountain, 69–70; at the Tivoli, 256
Tevis family, 186; home burns in 1906, 186
Thackeray, William M., entertains Charlotte Brontë, 12
Theater, memories of the, 210–11; see *also* Baldwin, California, Grand Opera House, Tivoli
Thompson, Joseph, and Melba at the Bohemian Club, 58
Thompson, Spanish Joe, of the Apollo bachelors, 83
Thumb, General and Mrs. Tom, 241–42
Tilden, Joseph, epicure and *bon viveur*, 132; at the Bohemian Club, 134
Tilden, Mrs. Joseph (Julia Foard), 132
Tivoli Opera House, 255–56
Tobin, Agnes, poet, 180
Tobin mansion on Nob Hill, 180
Tobin, Richard, 180
Toland, Dr. and Mrs., a legend of the plutocracy, 182–83; Mrs. Toland's carriage and the first hammercloth, 183
Torrence, Mrs. David, of Boston, 216
Toucey, the, launched at Mare Island, 119
Tricou, Henri, 81
Trilby craze, 254
Truet of the Vigilance Committee, 35
Tucker, Carroll, of Virginia, 23
Tucker, the Jeweller, and one-pound watches, 42
Turnbull, General and Mrs. Walter, entertain Patti, 232
Turner, Mr. and Mrs. Dan, of Mare Island, and Miss Alice Turner's wedding, 89
Twain, Mark, 162; and Mrs. Low at the lecture on Hawaii, 163
Twin Peaks, 52, 263

Union Pacific Railroad and the 'Big Four,' 180
Urquhart, Colonel and Mrs., parents of Mrs. James Brown Potter, in Oakland, 229

Vallejo, General, and John Sutter, 110; in his last years, 112
Van Buren, Martin, ex-President, visits Ireland, 20
Vanderbilts, the, and Mary Anderson, 220
Vanderbilt, W. K., Jr., marries Virginia Fair, 167
Vandewater, Mrs. John, her reception for Bayard Taylor, 140; drives 'Stevedore' on the Cliff House Road, 175
Van Ness, Mayor, his protest to the Vigilantes, 35

284 INDEX

Victoria Adelaide, Princess Royal, afterward Empress Frederick of Germany, 8
Victoria, Queen, opens Great Exhibition with Prince Albert, 5; presentation to, 7; at Crystal Palace, 8; driving in Hyde Park, 9; her daughter, Princess Louise, visits America, 96; a toast at Atlantic cable celebration, 119; Jubilee, 224; an American cousin, 225; and Albani, 247
Victoria, British Columbia, 67
Victoria, city, British Columbia, Lady Franklin's visit, 67
Victoria Regia blooms in Golden Gate Park, 239–40
Vigilance Committee (Vigilantes), and James King, of William, 27, 34–35; a French member, 34; how the Committee was formed, 34; Casey and Cora tried and hanged, 35–36; high place in public regard, 40, 43; brings law and order to the 'wickedest city,' 44; leaders of the Committee, 73; a call for reorganization, 197
Vigilance Committee headquarters, Fort Gunnybags, fortified with bags of sand, 34; the hanging of Casey and Cora, 36; a visit to, 40; banner from Trinity Church members, 40; Judge Terry a prisoner, 45–46
Virginia City, and the Placerville Road, 100–01; new silver lodes, 150; and Mrs. John W. Mackay, 188–89
Vokes, Rosina, English comedienne at the Baldwin, 228

Waldorf-Astoria, Peacock Alley anticipated, 33
Wales, Prince of (Edward VII), as a small boy, 8; approved by Miss McAllister, 76; Mrs. McCreery in his set, 138
Walkinshaws, the, drive a clarence, 173
Wallace, Judge William T., 83; a witty jurist, 255
Wallace, Mrs. William T., and a long-distance call, 255
Wallack, Mr. and Mrs. J. W., an interrupted performance at Maguire's, 93
Waller, Lady, of the Guinness family, 13
Walsingham, Lord, entomologist, hunts butterflies in San Rafael, 166

Warren, Miss Minnie, and Commodore Nutt, of Barnum's Circus, 241
Washington, George, and a decanter of wine, 133–34
Washington, John, sells Mount Vernon, 123
Washoe Indians, 109
Washoe mining district, 150
Waterspark, Lord, hunts bears on the Beale ranch, 171–72
Watkins, Commodore and Mrs., of South Park, 132
Weill, Raphael, recalls Rachel, 25; unique career as merchant, 57; host to celebrities, 57–58; as chef at the Bohemian Club, 134; and John W. Mackay, 190
Weller, Governor John, 87; the inaugural ball, 116
Wells-Fargo and Company, offices in Parrott Block, 78; explosion, 78–79; shot-gun messengers, 98–99; the Wells-Fargo treasure and highwaymen, 99–100; and Black Bart, 105–06
Whipple's, Steve, gambling-rooms and the Pacific Club, 78
Whistler, the Chase portrait of, and Billy Emerson, 211
Whiting, Admiral, marries Miss Afong, 223
White Sulphur Springs, 85–88
Whittell, Hugh, his epitaph, 129–30
Whittier, General, and his Beacon Hill reserve, 151
Wicklow County, Ireland, 21
Wiggin, Kate Douglas, establishes free kindergarten, 191
Wilde, Oscar, lectures in costume, 242
'Wild West,' 44–46; and Sir Robert Bridges, 170
Williams, Colonel Andrew, mayor of Oakland, 113
Williams, Mrs. Andrew, mother of Bret Harte, 113
Williams, Virgil, artist and friend of R. L. S., 95; executes a commission for R. B. Woodward, 176; at Stevenson's wedding, 245
Williams, Mrs. Virgil, a witness at Stevenson's marriage to Mrs. Osbourne, 245
Willows, the, public gardens, 61
World's Fair at Chicago, and a glass dress, 229; inspires the Midwinter Fair, 241

INDEX

Wood, John, comedian, is sued for divorce, 68
Wood, Mrs. John, at Maguire's and flowers from Judge Hager, 68
Wood, General Leonard, marries Miss Condit-Smith, 138
Woodward, R. B., art gallery and zoo, 176–77
Woodward's Gardens, 176–77
Wright, Mrs. Eben, and Mrs. Holladay, 216

Yale University, and William T. Coleman's son, 74
Yarde-Buller, Lady (Leila Kirkham), her wedding in Oakland, 114

Yellow Book, the, and *Fin de Siècle*, 253
Yerba Buena, first settlement at San Francisco, 43; Sutter's grant, 110
Yosemite Valley and Thomas Hill, 96, 104; the Ralston honeymoon, 199
Young, Brigham, and his wives, 161; his honor and qualities of leadership, 161
Yreka, a metropolis of northern California, 102
Ysaye at the Bohemian Club, 58

Zealous, H.M.S., divine service on deck for Lord Walter Campbell, 165

THE LEISURE CLASS IN AMERICA

An Arno Press Collection

Bradley, Hugh. **Such was Saratoga.** 1940

Browne, Junius Henri. **The Great Metropolis:** A Mirror of New York. 1869

Burt, Nathaniel. **The Perennial Philadelphians.** 1963

Canby, Henry Seidel. **Alma Mater:** The Gothic Age of the American College. 1936

Crockett, Albert Stevens. **Peacocks on Parade.** 1931

Croffut, W[illiam] A. **The Vanderbilts.** 1886

Crowninshield, Francis W. **Manners for the Metropolis.** 1909

de Wolfe, Elsie. **The House in Good Taste.** 1913

Ellet, E[lizabeth] F[ries Lummis]. **The Court Circles of the Republic, or The Beauties and Celebrities of the Nation.** 1869

Elliott, Maud Howe. **This Was My Newport.** 1944

Elliott, Maud Howe. **Uncle Sam Ward and His Circle.** 1938

Fairfield, Francis Gerry. **The Clubs of New York** and Croly, [Jane C.] **Sorosis.** 1873/1886. Two vols. in one

[Fawcett, Edgar]. **The Buntling Ball:** A Graeco-American Play. 1885

Fawcett, Edgar. **Social Silhouettes.** 1885

Fiske, Stephen. **Off-Hand Portraits of Prominent New Yorkers.** 1884

Foraker, Julia B. **I Would Live It Again:** Memories of a Vivid Life. 1932

Goodwin, Maud Wilder. **The Colonial Cavalier.** 1895

Hartt, Rollin Lynde. **The People at Play.** 1909

Lehr, Elizabeth Drexel. **"King Lehr" and the Gilded Age.** 1935

Lodge, Henry Cabot. **Early Memories.** 1913

[Longchamp, Ferdinand]. **Asmodeus in New-York.** 1868

McAllister, [Samuel] Ward. **Society as I Have Found It.** 1890

McLean, Evalyn, with Boyden Sparkes. **Father Struck It Rich.** 1936

[Mann, William d'Alton]. **Fads and Fancies of Representative Americans at the Beginning of the Twentieth Century.** 1905

Martin, Frederick Townsend. **The Passing of the Idle Rich.** 1911

Martin, Frederick Townsend. **Things I Remember.** 1913

Maurice, Arthur Bartlett. **Fifth Avenue.** 1918

[Mordecai, Samuel]. **Richmond in By-Gone Days.** 1856

Morris, Lloyd. **Incredible New York.** 1951

Neville, Amelia Ransome. **The Fantastic City:** Memoirs of the Social and Romantic Life of Old San Francisco. 1932

Nichols, Charles Wilbur de Lyon. **The Ultra-Fashionable Peerage of America.** 1904

Pound, Arthur. **The Golden Earth:** The Story of Manhattan's Landed Wealth. 1935

Pulitzer, Ralph. **New York Society on Parade.** 1910

Ripley, Eliza. **Social Life in Old New Orleans.** 1912

Ross, Ishbel. **Silhouette in Diamonds:** The Life of Mrs. Potter Palmer. 1960

Sherwood, M[ary] E[lizabeth W.]. **Manners and Social Usages.** 1897

The Sporting Set. 1975

Van Rensselaer, [May] King. **Newport: Our Social Capital.** 1905

Van Rensselaer, [May] King. **The Social Ladder.** 1924

Wharton, Edith and Ogden Codman, Jr. **The Decoration of Houses.** 1914

Williamson, Jefferson. **The American Hotel.** 1930

F
869
.S3
N4
1975

Neville
The fantastic city

38131

Date Due

NOV 3 '77	APR 9 '9		
NOV 27 '78			
APR 1 6 '79			
OCT 8 '79			
DEC 3 '79			
OCT 6 '80			
NOV 1 3 '80			
5 '81			
OCT 2 6 '81			
FEB 2 0 '84			
NOV 2 1 1986			

SKYLINE COLLEGE LIBRARY

Printed in U.S.A.